STRATEGIC STRESS MANAGEMENT

an organizational approach

STRATEGIC STRESS MANAGEMENT

an organizational approach

Valerie J Sutherland
and
Cary L Cooper

First published 2000 by
MACMILLAN PRESS LTD
Houndmills, Basingstoke, Hampshire RG21 6XS
and London
Companies and representatives
throughout the world

ISBN 0–333–77487–6

A catalogue record for this book is available from the British
Library.

This book is printed on paper suitable for recycling and
made from fully managed and sustained forest sources.

10 9 8 7 6 5 4 3 2 1
09 08 07 06 05 04 03 02 01 00

Designed and formatted by
The Ascenders Partnership, Basingstoke
Illustrations by *Ascenders*

Printed and bound in Great Britain by
Creative Print & Design (Wales),
Ebbw Vale

Contents

1

Change and the Need for Change

Need for an Organizational Approach to Stress Management

Many of us would subscribe to the adage, 'If it's not broken don't fix it'. However, there are many of us who also live with the nagging doubt, suspicion and fear that 'it' is not performing as well as it might or, indeed, maximizing its full potential. Thus, we conclude that 'it' needs fixing in some way. The 'it' referred to in this context is, of course, business success and effectiveness. In particular, the concern is for the health and performance of the organization. Therefore, this book addresses the ways in which we can maximize performance and health in the workplace by using an integrated, organizational strategy for the management of stress. It differs from other traditional stress management books in three main ways.

1. First, the approach recommended is a proactive model rather than using a reactive stance. Typically organizations tend to wait for something to happen before they adopt some form of stress management activity. It becomes acknowledged as a strategy needed to solve the ills of the organization. This implies that the employees have already become casualties or victims of exposure to workplace stress. They have become in need of treatment that tends to be both costly to administer and, all too often, ineffective in the long term.

2. Secondly, we would also suggest that any effective approach to the management of stress should be integrated into the organizational processes. It means that the process will become part of the way in which the business is managed on a day-to-day basis. Ultimately, it should be regarded as, 'the way in which we do things around here',

instead of being seen as some stand-alone activity that is introduced in response to a problem. We firmly believe that stress management activities can be a cost benefit to the business. However, in our experience, stress management activities tend to be classified as a necessary evil that is most certainly inconvenient to the running of the operations and the 'real' business. In addition they are perceived as an extra financial burden to the overstretched budget. Whilst such packages are offered by organizations for well intentioned reasons, the actions of senior management are often met with mistrust and resistance. Sadly, these initiatives rarely reach out to the people who really need them. Indeed, it is a common belief that stress management activities are intended for employees with problems and those labelled the 'non copers' within the organization. 'Stress' is viewed as something 'bad' and not wanted and so stress management activities introduced into this climate and culture are perceived in a negative light.

3. Typically in the past, stress management activities have focused on the individual in the workplace. Blame was firmly placed on the individual who was seen as having some sort of problem, or perceived as being unable to cope. Therefore, it was believed that the individual must change in some way so that the problem no longer existed. Empirical studies and evaluation of stress management programmes now clearly show the flaws in this simplistic line of thinking. For both humanistic and economical reasons a different approach was deemed to be necessary. This book offers a holistic approach to the management of stress. It is one that addresses the quality of life for the individual at work, the dynamics and interpersonal relationships of the work group or team, and the organizational structure and climate that shape the working environment. The approach offers many potential benefits to individual employees and business strategists if, in return, they take joint responsibility for the management of stress at work. It must be acknowledged that by optimizing the health of the workforce we ensure the good health of the organization. This becomes manifest in terms of maximum performance and productivity.

Endorsement for Change

The rationale for our approach to the management of stress in the workplace is endorsed at the highest levels:

National Government Level

The Government has identified the workplace as one of the three main locations for its proposed 'contract for health' with the British people (Health Strategy Unit, April 1998). In developing a healthy workforce, the aims are twofold. Namely, to improve its overall health, and to ensure that people are protected against specific harms caused by work. It notes that, 'people with a job spend a lot of time at their workplace, so a healthy workplace is vital to their health'. Thus, action will be achieved through Government strategies, for example, the Health and Safety Executive's (HSE) 'Good Health is Good Business' campaign. This states that *employers* should have excellent standards of health and safety management. They should take measures to reduce stress at work; try to create flexible working arrangements that are compatible with employees' home lives and provide child care strategies; ensure a smoke free environment and make healthy choices easy for staff (for example, provision for cyclists, healthy canteens, and so on). The *employees* should be able to support colleagues who are disabled or have problems, follow health and safety guidelines, and work with employers either directly or through trade union representatives to create a healthy working environment. This initiative involves Government working to foster a new culture of partnership in business between management and employees that will help impact on the problems of stress and insecurity in work (HMSO, 1988).

Institute of Employment

An Institute of Employment report prepared in 1997 argued that stress has become so big and confused an issue that it can prevent employers from looking at what is going on in their organizations. They suggested that organizations which view stress as a single issue will not be able to understand their employees' problems and manage workplace stress effectively. The Institute of Employment Studies' (IES) research and recommendations, drawing on eight studies, including Marks and Spencer, the Nationwide Building Society, Nestlé, the Post Office, and South West Water, found that, all to often attention is focused on the individual, rather than on the individual as an element within the work environment. It was found that unfocused stress management systems have only a limited impact. Good practice should include:

- Assessment and diagnosis of problem and concerns; why do organizations think they have a problem with stress (what is the evidence) and what do they mean by stress (what is the specific problem).

- Solution generation – what types of actions are appropriate? What are the aims? What does the organization want to achieve? What are the options for intervention? What are the goals of intervention?
- Implementation – if at all possible, in a way that allows for controlled comparisons. Plans must indicate the structure and timing of the intervention.
- Evaluation – the consequences of the intervention against expectations of positive and negative outcomes must be assessed. It must be decided how and when the intervention will be evaluated before any actions take place? It is important that any predetermined success criteria are specified and made public
- Ongoing monitoring and feedback – how can assessment findings be integrated with other management structures or policies? (IES Report, 331,1997).

European Foundation for the Improvement of Working and Living Conditions

In a recent report, the Foundation suggest that action to tackle absenteeism and ill health is given too low a priority by the majority of organizations within the European Union (EU). The Foundation stated that, 'The EU, national governments, employers' organizations and unions are insufficiently aware of the economic and human significance of absenteeism and of the potential for reducing it'. They report that the proportion of employees absent on temporary sick leave ranged from 3.5 per cent in Denmark, up to eight per cent in Portugal. Figures for extended or permanent disability range from three per cent in Ireland, up to 13.3 per cent in the Netherlands. Action to reduce absenteeism is still modest and can be put into four categories:

1. **Procedural measures** – whereby companies attempt to reduce absenteeism by tightening checks and procedures on absent workers. In some cases, financial incentives are used to reduce sickness absence rates.

2. **Preventive individual measures** – limited to encouraging individual employees to work and live in a safe and healthy way. Much of this activity is focused on providing information and training, the provision of protective equipment or the introduction of stress management

programmes. The emphasis in on healthy lifestyle activities such as anti-smoking campaigns, alcohol reduction, dietary advice, exercise, cancer screening and physiotherapy.

3. **Preventive work-related measures** – these aim to reduce the discrepancy between workload and capacity by reducing the workload. Ways of achieving this include making the workplace a safer environment, climate control, task rotation, better information systems, and better work organization and safety management. These are the healthy and safety improvement measures that tend to be under utilized. The Foundation reported on a Norwegian study of national absenteeism. They observed that the companies that had improved working conditions were the most successful in reducing absence, by on average 30 per cent per annum.

4. **Reintegration measures** – these aim to accelerate the return to work of sick employees and usually require support from managers, the occupational health and medical specialists, and reintegration activities such as offering specially adapted work.

Thus the Foundation recommends a comprehensive and systematic approach that addresses the needs of the workforce, employee participation and application to all workers (European Foundation of Living and Working, 1997).

Trade Unions

Many trade union organizations now provide their members with guidance for the management of stress at work. They are also becoming involved with stress-related court cases. For example, Unison, the public services union, recently stated that are dealing with around 7000 such cases (Johnstone, 1999). Of course, not all of these will go to court, but many claims for compensation will be privately settled before they reach this stage. The 'MSF', that is the UK union for skilled and professional people is also advocating an organizational approach to the management of stress. In the report, 'Preventing Stress at Work: an MSF Guide', it states that, 'stress is an organizational issue'. They state, that at the moment, the prevailing attitude among employers is that stress is an individual weakness. Thus any remedial action should be concentrated on the individual. However, they believe that the only effective approach to stress is to ensure that the focus is on the 'sick organization', rather than the 'sick individual'. Further, MSF advises that problems should be tackled organizationally, by identifying what it is about work that causes stress. Also, organizations should acknowledge that changes must be in the design of the workplace and the job itself if stress levels are to be reduced in the work environment. They recommend that Swedish legislation is followed and used as a guideline in the UK. These requirements include the following legislation:

- Working conditions shall be adapted to peoples' differing physical and mental aptitudes.
- The employee shall be given the opportunity of participating in the design of the work situation, and in the processes of change and development affecting their work.
- Technology, work organization and job content shall be designed so that the employee is not exposed to physical or mental strains that may lead to illness or accidents. Forms of remuneration and the distribution of working hours shall also be taken into account.
- Closely controlled or restricted work shall be avoided or limited.
- Work should provide opportunities for variety, social contact, and co-operation as well as coherence between different working operations.
- Working conditions should provide opportunities for personal and vocational development, as well as for self-determination and professional responsibility.

The MSF Union suggests that any approach to stress must follow a traditional health and safety model. This means that the organization must identify the hazard, assess the risk, take measures to eliminate or reduce the risk, and evaluate the effectiveness of the measures taken. Stress should not be seen as a weakness in the individual, but that we are all potentially at risk. Therefore, issues must be tackled from an organizational perspective (MSF, 1995).

In this chapter we continue by reviewing the reasons why organizational health and performance must be a topic for serious consideration. We suggest that this is not simply a journey of whimsy and indulgence because there are sound, practical business reasons why we need to have a firm understanding about our rationale for adopting an organizational approach to the management of stress at work. This scene setting is a quite deliberate and vital part of the diagnostic process needed before we are ready to put into place the various strategies and interventions that will ensure good organizational health. We will see that there is not just one problem, neither is there just one solution. Nevertheless, we believe that all organizations, from large multinational institutions right down to small-sized companies, and one-man businesses are able to benefit from adopting this new approach. In the final part of this chapter we will consider the changing face of the workplace and society itself, and the implications this has for a healthy workforce and healthy organization. At the end of this chapter, evidence for the unacceptable costs of mismanaged stress is presented.

The Changing Face of the Work Environment

It has been suggested that we have traded a certain future, perhaps of dubious, but known benefit, which was characterized as 'fifty years of work; fifty weeks each year, for fifty hours a week', for a style of living and working which would now be unrecognizable to our grandparents' generation. Indeed, the reality of the workplace in contemporary organizational life differs much from the work environment we would recognize from just two or three decades ago. In addition to the changing work environment, we also continue to face enormous changes to the nature of society itself. As we moved on from the postwar scenario, we readily embraced the 1960s. Eagerly we urged the limitless possibilities of change as we tried to move forward from the endless restrictions and confinements of tradition and a lacklustre postwar period. The era of the baby boomers soon became the fast pace world of the consumer society 'teenager' and, of course, the sexual revolution. This indulged group really believed that they invented the word 'sex'. A liberated generation pushed many of society's boundaries beyond the point of no return. Also at this time the pace of new technology moved at a dizzy speed. Harold Wilson, the Labour Prime Minister, proclaimed that we were living within the 'white heat of technology' that would transform our lives, and produce a leisure age of 20-hour working weeks. We faced a golden future!

However, this bubble finally burst and the reality of the 1970s emerged as one typified by industrial conflict, unrest and strife. Bitter battles were fought between the working classes and management as our strike ridden society slowly was brought to its knees. A no-win situation, from which many never recovered, developed. Normality in our working lives was gone forever as we moved into the 1980s and the emergence of the 'enterprise culture'. A decade of privatization, statutory constraints on industrial relations, mergers and acquisitions, strategic alliances, and joint ventures followed. One of the ways the big organization attempts to cope with global competition is to become a multinational company. The organization is no longer based in one particular country, but has plants or business arrangements in those countries that offer the most favourable conditions for its specific business. As Charles Handy has noted, the use of the internet and other methods of electronic communication has permitted the disappearance of the factual, though not nominal, headquarters of these multinationals (Handy, 1994). It means that different functions could now be performed anywhere in the world and where they were handled best (and cheapest)! Other organizations use reorganization or mergers as a way of adapting to a changing environment. The employees working in these organizations are simply left to complain about the constant reorganization that seems to take place for the sake of reorganization! As one manager working within a construction company told us,

> Just as we begin to see the light at then end of the tunnel (following yet another restructuring process) we realize that the light is only another train coming towards us, headlong and on our track!

Whilst it might be said that the purposes of a merger are to obtain scale enlargement or synergy, these have often been proven to have been nothing more than based on the personal ambitions of their initiators, rather than on factual necessity (Schabracq and Cooper, 1997). Nevertheless, the 1980s saw the biggest and most sustained wave of merger activity. This was estimated to have affected 25 per cent of the American workforce (Fulmer, 1986). A survey of 12 000 senior managers in 25 countries, across six continents, found that 45 per cent of companies employing more than 1000 people had been involved in merger, divestiture or acquisition activity in the two-year period, 1989–91. In the same period, 70 per cent had experienced major restructuring (Kanter, 1991). This wave of mania merger was facilitated by a number of factors. For example, capital was available within organizations and financial institutions, and many companies were for sale. Regulations on mergers were still fairly relaxed, but of key importance was the notion that market conditions brought a need to either consolidate or capture new markets. In rapidly changing conditions, strategic acquisitions become a more attractive and expedient alternative to the setting up of new outlets and provide an alternative means of eliminating competition. It was also felt that there was a need to share risk, particularly in capital intensive industries, and from a merger or joint venture it was possible to develop new products. A feeling prevailed that 'big was beautiful' and that only very large organizations could resolve the complexities of the contemporary business world.

Another, more worrying view was that mergers were seen as power games and provided an opportunity to create stimulation for the bored chief executive or senior management team! Acquisitive growth strategies continue to be popular, in spite of increasing evidence that they often do not enhance the financial performance of acquiring firms. Indeed, they may even have an adverse impact on innovation (Hitt, Harrison, Ireland and Best, 1998). Their popularity continued to rise steadily between the middle of the 1960s and the end of the 1980s but has slowed, somewhat, during the 1990s. The USA was the most active followed by Great Britain and Germany and in 1996 over $1 trillion (a million million) was spent in acquisitions globally (Lipin, 1997).

One of the key attributes observed in unsuccessful acquisitions is the changes in the top management team or structure. This leads to a loss or lack of strategic leadership and chaotic conditions within the company (Hitt *et al.*,1998). Research evidence also points to a high level of failure of mergers and suggests that the strains and pressures on the workforce far outweigh many of the benefits gained (Cartwright and Cooper, 1996). Estimates of merger failure rates vary from a pessimistic 77 per cent reported by some US studies (Marks, 1988), to approximately 50 per cent quoted by several UK sources (BIM, 1986; Hunt, 1988; Cartwright and Cooper, 1992). Studies of joint ventures reveal a high level of instability with almost 25 per cent being terminated within the first three years (Kogut, 1988). Merger and acquisition activities invariably result in job losses and a high rate of voluntary labour turnover. This results in a substantial outflow of talent and expertise from the organization. Some studies show executive turnover rates in the first three years post acquisition as high as 70 per cent (Unger, 1986; Walsh, 1988). Staff turnover is not confined to only senior positions within the organization. Typically an overall rate of staff turnover of at least 30 per cent in the first two years is experienced (Graves, 1981; Cartwright and Cooper, 1992). Costs to the organization, therefore, include recruitment, training, and loss of customer contact, goodwill and expertise.

Yet, in this free market, hothouse culture of the 1980s and early 1990s, competition, the supremacy of the individual, and 'youth' were idolised. Fortunes beyond avarice were won and lost by those who dared to reach out into this 'have it all' society. Whilst this entrepreneurial period improved our economic competitiveness at home and in certain international markets, it was not without tolls, such as strain and burnout. At this time, the word 'stress' became familiar in the vocabulary of working people. However, it also meant that 'stress' was thus seen only as a negative experience. In reality it was the mismanagement of the stressful situation, that was an inevitable part of modern-day living and working, that became deleterious in its consequences. Bad press and media coverage served to exacerbate the problem because individuals and organizations began to deny 'stress', their physical and psychological condition, and their symptoms of stress, until a crisis or breakdown situation had occurred. Before the 1980s ended a recession began which continued well into the 1990s. One of the key changes observed during this time was the privatization of the public sector industries and this laid the groundwork for potentially the most profound changes in the workplace since the Industrial Revolution.

Thus, the 1990s have been dominated by the impact of the recession and efforts to get out of it. Governments were striving to reduce budget deficits and thereby were squeezing more and more out of business. As the Western World fought to respond, to halt further losses in market share to their Pacific Rim competitors, gain access to new markets, and respond to market vacillations, we witnessed sweeping changes. One of the ways to respond to global competition was for the organization to become 'leaner and meaner'. Becoming meaner and leaner was achieved by processes variously described as, 'downsizing', 'rightsizing', 'delaying', 'becoming flatter' or 'process re-engineering'. This race to be more customer responsive, and reduce 'time to market', brought wave upon wave of change in the workplace, including the emergence of initiatives such as 'TQM'(Total Quality Management) and 'JIT'(Just-in-time Technology). In addition to these constraints were the problems associated with fluctuations in the demographic situation, rising expectations in the labour force, and an increasing reluctance for workers to accept certain jobs.

Change in the workplace appeared to be most endemic in the UK. One survey (1997) conducted by Coopers and Lybrand, management consultants, found, of the 254 firms polled in the UK, the Netherlands, Belgium and Sweden, that only the UK firms were more preoccupied with lay off than growth. Sixty-five per cent of the UK firms placed staff cuts high on their agenda, whilst 19 per cent said that both growth and downsizing were top priorities. The objective of this downsizing was to reduce the number of hierarchical levels as well as the number of employees. The reality for most people, whatever euphemism you cared to use, meant either job loss or constant change for those lucky enough to keep their job. Fewer people were doing more and more work, but feeling insecure because they did not believe that the job cuts were at an end. Whilst many of the changes were well intentioned, it became apparent that such organizational restructuring was widely highly stressful for employees

(Jick, 1985). The effects of job cuts were far ranging and the consequence undesirable in many ways, ranging from worry to job insecurity and uncertainty. The repercussions faced by the 'walking wounded' are discussed in more detail in Chapter 3, however, at this point it is relevant to observe that it is often the older employees who were made redundant. Organizations tried to get rid of their older workers, who were regarded, mistakenly as expensive, inflexible, hard to train, physically unfit, unhealthy and unproductive (Waldman and Avolio, 1986; Sterns and Alexander, 1988; Cascio and McEnvoy, 1989; Warr, 1995). For these same prejudices this group also finds it difficult to regain employment and this leads to higher social security costs and market loss in terms of the reduction in purchasing power of this group. The organization immediately loses a lot of experience and 'knowledge' and the employees left in the jobs feel a mixture of guilt and relief. However, they also express the impact of the loss of stability, permanence and wisdom born of experience. They are also well aware of what the future might face for them if they stay with the company. Many will respond by moving on to another company perceived as safer in terms of job security. This means that the organization can be faced with the unexpected high costs of re-hiring and training new staff and disruption to operations caused by labour turnover and instability. Conversely, job insecurity can present a quite different problem for the organization, in the form of 'presenteeism'. It would appear that employees vie to demonstrate organizational commitment by presenting themselves for work whether or not they are fit enough to do so. The ability to maintain a good record of employment and not be absent for any reason, is seen as a necessary credential for the individual who wishes to avoid becoming a redundancy victim in the next tranche of lay offs. This clearly has implications for health and safety in the workplace. There are also potential costs for the organization, such as poor performance from an employee who really should not be at work because he or she is unfit for work. Some cynics also suggest that the lay off of the older employee is done for more devious financial reasons. Organizations who adopt the practice of offering voluntary redundancy to employees aged 50 years or more, will be rid of a group of workers who might begin to suffer from symptoms of exposure to stress, caused by spending a great part of their lives in the same workplace. This, of course, is the group most liable to sue the organization for cumulative stress trauma!

During the 1980s and 1990s we also witnessed the massive expansion of numbers of women in the workplace, with a noticeable pushing, rather than shattering, of the glass ceiling further upwards. In reality, however, and in spite of equality of opportunity laws, women gained employment because they were cheaper to employ than men. Many families faced the prospect of the female acting as the major breadwinner in the family, whilst the male partner or spouse consistently failed to find, or keep a job. The changing role of men and women in the workplace and at home has added another dimension to the enormity of the changes taking place on factory floors, offices and technology culture of UK plc.

Many authors (Cooper, 1998; Cascio 1998) suggest that change is here to stay because of the business trends that drive it. Cascio (1998) believes that these include the growth of global markets and the global character of the economy, which continues to accelerate with the aid of the ever spiralling internet. The development in information technology has created 'commerce without borders' and continues to fuel the demand for a technology that can provide links with customers and access to information anytime, anywhere and at speed. These are vital if the organization is to be responsive to market changes and to gain and maintain competitiveness. Cascio also believes that change drives the need for continuous learning, and that thinking and inventing will be the most valuable assets in today's organizations. It produces the redefinition of careers and opportunities for new products and services. On the negative side of this equation is the increased stress produced. However, it is our argument that stress need not be damaging in its consequences since only mismanaged stress leads to a state of distress. (The concept and underlying theory of stress, the stress response, distress and reasons why 'change' is a source of stress are explained in detail in Chapter 3.)

Not all authors believe that the global competition we face has positive gain. Schabracq and Cooper (1997) describe this form of gruelling global competition as potentially very undesirable. Whilst it shows characteristics of a symmetrical escalation (Watzlawick, Beavin and Jackson, 1968), the competitive stakes become higher and higher because the situation is only influenced by positive feedback loops, and there are far more than two competitors involved. Ultimately such competition will lead to exhaustion or total breakdown of the conflicting parties. So, survival of the fittest becomes the name of the game and the pace and speed at which the players can adapt to the continually changing environment is the factor that will determine this survival. An ability to be flexible is the key characteristic for both the individual employee and the organization.

Nevertheless, Cascio suggests that the changes we have experienced have produced a revision of the psychological contract that binds workers to the organization and to each other. He compares the features of old and new contracts as shown in Table 1.1.

Every decade this century has brought its own unique changes to our

Table 1.1

Old Contract	New Contract
Stability	Change
Predictability	Uncertainty
Permanence	Temporariness
Standard work patterns	Flexible Work
Valuing loyalty	Valuing performance and skills
Paternalism	Self-reliance
Job Security	Employment security
Linear career growth	Multiple Careers
One-time learning	Life-long learning

(Cascio, 1998)

working environment. As we move into the new millennium two key changes will need to be addressed in order to ensure organizational effectiveness and profitability.

1. We must acknowledge the demographic changes that are taking place. This will result in a decrease in the number of economically active people, in relation to the number of those who have retired. The age structure of our working population is changing as life expectancy increases while the birth rate declines. Projections indicate that the number of workers per retired will continue to decrease. This has obvious implications and burdens for our welfare, health and pension systems and the organization of work. It is suggested that the current trend to retire at an early age will be reversed in order to cope with the problems of an ageing society. Thus, organizations will need to find ways to keep their workforce healthy, active and productive for a longer period of their lives. Early retirement for the 'stressed-out' or 'burnout' individuals, aged 50 to 55 years will no longer be acceptable as a standard practice or way of avoiding stress litigation procedures. Thus there is need to combat age barriers, to maintain older workers at work, and to support their continued health and productivity (Griffiths,1997). If projections about the demographic time bomb are correct, the first decade of the next millennium might be the golden age of the older worker, as organizations realize the true value of this human resource. Stress management activities will be necessary in ensuring that work is designed to minimize adverse impact on these employees. Worksite health promotion activities and training programmes will also help to optimize the full health and

productivity potential of this occupational group. However, the cultural barriers that currently exist to exclude older employees from job opportunities will need to be examined and addressed. These include both organizational policies and the attitudes of management. It is suggested that a stress audit can be adapted to address the issue of equality of opportunity in the workplace, with respect to the issue of ageism. This type of audit simply seeks to identify the barriers that exist, to prevent the individual developing their full career potential, and opportunities, by virtue of their age, gender, race or disability (Sutherland and Davidson, 1996). More details of this approach and method are described in the case study example provided in Chapter 6.

2. Whilst the potential to greatly improve communication between us exists, much of this electronic communications media, in the form of voice mail, email, video conferencing, internet links, interactive pagers and handheld organizers, can be potential sources of strain. This is known as 'technostress'. Rapid changing dimensions in modern technology will continue to bring dramatic changes to our work environment. For example, it is suggested that more and more of us will no longer be tied to a workplace. For some people, in certain jobs, the virtual workplace, in which employees operate remotely from each other, is already a reality. Technological developments have encouraged these changes and there is an urgent need to understand how we can optimize the performance, effectiveness and health of those individuals no longer under direct supervision in the work environment.

Nevertheless, it also means that employees, engaged in on site and off site working are now exposed to the pressures of electronic monitoring or computer-based monitoring. Issues surrounding this method of controlling employees and the impact of electronic monitoring are considered in Chapter 5. Meanwhile, we continue by examining the costs and consequences associated with the changing nature of the workplace.

The Changing Nature of the Workplace – Consequences and Costs

In the first part of this section we will review some the documented costs associated specifically with the impact of 'downsizing', 'mergers and acquisitions' and 'privatization'. In the last part of the chapter, the costs of mismanaged stress are presented. We firmly believe that organizations neither understand nor make enough effort to calculate the damaging costs of stress in the workplace. This part of the stress management process is vital for two main reasons. First, it is a key element of a 'diagnostic' phase in the process. It is essential that problem areas are *accurately* identified and that the potential impact of this is described in terms of business costs to the organization. Secondly, it is likely that the organization will require a budget for the implementation of an effective stress management programme that adopts an organizational approach. If the costs to the organization are well documented, the potential savings can be judged against the costs of the stress management activities. The North American experience has shown that stress management interventions ultimately provide cost savings for the organization (examples of the these will be provided in Chapter 7). However, they also require 'up front' expenditure before this investment benefit is realized. Thus, data on costs and cost savings are needed by those making a bid for funds since, in our experience, this type of activity tends not to be regarded as a priority in many organizations. This is because the organization has failed to understand and acknowledge the true costs to the business.

Downsizing

The rapid pace of change, fuelled by improved technology, has taken its toll in the form of downsizing in the workplace. The strain and burnout caused by the 'hot house' culture of the 1980s was also immensely costly to industry and society. It was estimated that mental illness was responsible for 80 million lost working days annually in Great Britain. This cost industry in excess of £3.7 billion (£3700 000 000). An additional 35 million days were lost through heart disease and strokes, which cost the average United Kingdom organization £2.5 million. Eight million days were lost through alcohol and drink related disease at an estimated cost of about £1.3 billion (£1300 000 000). In the UK, over ten per cent of gross national product was spent each year in coping with the manifestations of job generated stress (Cooper, Cooper and Eaker, 1988). Annually, the US industry lost 550 million working days due to absenteeism and it was estimated that 54 per cent of these absences were, in some way stress related (Elkin and Rosch, 1990).

Recent studies in the 1990s suggest that we are still paying a high price for the downsizing and changes to the nature of work. For example, the Health and Safety Executive's 1990 survey of self reported illness in England and Wales suggested that about 7500 employees missed work because of stress, caused or made worse by work. This cost British business more than £100 million. The impact of downsizing created a negative situation in one hospital environment. It was suggested that there were too many patients and too few nurses and this led to high levels of stress among hospital and community mental health nurses. The study, by Unison, of 500 members revealed that staff was struggling to maintain patient care standards in the face of constant organizational change. The main problems reported were the lack of facilities and resources, the high workload, the lack of time for planning and evaluating treatment, under staffing, a dangerous working environment, job insecurity and the awareness that patients were suffering because of the inadequate services. It is should be noted that 30 000 nurses left the profession in 1996 alone. In the face of strain and pressure an individual is likely to consider quitting as the only way of relieving these pressures (Mental Health Care: London, 1997 cited by Whitfield, 1997). Indeed, just one year later, in April 1988, Health and Safety Bulletin reported that a mental health trust had settled a widow's stress suicide claim. It was revealed that Richard Pocock, aged 50, worked as a mental health nurse in a UK hospital for over 20 years. In 1994 the NHS Trust told him that his ward was to close and he was forced to apply for another job within the trust. He worked for a few weeks in a managerial capacity for which he was unqualified and untrained. He struggled for a few weeks, telling his line manager that he was at his, 'wits end, useless and incompetent and with no choice but to run'. He found no support under what his union described as a 'vindictive, oppressive, ruthless and macho' style of management. Unable to cope any longer, he killed himself in January 1995. His widow claimed that the trust was negligent for failing to assess the risks to his health, particularly given its expertise in the field of mental health. It also failed to support him when his problems became apparent. It was accepted that Mr Pocock was a well-known member of staff, and that his deterioration under stress was obvious, and his suicide for foreseeable. A settlement of £25 000 was offered by the trust (which denied liability) and was accepted by the widow on behalf of the couple's three children (Health and Safety Bulletin, April 1998, p. 7).

Privatization

Other studies have examined specific changes in the nature of work due to privatization. One study on the effects of privatization observed that fear of unemployment was found to be linked to increased physical and psychological problems (Ferrie, 1997). The uncertainty created led to higher levels of longterm illness and an increased number of ill-health symptoms. This study was of 500 employees of the Property Services Agency (PSA), before and after privatization. The PSA is responsible for the design, building and maintenance of government offices and in 1992 became the first department to transfer to the private sector. Since this group of public sector employees was part of the Whitehall II project, data was available on a wide number of variables including blood pressure, ECG and cholesterol levels. In the run up to privatization most health variables deteriorated with body mass indices, cholesterol levels and ischaemia (restricted blood flow to the limbs). All of these rose above those of employees in other Whitehall departments. Two years after privatisation only 30 per cent of the original PSA sample were still working in the civil service and another 20 per cent had found work in the private sector. Half of those still employed perceived their jobs as insecure and reported psychological and physical health problems well above those who perceived themselves to be securely employed. Nelson and Cooper (1995) also observed some adverse impact resulting from privatization and reorganization within a regional water authority in Great Britain; 397 employees were surveyed on three occasions over a 20 month period. This was during the transition from a public to a private company and the reorganization that followed. For all three groups, namely, management, manual workers, and staff and administrative grade employees, job satisfaction levels systematically declined, and mental health symptoms and the incidence of psychosomatic symptoms of strain increased significantly in the period before and eight months after privatization of the organization. This decline was the greatest for those in the positions with the least amount of control and the highest levels of uncertainty, that is, the manual workers. The authors concluded

> ... privatization is a potentially stressful event for all concerned unless managed properly. Those who initiate the process may have staked their personal career on the successful outcome. Those responsible for managing and implementing the change process face an exhausting and often time-urgent challenge to make it work. However, for the vast majority of ordinary employees the adjustment and uncertainty that is often suddenly and unexpectedly thrust upon them are also likely to have adverse implications.

As Cartwright and Cooper (1992) suggest, for most of those affected, privatization will have been an unprecedented event in their lives. They are unlikely therefore to have developed any effective way of coping with the stress of the experience.

Mergers and acquisitions

Studies on the impact of mergers and acquisitions do not improve on this gloomy workplace situation. This type of major intraorganization change creates uncertainty and disequilibrium. A wide range of unproductive outcomes has been observed. These include lowered morale, job dissatisfaction, poor mental health, acts of sabotage and petty theft, absenteeism, and concomitant stress (Sinetar, 1981; Schweiger and Ivancevich 1985; Hall and Norburn, 1987; Cartwright and Cooper, 1993). These studies suggest that the stress-related physical and psychological health problems are likely to have a negative effect on the performance of a substantial number of employees continuing up to six months (Ashford, 1988) and even four years (Cooper and Payne, 1988) after the initial transition. One study of 166 employees involved in a cross section of 'friendly' or uncontested acquisitions, found that merger stress was caused by the uncertainty that prevailed and concerns about immediate merger-related issues. These included loss of identity, lack of information, fear of job loss, the departure of key personnel and colleagues and family repercussions (Schweiger, Ivancevich and Power, 1987). It is suggested that a lack of compatibility or fit between two merging cultures, the culture shock can result in poor person-environment fit and thereby have an adverse impact on job performance. Unmet expectations or cultural incongruity can result in both job dissatisfaction and distress. Different types of cultures imbue different values, attitudes and styles of management and work. If the merging cultures differ, ultimately one of them will tend to dominate and will thus cause strain and pressure for the work force and consequences for both individuals and the organizational merger outcomes. Thus exposure to merger or acquisition activity is a major and significant life event for most employees in the organizations involved. Handy (1985) suggests that when an organization ceases to exist or is fundamentally changed, the psychological contract that binds the individual to his or her organization is broken or becomes unclear. This contract has to be re-established or negotiated. Often, the psychological response to the news that their organization has been taken over, or merged with another, has been compared with the sense of loss experienced following bereavement of a close friend or relative (Schweiger, Ivancevich and Power, 1987; Marks, 1988). Employee reactions may, therefore, be expressed as a typical model of bereavement. First is the stage of disbelief and denial, followed by anger and resentment. Stage three in the cycle is where emotional bargaining begins with anger and ends up as depression. Finally, in stage four of the process, comes an acceptance of the changes brought to their lives. It is possible that fixation at any of stages one, two or three, will result in unproductive behaviour, or cause the employees to terminate their employment with the company. Schweiger and Ivancevich (1985) suggest that as stress arises more from the perceptions which employees hold about the likely changes themselves, the presentation of realistic merger previews (rather like realistic job previews) in the early stages of the process, are likely to avoid some of the negative impact of this major life-event change. Since exposure to stress often distorts communication at a time when demand for information is at its highest it is crucial that attention is paid to the distribution of information about the proposed changes. The axiom, 'a lie is half-way around the world before truth has got its boots on', is particularly worth remembering at this time. Communication in more than one medium is essential and the policy of, 'say what you are going to say, say it, and say it again' seems to be a useful strategy. This, of course, should be combined with opportunities for employees and management, at all levels, to be engaged in interactive 'question and answer' sessions. The human and financial costs of stress are generally well documented, but have been little considered in accounting for merger and acquisition failures. As research evidence continues to mount, organizations should begin to acknowledge that there are costs associated with the psychological impact of this type of business activity. It is to be hoped that they will include this as one of the factors in their business planning activities.

Changing patterns of employment

As more and more private sector companies have become publicly owned this has increased our appetite for the privatization of the public sector, and this has become manifest as 'outsourcing' and 'market testing'. Within the work environment we now have people working in a freelance capacity, or employed as part of a contract labour force. They work one of a variety of contracts, including very short-term contracts or 'zero-hours' arrangements. Employers refer to this as 'the flexible workforce' but in reality it means part time working for more and more people. In fact, from 1984 to 1994 the number of men working part time has doubled. Also, the number of people employed by firms of more than 500 employees has slumped to just over a third of the employed population. One in eight British workers is now self employed. Therefore, the need to have a 'portfolio of jobs' is just part of the means of earning a reasonable living! If employers increasingly recruit flexible workers, the likelihood is that more women will be employed, and will continue to displace men as the main breadwinner. Many women, have throughout their careers worked part time or on short term contract, whereas men have not. In 1984 there were more than four million women in part time work, but only 570 000 men. By 1994, there were five million women and 990 000 men in part time work. With two out of three families two-earner or dual career, the problem of who plays what role in the family and the conflicts surrounding work and domestic space, will upset an already delicate work-home balance.

We do not yet know the full impact of these changes in patterns of employment and some may ultimately be for the common good. However, there is some evidence to suggest that there is cause for concern about the quality of our working life. Worrall and Cooper (1997) are currently conducting a five-year longitudinal survey on the quality of working life among 5000 managers in the UK. Preliminary results show organizations to be in a state of constant change. It appears that 61 per cent of this national sample of managers have undergone a major restructuring over the previous 12 months. The consequences of these changes, among this group who are supposedly in control of events (and possibly driving the changes per se), were increased job insecurity, lowered morale and the erosion of loyalty and motivation. The changes reported included downsizing, delayering, outsourcing and cost reduction and did yield the expected increases in profitability and productivity. In negative terms, decision making was seen to be slower, and the organization was deemed to have lost the right mix of human resource skills and experience in the change process. Hours of working for this group also increased. It was found that 82 per cent of the managers surveyed regularly worked more than 40 hours a week; 38 per cent reported working in excess of 50 hours a week, and 41 per cent always, or often, worked at weekends. Poor communications and concern about future employability were the reasons for managers' insecurity. Sixty per cent stated that they felt 'in the dark' about the future of their organization's future strategies (Worrall and Cooper, 1997). It is suggested that, in the future, the trend will be for organizations to retain only a small core of full time, permanent employees who will work from a conventional office. The remainder of the skills needed are bought in on a contract basis. This comes either from individuals working at home and linked to the company by computers and modems, or by hiring people on short term contracts to do specific jobs or projects (Cooper and Jackson, 1997).

Job satisfaction

The rapidity of change in the workplace has taken its toll in many ways. For example, an Institute of Social Research (ISR) survey of 400 companies, in 17 countries, including eight million workers throughout Europe, found employee satisfaction levels in the UK dropped from 64 per cent in 1985 to 53 per cent by 1995. This was the biggest drop of any European country. For example, in the Netherlands a drop in satisfaction levels, in the ten year period was from 70 to 64 per cent; while in Germany it went from 67 to 61 per cent. Only in Switzerland did satisfaction levels increase during this period; from 65 to 69 per cent. The impact of downsizing and the rapidity of change also had effects on the family. More and more two earner families and couples emerged in a climate that was anything but 'family friendly'(Cooper, 1998). As unemployment levels increased, so did the divorce rate, and by 1991, the United Kingdom had the highest divorce rate in Europe, with over 171 000 divorces. Indeed, the proportion of people living in a one-parent family increased four fold between 1961 and 1991. In addition to the instability of the workplace, job insecurity (and unemployment for many), one other factor emerged as a detrimental factor to family and home life, namely, the need to *work long hours*. A survey, in 1995, reported that 25 per cent of British male employees worked more than 48 hours a week; one fifth of manual workers worked more than 50 hours; and one in eight managers worked more than 60 hours per week. Thus, organizations had 'downsized' and people were expected to work harder and for more hours each week.

Sickness absence

Job absence rates also rose in Great Britain during much of this decade and reached an all time high cost of £12 billion (£12 000 000 000) in 1996 (Confederation of British Industry, 1997). On average this sickness absence cost was equal to £533 business lost for every employee. The survey, which covered 691 organizations with a combined workforce of over 1.5 million people (that is, almost 7 per cent of the workforce) indicated that 187 million days were lost in 1996. On average, 8.4 working days were taken as sick leave by every employee and this represented 3.7 per cent of total working time in 1996 lost due to sickness. Sickness rates in the public sector were higher than for those in the private sector, and were respectively 10.2 and 7.3 days absent per year. On a regional basis, sickness absence for full time manual employees was lowest among firms in the South (6.5 days lost per employee), South East (8.5 days), and Wales

(8.8 days), and highest among firms in Northern Ireland (15.7 days), Great London (13.8 days), and the North West (12.6 days). For full time non-manual workers, absence was lowest in the North (4.0 days), South (6.2 days) and East Anglia (7.6 days), and highest in the South West (11 days), North West (9.5 days) and South East, Yorkshire and Humberside and East Midlands (9.3 days). The survey also showed that the majority of time off on sick leave was due to illness and 98 per cent of organizations said that most sickness absence was genuine. Taking time off for family responsibilities was the second most significant reason for absence.

This survey, jointly sponsored by BUPA and the MCG Consulting Group, prompted Dr David Constain, BUPA's assistant medical director to state,

> We are not surprised by the results of this survey. We work with a number of companies on workplace health programmes and these findings confirm BUPA's experience that very few of them have a comprehensive strategy for health. Companies need to improve their understanding of the cost implications of sickness absence and start to set themselves achievable targets for workplace health.

Likewise, Derek Burn, of MCG Consulting stated,

> Employees are too often considered to be an expendable resource. The increase in absenteeism reported among non-manual staff often arises from low morale and motivation, largely caused by uncertainty over job security and lack of investment in staff development. More organizations should view their staff as valuable assets. In organizations where the work-force is highly motivated, absenteeism can be as low as 1 or 2 per cent. Some enlightened employers are starting to recognise the value of the knowledge economy. This views people and the skills they have as an asset requiring investment that forms an important part of the capital of the business.

The CBI suggest that to cut the costs of sickness absence firms need to encourage their management to take a more active role in managing workplace attendance. This responsibility should be given to first line managers. The introduction of family friendly policies such as flexible leave, childcare support, and term time working may also help to reduce absenteeism.

The main causes of absence on sick notes (1996) compared to managers' opinions on the reason for the absence (reported by The Industrial Society – cited Personnel Today, 1997) were as shown in Table 1.2.

A study by the European Foundation for the Improvement of Living and

Table 1.2

Cause of Absence	Percentage: Recorded on the sick note	Percentage: In the Managers' opinion
Colds/Flu	93	64
Stomach upsets/ food poisoning	76	32
Headaches/migraines	59	22
Back problems	46	19
Stress/emotional problems/personal problems	43	52
Monday morning blues	2	32
Sickness of other family members/child-care problems	19	35

(Source: The Industrial Society, 1997 – cited Personnel Today, 1997)

Working Conditions (1997) provided a more detailed picture about sickness absence and the health of the workforce. This study, conducted in 1996, among the working population of the European Union (15 member states), surveyed 15 800 workers from all over Europe. They were questioned simultaneously about their working conditions and the sample is representative of both employed and self employed people. The findings highlight how pollution, noise, stress and musculo-skeletal disorders are among the rising occupational hazards in the EU. Specifically, the key findings were:

- the most common work-related health problems were:
  – back pain – 30 per cent of workers
  – stress – 28 per cent of workers
  – muscular pains in arms and legs – 17 per cent of workers;
- health problems were most often connected with poor working conditions;
- absenteeism due to work-related health problems affected 23 per cent of workers each year. This averaged out at four working days lost per worker; for the EU as a whole this represented 600 million days lost per year;
- the pace of work increased all the time. In 1996 more than half of workers were exposed to working at high speeds and deadlines that were too tight. Work was largely dominated by external constraints and the client had replaced the machine as the main factor dictating the pace of work;

- repetitive and monotonous work was still very common; 37 per cent of workers performed short repetitive tasks and 45 per cent performed monotonous tasks; repetitive work often went hand in hand with working at high speed; 49 per cent of workers with repetitive tasks were also required to work constantly at high speeds;
- 28 per cent of workers were exposed to intense noise and 45 per cent were exposed to painful or tiring working positions; more than half had no personal control over comfort factors at their workplace;
- only 32 per cent of employees had training provided by their company in the previous twelve months;
- the main feature of the organization of working time was its dispersion, that is, irregular hours, weekend work and night working;
- 49 per cent of workers worked more than 40 hours per week; 23 per cent worked more than 45 hours); health problems (backache and stress) increased with hours worked; 14 per cent of workers (mostly women) worked fewer than 30 hours per week;
- computers have become an important feature of the workplace and 38 per cent of workers used computers as part of their job;
- workers were gradually being given more autonomy over their work. Between 1991 and 1996, the percentage of workers with a measure of autonomy over their own pace of work increased from 64 to 72 per cent. This still means that 28 per cent of all workers (and 32 per cent of employees) have no personal control over their pace of work (these are mainly blue collar workers in manufacturing and workers in transport and hotel and catering sectors of industry);
- 9 per cent of workers claimed to have been subjected to intimidation at work (psychological violence), whereas 4 per cent of the workforce reported physical violence (that is, 6 million workers); 2 per cent (or three million workers) were subjected to sexual violence; thus violence in the workplace was not a marginal phenomenon. This finding was confirmed by a 1996 study in Great Britain by the British Retail Consortium (BRC). Their latest retail crime survey showed that the number of attacks increased by 4000 to 13 000 in the year to April 1997. Staff working in retail chemists faced the highest risk of violence during robberies (34 incidents per 1000 staff) compared to off-licence staff (26 per 1000 staff). Petrol retailing was the third riskiest sector with 24 attacks per 1000 employees (BRC, 1997).

Against such a background of mounting research evidence, clearly stress has a dysfunctional impact on both organizational and individual outcomes. Links have been demonstrated between exposure to mismanaged stress and:

- Ill health, causing sickness absence, early retirement or premature death, as a result of coronary heart disease, certain forms of cancer, mental breakdown, depression, anxiety; and delayed recovery from illnesses. There are many risk factors for cardiovascular disease, for example hypertension, high cholesterol levels, cigarette smoking or obesity. Research into occupational health suggests that the work environment can adversely affect cardiovascular health. In addition to exposure to the chemical aspects of unhealthy workplaces, it is also suggested that high levels of noise at work, long standing shift work (including night and early morning shifts) and sedentary work can adversely affect cardiovascular health (Siegrist, 1997). Whilst there are real, humanistic concerns about these problems, it should also be kept in mind that the financial burden of illness, early retirement or death is costly to industry, the business world and society. In addition, the costs of replacing staff are high. It is estimated, for example that over $700 million per year is spent by US employers, to replace the 200 000 men, aged 45–65 years, who die or are incapacitated by coronary heart disease (Cooper, 1985);
- poor health behaviours including alcohol and drug abuse problems (including cigarette smoking), bad dietary habits, such as bingeing, crash dieting or bulimia; and lack of exercise;
- increased vulnerability to accidents and delayed recovery from accidents;
- job dissatisfaction;
- poor job performance and productivity and the dysfunctional impact of presenteeism (where employees are not really fit enough to be at work, but fear the consequences of being absent);
- unsatisfactory employee relations;
- ineffective management or style of leadership;
- high labour turnover;
- increased claims for compensation and increased insurance premiums; in America the high costs of employee health care have caused individual insurance premiums to rise by more than 50 per cent in the past twenty years. In the same period (1974–94), the employer's contribution has increased by over 140 per cent (Cooper, 1985).

Finally, last but not least, the issue of:

- stress litigation costs.

Before we address the issues surrounding stress and the litigation process in Chapter 2, it is worth listing the deleterious and costly behaviours that manifest in response to stress in the workplace. Employees under stress are more likely to:

- arrive late to work and/or take an early departure;
- take extended lunch, coffee and tea breaks;
- make more errors, resulting in the need to redo work; due to slow and poor decision making, poor concentration or impaired judgement;
- have more rejects in quality inspection;
- have increased equipment breakdowns that are sometimes the result of sabotage;
- miss deadlines;
- have accidents at work; more work-related travel accidents (that is, road traffic incidents that cause damage to vehicles and injuries to employees);
- engage in petty theft;
- interpersonal conflict with other people at work; this includes petty bickering and the creation of a climate of unsubstantiated, time wasting rumours and mistrust at all levels;
- be moved around as a result of departmental transfers. For example, a manager might try to get rid of the 'stressed' employee, before they become a serious and potentially costly problem, by transferring them to another 'unsuspecting' manager or colleague;
- be less innovative and creative.

It is clear, that the overall cost of mismanaged stress to organizations, individuals and society itself is immense. Therefore, the potential rewards for effective stress management in the workplace are also very high in both humanistic and business terms.

Structure of the Book

In Chapter 2 we consider issues surrounding the stress litigation process in the workplace. That chapter includes the implications for employer's liability insurance and the requirements for health and wellbeing standards at work. In addition to the health and safety consequences for public and private sector organizations, the potentially high and damaging costs of stress litigation are, and should be, a serious cause for concern for human resource professionals, in their role of preventing and treating stress at work.

In Chapter 3 the nature of stress is examined, whereas in Chapter 4, 'hot spot' stressors experienced by specific occupational groups are considered. In Chapter 5 the issue of rapid technological development and change is considered, in addition to the topic of computer-based work monitoring, as potential sources of stress at work.

Chapter 6 provides guidance on how to conduct a stress audit and includes examples of three case studies of psychological risk assessments. Finally, in Chapter 7 , options for the management of stress are described, with examples of each type of intervention, their effectiveness and potential weaknesses.

Stress and the Law

The current cause for agitation and concern among employers and their insurers is the possibility of workplace personal injury claims being initiated. This can happen when the employee suffers a breakdown in health, caused by continual stress at work, over a long period of time (Buckingham, 1992; Lapper, 1994). In the USA 'cumulative stress trauma' cases are common and in the 1980s these cases tripled (Karasek and Theorell, 1990). Although the Worker's Compensation Scheme in the USA differs from the compensation system in the UK, there are indications that litigation based on cumulative trauma or chronic stress will become a significant issue in UK law.

Statute and common law require employers to uphold a duty of care, and to ensure, so far as is reasonable and practicable, the health, safety and welfare of their employees. The employer must not by act or omission conduct himself in a way that would cause injury to the employee. If this duty of care is breached and an employee suffers foreseeable damage in the form of personal injury, then the employee may sue the employer in a tort of negligence (that is, a civil wrong as opposed to a criminal offence), in order to obtain compensation for the loss sustained. In the following sections we describe three different cases. The first, *Johnstone v. Bloomsbury Area Health Authority*, was eventually settled prior to trial after much media attention. The next case went to court and established the law on stress-related injury. This was the case of *Walker v. Northumberland County Council*, in 1994. Ultimately an out-of-court settlement of £175 000 was made with no admission of liability by the defendant. Recently, a third case made legal history when a former council housing officer was awarded £67 000 compensation for stress at work. Birmingham City Council admitted liability for the illness that led Beverley Lancaster to retire early on medical grounds (Johnstone, 1999).

Johnstone v. Bloomsbury Area Health Authority

The case of *Johnstone v. Bloomsbury Area Health Authority* (IRLR 118, 1991) was the first such reported case. Dr Chris Johnstone was employed as a senior house officer and claimed that the job required him to work excessively long hours that could exceed 88 hours in some weeks. Thus, he claimed, his employer was acting in breach of contract of their duty of care. Therefore, this case raised the question of whether the individual could be obliged contractually to work so many hours in excess of his standard working week as foreseeably would injure his health, and thus be contrary to the implied duty of care to provide a safe system of work. According to Dr Johnstone, exposure to long hours of working led to his symptoms of depression, stress, and even being physically sick from exhaustion. He had difficulties sleeping and eating and claimed to frequently experience suicidal feelings. Things came to a head when he fell asleep at the wheel of his car and drove into a tree when on holiday, following a 110 hour working week. He was not injured but he returned to work, resigned from his job and brought a case against his employer. In the end, and at the eleventh hour, this case was settled prior to trial. Dr Johnstone settled out of court for compensation from his employer. He received the 'token' sum of £5500 plus costs. Thus, the precise contractual position of this remains unclear. However, it can be said that it is unlikely the court will uphold a clause of a worker's contract. It means that employees are effectively exposed to a system of work that will cause them or others a potentially serious injury or illness (Buchan, 1996).

Walker v. Northumberland County Council

A considerable amount of publicity also surrounded the first real case of 'stress litigation' which successfully went to trial. It seems appropriate to describe the background to this judgment and the outcome as a means understanding this complex scenario. In *Walker v. Northumberland County Council*, the High Court held the employer liable for the psychiatric damage suffered by a fifty-year-old employee, after it failed to take reasonable steps to avert a second nervous breakdown suffered by the individual. Mr John Walker was employed as an area social services officer for Northumberland County council from 1970 until 1988, and dealt with child care cases, particularly child abuse allegations. This was a middle management position and Mr Walker was responsible for one of five divisions, which during the 1980s witnessed a considerable increase in population. The resulting number of referrals and cases were not matched by an increase in the number of field social workers. From 1985, John Walker and his colleagues had tried to persuade their superiors of the need to restructure in the absence of increased resources. Towards the end of 1985, Mr Walker expressed his concerns and said that he could not continue to shoulder the same workload. Whilst his supervisor was sympathetic, the requests for a transfer or the splitting of the division into two separate management areas were rejected. The pressure of work continued to grow and Mr Walker tried to do some reorganizing of his own. However, an experienced team leader was moved away from the area, and replaced after some delay with only a part time member of staff as cover. Requests for staff overtime payments were refused. The supervisor suggested that the best way to handle the situation was by, 'all of your team leaders and, if necessary, yourself, mucking in together, until a replacement was appointed'. John Walker had a nervous breakdown in November 1986.

On medical advice he stayed away from work until 4 March 1987. However, his psychiatrist had advised him not to return to his former level of responsibility and this issue was discussed with his supervisor prior to his return to work. Again, sympathy was offered, but the expectation was that he should return to his old job. The issue of splitting the division arose and again it was rejected. The provision and assistance of another senior officer proved to be only a temporary and short lived secondment of one month. Weekly visits by his boss and the promised help in chairing case conferences did not materialize. It took Mr Walker until May to clear the paperwork backlog and meanwhile the number of pending cases continued to rise. Symptoms of stress returned and on 8 September 1987 he told his supervisor that he could not continue; he was having to postpone urgent work and was concerned that his judgement was impaired. On 16 September, on medical advice he took sick leave, having been diagnosed as suffering from stress-related anxiety. He suffered a second mental breakdown and in February 1988 he retired from his post for reasons of permanent ill health.

John Walker sued his employer for damages for the psychiatric ill health he had suffered. In court it was stated that he had, in effect, been severely mentally wounded and rendered incapable of ever returning to the work that had been his career for 20 years. He was, thereafter, unable to be employed in a job that required him to take the burden of responsibility and suffered permanent damage to his self-confidence. Mr Walker's case was that his immediate superiors knew that social work is particularly stressful and could give rise to mental illness. His growing workload was such that they ought reasonably to have foreseen that, unless steps were taken to alleviate these pressures, there was a real risk of mental illness. Whilst the employer accepted that it should have provided a safe system of work to protect Mr Walker from foreseeable risks, subject to practicability, they argued that it was not in breach of duty. It was NOT reasonably foreseeable that the work would be so stressful as to cause a significant risk of mental illness. The court found that the supervisor knew that John Walker had a very difficult management position, was a very conscientious worker, and under considerable pressure and stress, and was expecting reorganization. The nature of this work was identified as 'stressful' by the court.

However, the issues of 'foreseeability' and 'causation' need further expansion. The court considered the issue of 'reasonableness' and stated that an employer's duty calls for no more than a reasonable response. This would be judged on the nature of the employer-employee relationship, the risk of a reasonably foreseeable injury occurring, the seriousness of an injury, and the cost and practicality of averting the risk (taking into account the employers' resources and facilities). It was concluded that the consequences of an injury to Mr Walker were serious, and there was clearly some risk that a breakdown might occur as a result of his work. What was questionable was the size of that foreseeable risk. There was no evidence that social services area officers with heavy workloads or others in middle management were especially vulnerable to stress related illness. Thus, the court had to decide if Mr Walker was exposed to any greater risk than his peers and should his employer have been alerted to the fact prior to his first breakdown? The court was not persuaded that the employer (or superior) ought to have realized that this employee was at significantly greater risk of stress-induced mental illness. The council could not have reasonably foreseen that, prior to his breakdown in 1986, Mr Walker was exposed to a significant risk of mental illness. Yet, the court believed that if he was again exposed to the same workload as in 1986, there was a risk that he would succumb to further illness, which would have been likely to end his career as an area manager and in social services. Thus, by April 1987, the court believed that it was established that Mr Walker was exposed in his job to a reasonably foreseeable risk to his mental health. This was significantly greater than that anticipated in the ordinary course of an area officer's job. When he returned to his job after his first illness, the council had to decide whether to continue to employ him, even though he made it clear that he needed some assistance. They continued to employ him but had provided no effective help. This action was unreasonable and so the council was in breach of its duty of care (HSE, 1995).

Lancaster v. Birmingham City Council

Beverly Lancaster started working for Birmingham City Council in 1971 as a junior clerk. By 1978 she was employed as a senior draughtsman in the architecture department and supervized ten members of staff. Following the birth of her first child she changed to a part time working, job share arrangement. Following various organizational restructuring initiatives and job changes, Mrs Lancaster finally ended working as a housing officer where she had to deal with 'rude and demanding' council tenants (Johnstone, 1999). Mrs Lancaster began to suffer panic attacks, anxiety and depression, for which she received medical help. She retired from work and claimed that her health had suffered due to the council's negligence. They had failed to assess her ability to do the job in the housing department and she had not received the training necessary to do the work of a housing officer. Clearly, she also experienced severe work overload conditions and felt unable to meet the demands placed upon her. Birmingham City Council admitted liability for the illness that led Beverley Lancaster, aged 44 years, to retire early, on medical grounds. The £67 000 compensation payment, awarded by a county court judge, covered the loss of wages, loss of future earnings and the costs of prescription charges. Mrs Lancaster claimed that the work conditions caused her ill health and damage to her self-esteem. This would limit her chances of finding satisfactory employment in the future.

Common Law Liability – Negligence

An employer, therefore, has to address three basic questions before being in a position to decide whether it has been negligent towards an employee (DLA, 1999).

1. Is a duty of care owed towards the employee and what is that duty of care?

   A duty of care exists where one ought to exist by virtue of the relationship between the parties. A duty of care always exists in the employer and employee environment where one person has control over the other. The position at common law in the tort of negligence is that an employer owes a general duty towards all employees, to take reasonable care so as to avoid injury, disease and death occurring at work. An employer's actions are judged in accordance with the standard of the reasonable man or the 'ordinary prudent employer'. Therefore, the employer must be able to foresee the existence of a risk to the employee. Also, they must be able to assess the magnitude of that risk in terms of the seriousness of an injury, and the likelihood of the injury occurring. Finally, the employer must take reasonable steps and precautions so as to prevent the injury happening.

2. Has a breach in the duty of care occurred?

3. Did damage, injury or loss result from or was it caused by that breach in the duty of care?

So, in the John Walker case, whilst the first breakdown may not have been foreseeable it would be difficult to argue that the second breakdown could not have been foreseen. It is important to acknowledge that Mr Walker was a fairly normal person. He did not work long hours; he did not have pressures outside work that might have led to a breakdown; and he did not have a personality that might have rendered him more vulnerable to a stressful work environment. Even so, it remains that the employee must prove that the employer has been negligent, and that on the balance of probability an injury was caused by the conditions at work. Indeed, in relation to the issue of causation, a breach of duty must materially contribute to the injury. In Mr Walker's case there is no evidence to suggest that home pressures contributed to his mental breakdown. Social worker, John Walker was paid £175 000 in damages after his protracted legal battle. The High Court ruled that his employer was responsible for causing a nervous breakdown, brought on by stress and his 'impossible workload'.

A Successful Personal Injury Claim

It is suggested that there are four crucial issues that will determine the extent to which stress at work will give rise to a successful personal injury claim (Earnshaw and Cooper, 1994).

1. Can the employee establish that he or she has suffered a stress-induced illness? Medical disagreement exists about conditions such as upper limb disorder, or repetitive strain injury (RSI) as it is commonly described, and myalgic encephalomyelitis (ME), or post-viral fatigue syndrome. This indicates that it is not a straightforward matter. Whilst it is accepted that exposure to stress can cause changes in behaviour in

the form of moodiness, aggression and irritability, and that it can lead to, or be a contributory factor in illness such as ulcers, migraines, heart disease and certain cancers, non-stress triggers of such conditions do exist. In personal injury, stress is not an illness nor is it compensatable as such. Stress is a cause, of for example, 'psychiatric illness', which is a personal injury. Therefore, in personal injury claims based on stress, it will be necessary to establish that a plaintiff has suffered a recognized stress-related illness such as a nervous breakdown, an eating disorder, or irritable bowel syndrome. The allegation that the individual is suffering from 'stress' will not be sufficient. Psychiatric illness will embrace all forms of mental illness, neurosis and personality change, but there is no need for the victim to have suffered physical harm as well as psychiatric harm. Where the victim is the participant in an incident and not merely a witness, the defendant has to take the victim as he finds him. That is, the principle of 'eggshell personality' applies equally with the 'eggshell skull' principle.

2. Can it be shown that there is link between the alleged stressful workplace condition and the behavioural change or illness that is manifest? For example, a heart attack can be the consequence of some circumstance unrelated to the workplace, such as smoking, diet, Type A personality or hereditary factors, rather than the result of workplace stress. The courts will face difficult decisions if it is revealed that the plaintiff has financial problems, difficult personal relationships outside work, or problems in trying to balance the demands of home life (child care, elder care, and so on) while dealing with a stressful job at work. In the case of John Walker, the court ruled that this individual did not have such problems and that his mental breakdown was due solely to the pressures and strains of his job. Not many people would be able to present and hold up for close examination a stress-free private life, which would then be under the scrutiny and judgment of the court. This issue of causation will lead to questions in the witness box about an employee's private life and family background. It is an experience that is likely to be distasteful and distressing. If this questioning becomes a recognized feature of stress litigation, it could well deter potential litigants, in the same way that rape victims have become reluctant to pursue cases against their attackers (Earnshaw and Cooper 1994).

3. For an employee to succeed in a negligence case against an employer, it must be shown that the damage suffered by the employee was foreseeable, and foreseeability must be established in each case. So, it

must be shown that the employer could foresee a stress-based illness. As research evidence mounts up, the sources and consequences of stress in certain jobs will become documented and given publicity. However, the Health and Safety Executive (HSE) have now produced a research report (Cox, 1993), and guidelines for employers (HSE, 1995). These urge that stress at work should be recognized officially as a health and safety issue. These documents identify the causes of stress at work and make recommendations for action. Therefore, it seems likely that employers in the future will find it more difficult to argue that they could not foresee that an employee in a given job would suffer from stress. The case of *Petch v. Customs and Excise Commission* (ICR 789, 1993) shows how a plaintiff may fail to meet the requirement of 'foreseeability'. Mr Petch was an Assistant Secretary in the Civil Service and suffered a mental breakdown in October 1974. The judge found that this man was, in fact, a manic depressive, and on the issue of causation he stated,

There were undoubtedly two causes for his breakdown in October of 1974; one was his basic personality, which was that of manic depressive, and the other was undoubtedly the pressure of work, both in the load that he carried and also in the nature of the conflict of personalities which produced his breakdown. I do not think that any fair-minded person looking at this case would come to the conclusion that the plaintiff might have suffered that breakdown, even if not subjected to the undoubtedly heavy pressures which were laid on him.

However, the judge went on to find that until his breakdown the plaintiff, '... showed himself not only able to cope with the existing workload but enthusiastic to take on more... It seems to me that the plaintiff revelled in his work and enjoyed every minute of it'. Witnesses testified that Mr Petch was the last person they would have expected to break down under the pressure of work. The judge held that unless senior management was, or ought to have been, aware that this employee was showing signs of impending breakdown, or that a high workload carried a real risk that he would suffer such a breakdown, they were not negligent in failing to avert it. Thus, the plaintiff's breakdown was *not* foreseeable.

4. What should a reasonable employer do to satisfy the duty of care? There are three kinds of statutory duty and these describe the extent to which an employer can give more weight to some duties than others:

(a) Absolute duty – duties are made absolute where the risk of injury is inevitable and safety precautions are not taken. Such a requirement has been enforced even when employers have shown that the action would make the task incapable of being conducted.

(b) Practicable – carrying out a statutory duty so far as it is 'practicable' means that it must be carried out if, in the light of current knowledge, technology and invention, it is feasible, even if it is difficult, costly or inconvenient.

(c) Reasonably practicable – a less strict duty in that it involves a cost/benefit analysis and trade-off. Thus it is a matter of 'balance'. If the benefits to be gained are minimal compared to the costs of achieving them, the employer may be able to take the risk of not taking any action. Any decision to take a risk should be informed on. Indeed employers will need to keep up to date with official health and safety requirements in order to ensure that their actions remain within the law.

Section 2 of the Health and Safety at Work Act 1974 (HSAW) sets out the general duty of ensuring health, safety and welfare at work, namely,

- to provide and maintain a safe plant and safe systems of work,
- to make arrangements for the safe handling, use, storage and transport of articles and substances,
- to provide information, instruction, training and supervision to ensure health and safety,
- to maintain the place of work and the means of access and egress in a safe manner,
- to provide and maintain a working environment which is safe and without risk to health, and adequate facilities and arrangements for the welfare of employees.

All these requirements are subject to this 'reasonably practicable' provision outlined above and so require an employer to balance the costs and benefits to be gained. However, we should also acknowledge that there is always the possibility of there being nothing, or nothing as yet known, which the employer could have reasonably done. This was the case for *Mughal v. Reuters Limited* (IRLR 571, 1993). Mr Mughal was a journalist employed by Reuters Limited, who claimed against his employer on being diagnosed as suffering from repetitive strain injury (RSI). In addition to stating that, 'Repetitive strain injury had no place in the medical books... it has no pathology and no clinical symptoms that can be pointed to as confirming that a patient is suffering from it', Judge Prosser also commented, that in any event there had been no breach of duty by the defendants in the arrangements made for keyboard operators. It was his belief that, since there was no one correct method of sitting or posture, employers could do little more than provide British Standard equipment, and then leave individual operators to find the position most comfortable for them. It should, however, be noted that Judge Prosser was heavily criticized for his judgment in this instance and, indeed, other cases of RSI have subsequently been awarded compensation because this injury has been acknowledged as a stress-related injury.

Managing Stress – Complying with Health and Safety Law

Although there is no single piece of legislation that requires employers specifically to prevent stress or regarding the management of stress at work, the following legal framework describes an employer's legal responsibilities:

1. By the Health and Safety at Work Act 1974, section 2(1) employers are required to ensure the health, safety and welfare at work of their employees, so far as is reasonably practicable.

2. Under section 2(6) of the Health and Safety at Work Act 1974 and under regulation 4A of the Safety Representatives and Safety Committees Regulations 1977, employers have a duty to consult trade union safety representatives in good time about health and safety matters. This includes the introduction of any measure that may substantially affect members' health and safety, and about the health and safety consequences of the planning and introduction of new technologies into the workplace.

3. European Directive 1992, The Six Pack – The Framework Directive, which states that member states are required to introduce parallel legislation into domestic law. It states, 'Health and safety is an objective which should not be subordinated to purely economic considerations'. This movement means a major change in the way in which employers are required to manage health and safety issues. These regulations envisage the employer adopting a proactive approach to health and safety, rather than investigation after complaints are made or 'something happens' and harm is caused to an employee.

Thus, the Management of Health and Safety at Work Regulations 1992, provide:

– Regulation 3 requires every employer to make a 'suitable and sufficient' assessment of the risk to health and safety of its employees... for the purposes of identifying the measures he needs to take to comply with the requirements and prohibitions imposed upon him by or under the 'relevant statutory provision';

– Regulation 5: 'Every employer shall ensure that its employees are provided with health surveillance as is appropriate having regard to the risks of their health and safety that are identified by the assessment.'

The occupational health principles to be applied are set out in the Approved Code of Practice to the Regulations. It includes adapting work to the individual, especially as regards the design of workplaces, the choice of work equipment, and the choice of working and production methods. Employers should have a coherent policy that considers the way work is to be organized, working conditions, the working environment and any relevant social factors. Although it is not explicitly stated, the duty to protect health should be taken as referring to physical and mental health. When identifying hazards in the workplace, the employer should include potential causes of stress such as anxiety and psychosocial hazards.

– Regulation 11 requires employers to consider the capabilities of their employees as regards health and safety before entrusting tasks to them. This involves consideration of an individual's ability to undertake the job and that the demands of the job do not put the employee at risk.

4. Regulation 2 of the Health and Safety (Display Screen Equipment) Regulations 1992 requires employers to analyse DSE workstations and assess the health and safety risks to users. The principal risks involved, according to the accompanying HSE Guidance to the Regulations, include mental stress.

Following the *Walker* decision there was consternation that the 'flood gates' would open and employees would rush to bring claims against their employers. Whilst it was seen initially as a victory for employees, it is clear that stress cases can be won, but it is not easy to do so. Compensation will be awarded if a risk to injury was established and nothing had been done to reduce or eliminate that risk. Employees will need to have evidence of risk that puts an employer on notice of that risk. Once the employer is sufficiently aware of a problem, they are under an obligation to respond in order to protect the employee. If an employer responds and takes the necessary steps it is unlikely that the employee will have a claim in damages because the employer will have taken reasonable steps to avoid a breach of the duty of care. Nevertheless, evidence of risk might be obtained from medical records that indicate that an employee has a medical history of vulnerability to stress. A plaintiff has to show that 'he or she was at materially greater risk of stress induced mental illness ... (than a normal ... would be)'. The defendant will, of course, try to show that the plaintiff's personality is relevant (as in the case of *Petch v Customs and Excise Commission*) and that people have a different capacity to absorb stress. Even if the employer fails to take necessary steps the employee may still be without compensation unless it can be shown that the employer knew or ought to have known of the particular risks of the individual developing a recognized psychiatric illness.

Certain existing company documentation such as personal files, appraisal records or sickness absence data might be helpful to indicate evidence of risk that should put an employer on alert. However, as we have stated, to win a stress case, the issues of foreseeability and causation must be proved in each case presented. Questions that will be asked are likely to include:

1. Was the employer aware of key documents on stress, for example, HSE reports?

2. Was a risk assessment conducted?

3. What internal procedures and monitoring processes are in place to deal with stress?

4. Is there an adequate health record system?

5. Details about manning and training records, job descriptions, and the resourcing of jobs.

6. Details on cost and practicability, in order to measure the 'reasonable response' in terms of the magnitude of the risk of injury, the seriousness of the consequences, and the cost and practicality of preventing that risk.

Employers will need to know, and to provide documentation to show that they know how safe is the system of work. It is equally important that complaints and warnings from staff about potential injury due to the work environment are treated seriously and are monitored and dealt with in a systematic and timely manner. The prevention of problems and the avoidance of the stress litigation process is preferable and less costly in the long term. When an employee wins a stress case, in addition to the financial burden of compensation claims, the court costs and unwanted publicity for the organization, there is also the prospect of increased employer's liability insurance premiums.

A Duty of Care – Employer and Employee

The Health and Safety at Work Act 1974 (HSAW), section 2 describes the general duties of care under the Act in respect of health and safety in the workplace. It is important to keep in mind that both the employer and the employee have duty of care responsibilities. Whilst the employer holds primary duty of care responsibilities, it is acknowledged that an employer can not properly carry out these duties without the co-operation and the assistance of the work force. Thus, section 7 of the Act states that the employee at work has a duty to take reasonable care for the health and safety of himself and of other persons who may be affected by his acts or omissions at work; and as regards any duty or requirement imposed on his employer or any other persons by or under any of the relevant statutory provisions, to co-operate with him so far as necessary to enable that duty or requirement to be performed or complied with. It must be kept in mind that the behaviour, health and wellbeing of an employee can be directly and adversely affected by exposure to mismanaged stress. This can also spill over to impact on relationships with colleagues, superiors and business contacts (customers and clients), and thereby have effects on productivity and performance.

In addition, this 'duty of care' responsibility for employees has implications for the implementation of a stress management policy within the organization. It is our firm belief that the management of stress in the workplace can only be successful if it is the joint responsibility of both the employer and employee. It must become a process and, 'part of the way we do things around here'. A stress management policy is, therefore, by definition part of the health and safety policy for the organization. Since this has to incorporate the mental health of employees and how potential pressures at work can be minimized, it is important that a policy on stress is written into a formal document.

A Policy for Stress Management

The objective of a policy for stress is to protect the health, safety and welfare of employees.

An effective policy on stress should recognize that stress is a health and safety issue. It should be developed jointly and agreed with trade union assistance and co-operation. The policy must apply to everyone in the organization and be endorsed from the most senior level within the company. Overt commitment to a policy on stress must be in evidence and it should guarantee a non-judgemental approach. It must include:

- a statement of intent;
- an outline of the responsibilities of the employer and the employee;
- a description of how the policy is organized and operationalized; specifically it should identify the chain of command and state who is responsible and for what and when. It should show how the policy and the responsibilities described therein are managed, monitored and evaluated;
- a description of the specific systems and procedures in place to either eliminate, minimize, control or treat stress in the workplace. This might include, for example, audit and risk assessment procedures; recruitment and training options; medical services; lifestyle management practices; management systems; organizational development plans; access to referral services such as counselling or employee assistance providers.

Thus the objectives of a policy on stress should be:

1. to prevent stress by identifying causes of workplace stress and eliminating (or minimizing) them, that is, to deal with the source of stress;

2. to control stress by ensuring that the stress response does not cause negative impact on the individual, that is to deal with the response to stress;

3. to rehabilitate employees who are suffering from exposure to stress through the provision of a confidential counselling service. That is, to deal with the symptoms of stress.

It is important that a policy on stress is reviewed on a regular basis since there are likely to be changes both within the organization and to the legislative requirements relating to stress in the workplace.

Implications for Employer Liability Insurance

In the last section of this chapter we consider the implications for employer liability insurance and the premiums that an organization is likely to pay. Understanding the relationship between medical, workplace conditions and legal factors, is an important part of the job of the underwriter who needs to assess the risk and the premium required to provide the employer with adequate insurance protection. The aim of this section is to provide employers with an insight on how they can avoid becoming involved with their insurers because one of their employees is making a claim against them for cumulative stress trauma compensation.

Williams, (1997) suggests that four ingredients need to be in place for litigation to take place. These include:

- a disenfranchized victim,
- a responsible party,
- a lawyer,
- a fund of accessible money, such as insurance company funds.

If one of these ingredients is missing then litigation is unlikely to proceed. For litigation to be successful negligence must be proved (as already described above). Therefore, it is only when claims costs begin to mount up that the insurance company takes action by increasing the premiums to be paid. Indeed, the evidence so far, from the awards made for cumulative stress trauma, suggests that compensation is likely to be substantial compared to the average cost of £5000 for an employer's liability claim (inclusive of costs and expenses). For example, John Walker (*Walker v. Northumberland County Council* [1995] Ael ER 737) was awarded £175000, plus costs. Tania Clayton, the fire fighter who suffered a life of 'sexist hell' and consequently received treatment in a psychiatric hospital, and is now, 'unemployed and unemployable'(*Clayton v Hereford and Worcester Council*), received an award of £200000 compensation. These awards are more likely to be very high when the victim becomes unemployable. For example an unemployable manager earning £30000 per annum, with an assessment of a ten year loss will receive £300000 on a full liability basis. Also, it is estimated that 40 per cent or more of the average employer liability claims cost goes to meet costs and expenses, and so this is a lucrative business for the lawyers. They will be more than keen to help a distressed victim into the courts.

Thus it seems that successful claims will be costly. Therefore, the first step in avoiding the claim situation and the inevitable increase in insurance premiums is to 'manage the risk' by being proactive rather than waiting for 'something to happen'. However, as Williams points out, 'It is difficult enough to manage something when we can see it, touch it or feel it. It is very difficult to manage stress, since it can be hard to see, touch or feel its consequences until it is too late'. Whilst these duties might be difficult to discharge the employer must still take reasonable steps to remove risk of psychiatric injury to employees. Clearly, John Walker received his compensation because his employer should have foreseen that he was at risk. This employee complained vociferously to his employer and documented his concerns at length. However, Mr Petch (*Petch v. Customs and Excise Commission*, 1993 ICR 789), was not successful in making a claim because the Court of Appeal was not satisfied that he exhibited signs of stress that might have made his mental breakdown reasonably foreseeable to his employer. Employers, therefore, ignore the signs of stress and changes in an employee's behaviour to their peril, and cost! The most effective way of keeping your insurance premiums down is to manage and control stress in the workplace. As Williams advises, 'You cannot prevent the disenfranchised victim from seeking legal advice; nor do you control the issue of litigation once the damage is done. By causing the conditions which result in injury, you lose control of the legal consequences'. Some companies have found that substantial premium savings can be made if they can demonstrate that risk is properly controlled by the implementation of a well-managed and effective stress management programme. These savings can be used to fund further activities, and so a virtuous circle can begin to the financial benefit of all parties concerned. As Williams advises, prevention is cheaper than cure. In Chapter 3 we examine how and why exposure to stress is likely to cause harm and injury, and how to spot the signs of distress that might be manifest.

3

What is Stress?

To successfully manage a stress situation we must first define what we mean by 'stress' and identify what causes it in order to recognize the effects of exposure to stress. We have already examined the deleterious costs of mismanaged stress in Chapter 1, and acknowledged the implications of the stress litigation process and the consequences of increased employers' liability insurance in Chapter 2. Now we need to understand how and why stress is damaging in its consequences.

In order to do this we will refer to a theoretical framework and describe certain models of stress. Thereby, we can explain how and why exposure to certain conditions and situations can have an adverse impact on performance, health, well-being and quality of life. It is important that we understand how and why exposure to a constantly changing work environment might be manifest in terms of poor performance, productivity and ill health. Until we can identify the source of stress it is unlikely that stress management activities will be successful. Therefore, it is necessary:

1. To recognize our response to stress in behavioural, emotional and physical terms; also to understand how models of stress evolved to influence our thinking about the stress response and stress management strategies.

2. To understand the differences between adaptive and maladaptive stress coping strategies.

3. To define and clarify what we mean by the word, 'stress'.

These steps are all vital to the effective management of stress and so will be discussed in the first part of this chapter. However, it is also important that we:

4. Identify potential sources of stress in our environment.

In Chapter 4 we will use a model of stress to discuss the prevalent sources of stress for both white and blue-collar occupational groups of managers and other employees working in contemporary society.

The Origins of Stress Rresearch

From our discussions so far we seem to have assumed that 'stress is what happens to people'. This is misleading and likely to be the cause of errors in our understanding about the nature of stress. Thus it is useful to review the various models of stress to help to explain the ways in which stress is perceived and operationalized. It is important to understand the origins and the evolution of the various models of stress, and how they have influenced our attempts to manage stress in the workplace.

First, pause for a moment or two, and write down the words or phrases that immediately come into your mind, when you think about what the word 'stress' means to you. If we ask a group of people to take part in this exercise, the list of words produced invariably has three key characteristics.

1. Most of the words or phrases are expressed in 'negative' terms. That is, 'stress' is perceived as something bad or not wanted. For example, words or phrases such as, 'depression', 'feeling out of control', 'overworked', 'migraine or headaches', 'time pressures', 'panic attacks', 'anxiety', 'cannot sleep', are commonly used to express what stress means to us personally. Mostly, stress is regarded as a negative experience for the individual.

2. The list usually contains expressions or words that describe 'symptoms' of exposure to a stressful situation. That is, people describe stress as, 'feeling anxious', 'depressed' or having headaches or panic attacks. The stress is being explained in terms of the feelings and reactions that the individual is experiencing. Therefore, stress is being described in terms of a 'response-based' model and approach to managing stress.

3. The lists rarely contain words that can be described as 'the source of the stress' or the 'stressor'. In our example in point 1 above, being 'overworked' and 'time pressures' are workplace stressors. However, these work conditions and situations need to be explained in more detail before we are able to use this information to effectively manage the potentially stressful situation. By refering to the source of stress or

'stressor', we are describing stress in terms of a 'stimulus-based' model, as an approach to managing stress.

However, it was realized that these models were too simplistic and not adequate to understand the complex nature of stress and the stress reponse. Clearly, a better model was needed for further research into the study of stress. Also, the broad application of the stress concept to medical, social and behavioural science research over the past 60–70 years, compounded the problem. Each discipline investigated and attempted to explain stress from its own unique perspective. The historical origins and the early approaches to the study of stress are outlined below to show how a contemporary 'interactive' model of stress evolved.

A response-based model of stress

As we have seen, when asked to provide alternative words to the term 'stress', associations tend to be in terms of response-based meanings that take the form of strain, tension or pressure. The lay person readily identifies with the expressions, 'being under stress', and, 'I feel very stressed', and can usually identify the manifestations of the stress response. Therefore, the response-based approach to understanding stress, in seeking to define an intangible phenomenon, views it as an 'outcome'. In research terminology this is described as the 'dependant variable', where the main conceptual domain is the manifestation of stress. Figure 3.1 illustrates a response-based model of stress.

The origins of response-based definitions of stress are found in medicine and are usually viewed from a physiological perspective. This is a logical stance for a discipline trained to diagnose and treat symptoms, but not necessarily the cause of the condition. For example, John Locke, the seventeenth century physician and philosopher proposed that intellectual functioning, emotion, muscle movement and the behaviour of internal organs were the product of sensory experiences processed by the brain. From these early notions the study of stress from a physiological perspective developed. Links were established between life experiences, emotions and the importance of hormonal and chemical actions in the body.

Thus, emotional stress as a causal factor in ischaemic heart disease was proposed by Claude Bernard as early as 1860. Osler (1910) later identified the high incidence of angina pectoris with the hectic pace of life among Jewish businessmen. In the 1930s, the psychoanalyst, Franz Alexander, and Frances Dunbar, a physician, reported on the relationship between personality patterns and constitutional tendencies to certain organic disorders. That is, they described a psychosomatic theory of disease (Warshaw, 1979). Claude Bernard was the first person to suggest the notion that the internal environment of a living organism must remain fairly constant despite exposure to external changes. This concept of stability or balance was later developed and described as 'homeostasis' by Walter Cannon (1935). In systems theory this would become known as dynamic equilibrium, whereby the co-ordination of physiological processes maintains a steady state within the organism. The theory states that natural homeostatic mechanisms normally maintain a state of resistance but are not able to cope with unusually heavy demands. Under homeostatic principles it is acknowledged that there is a finite supply to meet demand.

The earliest report of a systematic study on the relationship between life events and bodily responses is probably attributed to Wolf and Wolf (1943, reported by McLean, 1979). Their observations and experiments with the patient, Tom, provided an opportunity to observe changes in stomach activity in response to stressful situations. These researchers were able to document the changes in blood flow, motility and secretions of the stomach, with feelings of frustration and conflict produced under experimental conditions. Sadness, self-reproach and discouragement were found to be associated with prolonged pallor of the stomach mucosa and a hypo-secretion of acid. Hostility and resentment were associated with a high increase in gastric secretion and acidity. From the results of this research our understanding of the relationship between engorgement of the stomach lining, lowered resistance to psychological trauma and the

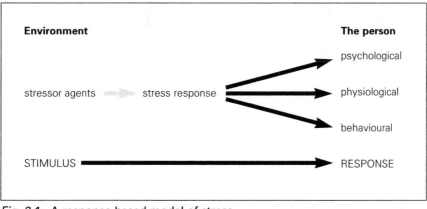

Fig. 3.1 A response-based model of stress

incidence of gastric ulcers was formed. As McLean, (1979) suggested, the study of Tom inaugurated the scientific study of psychosomatic medicine.

However, it is the work of Hans Selye in the 1930s and 1940s that really marked the beginning of a response-based approach to the study of stress. In 1936, Selye introduced the concept of stress-related illness in terms of a 'general adaptation syndrome' known as the 'GAS'. He suggested that, 'stress is the non-specific response of the body to any demand made upon it' (Selye, 1956) ... and that all patients, whatever the disease, looked and felt sick. This general malaise was characterized by loss of motivation, appetite, weight and strength. Most of Selye's experiments were with animals and so he was able to demonstrate internal physical degeneration and deterioration as a result of exposure to stress. According to Selye, '... the apparent specificity of diseases of adaptation is ascribed to conditioning factors such as genetic predisposition, gender, learning experiences and diet, etc.'. Response to stress was, therefore, deemed to be invariant to the nature of the stressor and followed a universal pattern. Three stages of response were described within the GAS (see Figure 3.2). The alarm reaction is the immediate psycho-physiological response and at this time of initial shock, our resistance to the stressor is lowered. After the initial shock phase, the counter shock phase can be observed and resistance levels begin to increase. At this time our defence mechanisms are activated, forming the reaction known as the 'fight or flight response' (Cannon, 1935).

The 'fight or flight' response prepares our body to take action. Increased sympathetic activity results in the secretion of catecholamines that make

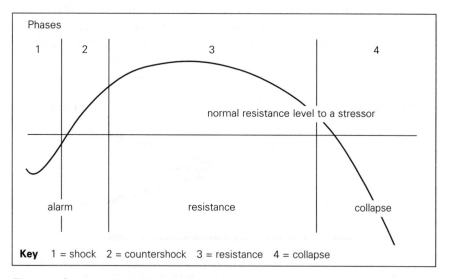

Fig. 3.2 General adaptation syndrome (the 'GAS')

the body ready to act. The internal physiological changes initiated by hormones provides us with energy from the metabolism of fat and glucose. This causes increased delivery of oxygen (another energy source) to muscles through an increased number of red blood cells in the circulation, increased blood flow to the muscles, with reduced blood flow through the skin and the gut. So, our breathing becomes more rapid, the heart beats faster and our blood pressure increases. The spleen contracts and blood supplies are redirected from the skin and viscera to provide an improved blood supply to the brain and skeletal muscle. Glucose stored as glycogen in the liver is released to provide energy for muscular action; blood coagulation processes become enhanced, and the supply of blood lymphocytes is increased to combat the impact of injury and infection from wounds.

Table 3.1 overleaf illustrates the physiological changes experienced when we are in the alarm stage of the stress response. The table is provided to explain the effects we experience in response to stress. In summary, this includes:

- the release of adrenal hormones and free fatty acids;
- lipid changes, for example, in cholesterol and triglyceride levels;
- changes in various catecholamines, for example thyroxin in urine and blood.

Thus the actions of adrenaline, noradrenaline and cortisol combine to produce a variety of actions as part of the 'fight or flight' response.

Stress, and the stress responses, in an evolutionary sense are good for us, and have been necessary for the development of our society. Indeed, 'social' Darwinism could be defined as the 'promotion of the fittest' assuming that the individual survives the rat race in the first place (McCloy, 1995). The response to stress was meant to be both adaptive and vital for survival. In the past we had simple choices to make. Either to stand and fight an enemy, or run away from a threatening and potentially dangerous situation. However, in contemporary society we face a dilemma because neither of these options is appropriate behaviour in the workplace. In the work environment there is no opportunity to indulge in physical action and thereby dissipate the physiological effects that then become dominant and can cause distress. We cannot physically fight to escape workplace stress, but neither can we turn and run away from the situations that we must continue to meet, without losing face, every day at work. Therefore, it is suggested that our bodies are continually primed to take actions that we are denied. Since many of us also lead increasingly sedentary lives at work and at home, we are denied both the aggression

Table 3.1 The Physiology of Stress and Stress Response

Organ or Tissue Involved	Reaction
Lungs	Airways dilate and breathing becomes more rapid and deeper
Heart	Increased rate – the heart beats faster and harder; we can experience palpitations and chest pains
Legs/arms	An experience of muscle tension or tingling in the arms and legs as the electrical balance of the cells in the muscles undergoes change
Liver and fat tissue	Mobilization of glucose and fats for energy to fuel muscles
Brain	Increased mental activity to be alert for quick decision making
Skin and sweat glands	Increased sweating; hands and feet (extremities) often feel cold as blood supplies are diverted to the brain and muscles; hairs stand erect and we experience 'goose-pimples'
Salivary glands	Decreased flow of saliva; the mouth feels dry
Gut muscles	Gut activity is slowed; blood supply is reduced and we might experience indigestion or the feeling of a 'knotted' stomach because digestive processes stop or slow down
Spleen	Contracts and empties red blood cells into the circulation
Kidneys	Reduced urine formation
Ears	Hearing becomes more acute; people under extreme stress often report feeling very sensitive to noise
Eyes	Pupils dilate as an aid to keen vision; vision can become blurred if oxygenated blood is impeded in getting to the brain as blood vessels in the neck constrict
Blood	The action of cortisol produces an increased ability for blood clotting; the immune system is activated to prevent infection

release and the physical activity necessary to quickly remove the build-up of hormone and chemical secretions. Fats released to fuel muscle actions are not used and so we have elevated blood lipids. The fat deposits that are not used are likely to be stored on the lining of our arteries. This means that our blood pressure increases as the heart works harder to pump blood around the body through these smaller capillary openings. If one of the clots breaks away from the lining of an artery and finds its way to the heart or the brain, it will cause a stroke, or heart attack (thrombosis). Coronary heart disease can, therefore, be caused by indirect effects, namely the stress-physiological consequences of sustained active distress on increase of blood pressure, on elevation of blood lipids and blood platelets, and on impaired glucose tolerance and related metabolic processes (Siegrist, 1997). Recent studies have documented associations between high levels of psychosocial stress and the prevalence of hypertension, high levels of blood lipids not attributable to diet, and of high fibrinogen (a soluble protein in blood plasma, converted to fibrin by the action of the enzyme thrombin when the blood clots). In addition to diseases of the heart we are also likely to suffer from ulcers, troubles with the gastrointestinal tract, asthma, colds and flu, and various skin conditions such as psoriasis, caused by exposure to mismanaged stress. These problems can be exacerbated because we often resort to using maladaptive stress coping strategies in response to stress rather than adaptive, positive stress management techniques (this issue will be discussed in more detail later on in this chapter).

In the third phase of the GAS we observe resistance to a continued stressor, and where the adaptation response and/or return to equilibrium replaces the alarm reaction. If the alarm reaction is elicited too intensely or too frequently over an extended period of time, the energy required for adaptation becomes depleted, and the final stage of 'exhaustion', collapse or death occurs. Resistance can not continue indefinitely, even when given sufficient energy because, as Selye says, 'Every biological activity causes wear and tear .... and leaves some irreversible chemical scars which accumulate to constitute signs of ageing' (Selye, 1983).

Although the non-specificity concept of stress-related illness and the GAS model had far reaching influence and a significant impact on our understanding of stress, it has been challenged. Research indicates that responses to stimuli do not always follow the same pattern. They are, in fact, stimulus-specific and dependant on the type of hormonal secretion. For example, anxiety-producing situations seem to be associated with the secretion of adrenaline (for example, waiting for an appointment with the dentist; or sitting and waiting for a written examination to commence). Response to these experiences produces the feelings of fear and dread that make us want to just run away from the situation. Noradrenalin is released, however, in response to aggression or challenge producing events. These situations stir feelings of elation and excitement as we prepare to 'fight' or take the plunge of the parachute sky-dive or bungee jump.

The GAS model makes no attempt to address the issue of psychological response to events, or that a response to a potential threat may, in turn, become the stimulus for a different response. It is acknowledged that this model is too simplistic. Whilst the framework of the GAS can explain our response to certain stressors, such as the physical effects of heat and cold, is not adequate to explain response to psychosocial stress (Christian and Lolas, 1985).

Kagan and Levi (1971) extended the response-based model of stress to incorporate psychosocial stimuli as causal factors in stress related illness. Response to stress is viewed as the product of an interaction between the stimulus and the psychobiologial programme of the individual. That is, genetic predisposition and experience or learning. The term 'interaction' is used in this instance to mean 'the propensity to react in accordance with a certain pattern' (Kagan and Levi, 1971). Since their model also incorporates the concept of feedback it cannot be considered a simple, stimulus-response model of stress. An additional problem associated with this approach is that stress is recognized as a generic term, which subsumes a large variety of manifestations (Pearlin *et al.*, 1981). Disagreement exists about the real manifestation of stress and the level in the organism or system that most clearly reflects the response. Pearlin asks, for example, if the response is in the single cell, in an organ, or throughout the entire organism; is it biochemical, physiological or emotional functioning? Is it at the endocrine, immunological, metabolic or cardiovascular level, or in particular diseases, physical and psychological? Resolution of this problem is not easy because the findings of replication research are likely to be confounded. Individuals adapt to any potential source of stress and so a response will vary over time (for example in the assessment of noise on hearing and performance).

A stimulus-based model of stress

Historically this approach, which links health and disease to certain conditions in the external environment, can be traced back to Hippocrates (fifth century BC). The Hippocratic physician believed that characteristics of health and disease were conditioned by the external environment (Goodell *et al.*, 1986). It is the belief that some external force impinges upon the organism in a disruptive manner. Indeed, it is also suggested that the word stress derives from the Latin word, 'stringere', meaning to bind tight. The stimulus-based psychological model of stress has its roots in physics and engineering. The analogy being that stress can be defined as a force exerted, which results in a demand or load reaction that causes distortion.

Both organic and inorganic substances have tolerance levels, which if exceeded, result in temporary or permanent damage. The aphorism, 'it is the straw that breaks the camel's back', is a view consistent with a stimulus-based model of stress. An individual is bombarded with stimuli in the environment, but just one more, apparently minor or innocuous event, can alter the balance between coping with the demand, and a breakdown in coping and of the system itself. Figure 3.3 illustrates this model of stress that treats a potential stressor as an independent variable that will cause a certain effect (that is, an outcome, or symptom).

Rapid industrialization provided an impetus for the increasing popularity of this particular model of stress. Much of the early research into blue-collar stress at work adopted a stimulus-based model when trying to identify sources of stress in the work environment. Considerable attention was paid to our actual physical working conditions and task circumstances, such as exposure to heat, cold, light levels and social density. Thus, workload conditions, either overload and underload were explored and understood within this framework. (Note – the inverted 'U' hypothesis is discussed later in the section on work load as a source of stress.) However, it was realized that purely objective measures of environmental conditions are inadequate and do not fully explain the response to stress observed. Also, individual differences, including variability in tolerance levels, personality traits, past experiences (learning and training), needs, wants and expectations, seemed to account for the fact that two individuals, exposed to exactly the same situation, might react in completely different ways. A stimulus-response model of stress does not explain this and thus it is a major weakness of the model. In fact, Lazarus

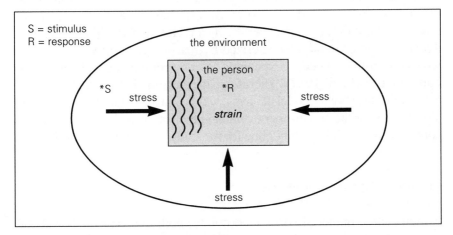

Fig. 3.3 A stimulus-based model of stress

(1996) stated that no objective criterion was good enough to describe a situation as stressful, only the person experiencing the event could do this.

Although this model does have limitations, it has some appeal in organizations seeking to identify common stressor themes or patterns of stress that might affect the majority of the work force. However, rarely and ill-advisedly would any subsequent stress management intervention be carried out without exhaustive consultation with the personnel effected.

Nevertheless, organizations do use a response-based model of stress to guide their stress management programme. They view the problems of stress as something inherent to the person and this allows them to transfer responsibility to the individual. It means that they introduce a programme that aims to help the employee cope with stressor situation but usually does nothing to actually remove or eliminate the origin of the stress. Other organizations favour a stimulus-based model of stress and they attempt to manage the stress situation without taking into account the needs of the individual concerned. Both of these models have limitations and weaknesses. Industrialization brought many problems associated with physical and task-related sources of strain and pressure. Poor working conditions caused diseases such as tuberculosis and pneumonia that often led to early death. Legislation regarding health and safety requirements in the workplace resolved many of these unsatisfactory conditions. However, contemporary industrialization and new technology brought different problems which caused new forms of illness, These include, for example, upper body limb disorder, often known as repetitive strain injury (RSI), and psychological ill-health (for example, the problems of sick building syndrome), or increased accidents at work. Our expectations for quality of life have brought a new meaning to the concept of health. It not only means an absence of disease or infirmity, but a satisfactory state of physical, mental and social well-being (WHO, 1984). Well-being is a dynamic state of mind, characterized by reasonable harmony between a worker's ability, needs, expectations, environmental demands and opportunities (Levi, 1987). Therefore, it is acknowledged that an inter-active or transactional model of stress, which considers the stressor source, a perception of the situation or event, and the response, is the most useful approach for providing a guideline for the study and management of stress.

An interactive model of stress

An interactive model of stress incorporates both the response-based and the stimulus-based models of stress. Figure 3.4 provides an illustration of the way in which stress is perceived and how a response is subsequently modified by individual differences. There are five key characteristics associated with this model of stress.

1. **Cognitive Appraisal:** stress is regarded as a subjective experience contingent upon the perception of a situation or event. That is, 'stress is not simply out there in the environment' (Lazarus, 1996). As Shakespeare's 'Hamlet', says, 'There is nothing good or bad, but thinking makes it so'.

2. **Experience:** the way a situation or event is perceived depends upon familiarity with the circumstances, previous exposure to the event, learning, education and training (that is, the individual's actual ability). Related to this is the concept of success or failure in coping with the demand on previous occasions. Therefore conditioning and reinforcement is an important part of an interactive model of stress.

3. **Demand:** pressure or demand is the product of actual demands, perceived demands, actual ability and perceived ability to meet that demand. Needs, desires and the immediate level of arousal all will influence the way in which a demand is perceived.

4. **Interpersonal influence:** a potential source of stress is not perceived in a social vacuum. The presence or absence of other people or work colleagues will influence our perception of stress. Thus, background and

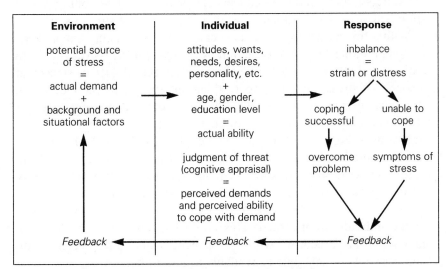

Fig. 3.4 Stress Perception – an Interactive Model of Stress

situational factors will influence the subjective experience of stress, our response and the coping behaviour used. The presence or absence of other people can have both a positive and negative influence. For example, the presence of work colleagues can be a source of distraction, irritation or unwanted arousal. Conversely, the presence of work colleagues can also provide a support network that helps to boost confidence and levels of self-esteem, provide confirmation of values and a sense of personal identity and self-worth. Through the process of vicarious learning, increased awareness and an understanding of potential consequences can also be gained.

5. **A state of stress:** this is acknowledged as an imbalance or mismatch between the perceived 'demand' and the perception of one's ability to meet that demand. The processes that follow are the coping process and the consequences of the coping strategy applied. Therefore, the importance of feedback at all levels is specified in this model of stress. Successful coping restores any imbalance, whereas unsuccessful coping results in the manifestation of symptoms of exposure to stress. The response may produce either short-term stress manifestations in the form of maladaptive coping strategies such as, 'light-up another cigarette'; 'need alcohol', or 'take a sleeping pill', or long-term effects such as heart disease, certain forms of cancer or ulcers. Obviously, it is acknowledged that the short-term consequences of exposure to stress and maladaptive coping strategies can also be causal factors in the aetiology of these long-term diseases (for example the link between cigarette smoking and lung cancer). Thus, a method of coping with a source of stress can ultimately become the source of stress itself!

   Within this model of stress, an accident at work can be both a short-term and a long-term manifestation of exposure to stress (having both a direct and indirect impact on behaviour). McGrath (1976) states that a source of stress must be perceived and interpreted by the individual. It is also necessary to perceive that the potential consequences of successful coping are more desirable than the expected consequences of leaving a situation unaltered. For example, an individual who chooses to use palliatives as a coping strategy (perhaps as an 'escape' from reality) views this type of short-term, immediate response as less costly or more personally desirable than trying to alter the demand. Of course, it might not be possible for them to actually alter the demand at the level of the individual concerned. This could happen, for example, if an individual is forced to work permanent night shifts because no alternative work schedule is available to him or her.

In summary, an interactive model of stress acknowledges that situations are not inherently stressful, but are potentially stressful, and it is necessary to take account of:

- the source of stress
- the mediators or moderators of the stress response
- the manifestation of stress.

One example of an interactive model of stress is known as 'the person environment fit' approach to understanding stress (French, 1973; Cooper, 1981). 'Fit' is assessed in terms of the desired and actual levels of various job conditions. The main weakness of this model is that it infers some static situation, whereas, in reality response to stress is a dynamic process. However, the model is useful where certain personality traits are relatively stable. For example, Kahn, *et al.*, (1964) found that introverts under stress from role conflict will tend to reduce contact with other people and will further irritate work colleagues by appearing to be too independent. Role senders, attempting to define the role will increase their efforts thereby adding to the strain. This means that the introvert's coping strategy of defensive withdrawal is ultimately maladaptive. An understanding of such differences between introverts and extroverts can help to avoid potentially stressful interpersonal conflict situations. Kahn *et al.*, also noted that 'rigid' personality types tended to avoid conflict. They rely on compulsive work habits and show increased dependence on authority figures when under threat. 'Flexible' people, however, are more likely to respond to a conflict situation by complying with work demands and seeking support from peers and subordinates. This compliance strategy can lead to work overload problems. Also, reliance on those of equal or lower status does not help to resolve the stressor situation because it is often the boss or superior who sets out the work expectation that is the source of stress. Thus, the 'rigid' and the 'flexible' personality types create very different problems in the workplace in response to stress and may ultimately be more suited to some work environment more than others.

Stress – Myth, Reality or Whipping Boy?

As we have seen, a variety of models have been offered in an attempt to increase our understanding of the nature of stress. The most recent 'transactional' models of stress are indicative of the complexity of the concept. In reality, however, models still tend to oversimplify the problem to the extent that the issue of stress can seem to become trivialized. As Schuler (1980) says, 'it is too all encompassing a phenomenon, too large to investigate'. Yet this has not deterred interest into the topic. However, this high level of interest and popularity is not always positive. Indeed, incorrect usage of the word 'stress' is common and it is now used interchangeably to refer to a state or condition, a symptom, or the cause of a state or a symptom. There are problems of definition and about the meaning of the word, 'stress', and if indeed it exists. We have asked, should the word 'stress' should be used at all! The words, 'stress', 'pressure' and 'strain' are readily used in an interchangeable way to describe feelings, emotions or situations. The lay person seems quite able to identify with the concept of stress and has an appetite to know more. This need is served too eagerly by the press and media. Without a doubt, certain individuals hope to make a quick profit from 'being stressed' at work.

This situation creates problems for us in the effective management of stress because stress is often wrongly blamed for *all* our ills. It is now seen as the cause of *all* our problems. It has become a 'whipping boy' and it is certainly misunderstood. Many of us continue to view stress only in negative terms or even prefer to deny that any problem exists. Prevalence of this view is likely to be detrimental to the effective management of stress in the work environment because it is synonymous with not coping. One outcome is that staff will tend to hide their work problems and health condition until they become victims of exposure to stress. What they really need is encouragement to try to actively and positively manage the strains and pressures that are an inevitable part of modern day living and working.

So, it is vital that we acknowledge that *not all stress is bad*. Hans Selye, the acknowledged 'father' of stress research said that the only person without stress was a dead person. By this Selye meant that stress is an inevitable part of being alive, and should be viewed as 'stimulation to growth and development...it is challenge and variety, it is the spice of life'. Hans Selye used the word 'stress' to describe a state of arousal in the nervous system. So, it is any stimulus, event or demand impacting on the sensory nervous system. When an imbalance exists between a perceived demand (that is, the stimulus) and our perceived ability to meet that demand, we will experience a state of stress (that is, distress or pressure). Stress, therefore, is unwanted pressure and is manifest when we feel that a situation is out of our control or when we feel unable to cope with the event. It is a subjective experience that is 'in the eye of the beholder'. An understanding of this explains why, in a given situation, one person might be highly distressed, yet another seems to prosper and thrive.

In organizational life it is likely that we are now denied a natural outlet and expression of the stress response since we can not 'fight' or 'flee'. We are physiologically primed to take actions that are inappropriate and the sedentary nature of the job further exacerbates this problem. Whilst our response to stress is, in the first instance, physiological, complex emotional and behavioural reactions also take place. These can lead to potentially damaging health outcomes. Understanding the nature of stress in these terms helps us to think positively and proactively about stress, instead of taking a defensive, self-blaming stance. It implies that each of us, at various times during our life, may be vulnerable to stress.

Adaptive versus maladaptive ways of coping with stress

Since it is mismanaged stress that is damaging in its consequences it is apparent that we need to manage a potentially stressful situation in an active and positive manner. It is important to do this without resorting to maladaptive ways of coping. By this we mean avoiding:

1. excessive use of alcohol or nicotine;

2. dependence on other drugs, such as tranquillizers, sleeping pills, 'pep' pills and caffeine;

3. being tired all the time so failing to take adequate levels of exercise or engaging in fulfilling social and recreational activities;

4. indulgence in 'comfort' eating because we feel sorry for ourselves; especially when we binge on those foods high in sugars and fats which have empty calories and with low or poor nutritional value;

5. procrastination.... putting off dealing with a situation because it is threatening or difficult. This usually causes the situation to escalate and leads to even larger problems to tackle;

6. becoming angry and aggressive with ourselves and others; this is a particularly damaging strategy if we persist in 'bottling our anger up inside'. A quietly seething time-bomb becomes dangerous and unstable and can cause irreparable damage when a situation finally leads to a major eruption or explosion that is completely out of control.

All of these maladaptive coping strategies render us *less fit* to cope with the demand. Members of an organization are unlikely to come forward and deal with problems that exist within an organization if there is a fear of being identified and labelled as a 'non-coper'. Research evidence is clear, mismanaged stress arising from certain conditions and situations in the workplace, or at home, is likely to have an adverse impact on performance, health, well-being and quality of life.

Implicit in a contemporary approach to understanding the manifestations of stress are the assumptions that stress is a subjective experience and that the outcomes or symptoms of distress may be physical, psychological, or behavioural. This means that establishing causation is difficult because the relationships between exposure to stress and ill-health are not simple. Factors to consider include:

- The aetiology of disease.
- Subjectivity of response to stress and illness
- Unwillingness to accept a situation, or to deny the real reasons for one's plight.
- An inability to recognize the difficulties we are in when in a state of distress (that is, unwell, anxious, depressed).

These are just some of the reasons why it is difficult to identify the root cause of a problem.

Definitions of stress

A review of the various models of stress guides us in providing an adequate definition of stress. It would seem that an understanding of stress must be in terms of an interactive process model. It is a dynamic process in which time plays a vital role. It is apparent from the examination of simple dictionary definitions of stress that they also can be traced back to the various schools of thought about the mechanism and nature of stress. For example, in the seventeenth century, stress (derived from Latin) was used to mean hardship, straits, adversity or affliction (Shorter Oxford Dictionary, 1933). By the eighteenth and nineteenth centuries, the use of the word stress had broadened to indicate 'strain, pressure or strong effort'. This was intended to include terms to describe the laws of physics and engineering, in addition to person, or a person's organs and mental powers (Hinkle, 1973). Within the fields of physics, stress was used to refer to an object's resistance to external pressure. This model was adopted by the social sciences. However, as Cox (1985) pointed out, an engineering analogy is too simplistic. He said, 'We have to accept some intervening psychological process which does mediate the outcome ... stress has to be perceived and recognized by man. A machine, however, does not have to recognize the load or stress placed upon it'.

Recent dictionary definition actually associates the word stress with disease. For example, the Concise Oxford Dictionary, 1984, new edition, describes stress as, '... suffered by managers, etc; subject to continual stress'. Medical dictionaries have included both a response-based and a stimulus-based approach to stress when providing guidance on definitions of stress. For example, Steadman's Medical Dictionary (1982, 24th ed.) states:

1. Stress is the reactions of the animal body to forces of a deleterious nature, infections, and various abnormal states that tend to disrupt its normal physiologic equilibrium.

2. Stress is the resisting force set up in a body as a result of an externally applied force.

3. In psychology, stress is a physical or psychological stimulus which, when impinging upon an individual produces strain or disequilibrium.

The Encyclopaedia and Dictionary of Medicine, Nursing and Allied Health (Miller and Keane, 1978, 2nd ed.) suggest that stress is,

the sum of all the non-specific biological phenomena elicited by adverse external influences including damage and defence. Stress may be either physical or psychologic, or both. Just as a bridge is structurally capable of adjusting to certain physical stresses, the human body and mind are normally able to adapt to the stresses of new situations. However, this ability has definite limits beyond which continued stress may cause a breakdown, although this limit varies from person to person ... for example, peptic ulcers may result from prolonged nervous tension in response to real or imagined stresses in people who have a predisposition for ulcers.

However, within our conceptualization of stress, a person-environment fit model also acknowledges that 'underload' as well as overload can be a stress agent. Levi (1987) takes account of this when he describes stress as a poor-fit. That is, 'the interaction between, or misfit of, environmental opportunities and demands, and individual needs and abilities, and expectations, elicit reactions. When the fit is bad, when needs are not being met, or when abilities are over- or under-taxed, the organism reacts with various pathogenic mechanisms. These are cognitive, emotional, behavioural and/or physiological and under some conditions of intensity, frequency or duration, and in the presence or absence of certain interacting variables, they may lead to precursors of disease'. This definition is consistent with a contemporary, interaction approach to the study of stress. Implicit in Levi's definition is the view that stress can have both positive and negative consequences. That is, stress can be a motivator to growth, development and adaption; it can be challenge and variety ...it can be the spice of life (Selye, 1956).

Therefore, a distinction must be made between stressors that cause distress and that which result in 'distress' (that is, a positive stress response), because stress is inevitable, distress is not (Quick and Quick, 1984). This is most important in the work environment. Beehr and Newman (1978) acknowledge this and provide our ultimate definition of job stress as

> ... a situation wherein job-related factors interact with a worker to change (that is, disrupt or enhance) his or her psychological and or physiological condition such that the person (that is, mind or body) is forced to deviate from normal functioning. This definition also serves to define what we mean by 'employee health'; namely a person's mental and physical condition. We are referring to health in its broadest sense – the complete continuum from superb mental and physical health all the way to death. Note that we are not excluding the possibility of beneficial effects of stress on health (p. 670).

Before we review various sources of stress in Chapter 4, it is useful to acknowledge how and why change is a significant and pervasive source of stress. It is considered at this point because of the major impact it can have on organizational life and has some effect on all the other stressor categories.

Change as a Source of Stress

Research evidence indicates that a wide variety of workplace conditions cause stress, strain or pressure that are associated with a wide range of physical and psychological ill-health problems. However, for many people at work the changing nature of the work environment is a potent source of stress and pressure. This must be managed in a positive way if we are to remain both healthy and productive. Clearly, constant change has been the dominant theme of organizational life in the 1990s and this pattern seems likely to sustain as we move into the next millennium. While we endeavour to meet the demands associated with predictable life event changes, we must continue to face the endless reshaping of our work structure and climate, embedded in the changing nature of society.

Change, it is said, brings progress and improvement to our quality of life, and stimulation and variety that relieves us from boredom. So, why would we wish to make changes for the worse? It seems that our work environment has become a world of rapid, discontinuous change that requires us to live in a state of transience and impermanence. The situation is potentially damaging because energy is needed and expended by constant adaptation to stimulation from the external environment. In this way, 'change' becomes a powerful stressor agent because it necessitates adaptation whether it is perceived as a negative or positive experience. Whether we welcome the change, fear it, or actively try to resist it, adaptation or adjustment requires energy (Selye, 1956). Samuel Johnson, quoting Richard Hooker, suggested that, 'Change is not made without inconvenience, even from worse to better'. As Selye advises, our energy resources are not infinite, and so breakdown of the system, in part or total, will ultimately occur. In Selye's view, impairment of function and structural change are wholly, or in part, linked to adaptation to stimulation, or as he described this, 'arousal'. Exposure to a continued state of arousal will result in wear and tear on the body which in the extreme leads to exhaustion, collapse and finally death of the system. It we accept this theory we can concur with Hans Selye's hypothesis that the only person without stress is a dead person! Of course, we are not in the position to actually test his hypothesis and are happy not to have this opportunity. Instead we prefer to accept Selye's view that stress is 'stimulation to growth and development ... challenge and variety ... the spice of life'.

However, too often we try to cope with the demands of exposure to change by resorting to maladaptive ways of coping. That is, we drink alcohol because we believe it gives us confidence or helps us to sleep or relax; we drink lots of strong coffee to gain the 'buzz' necessary to sustain long hours of working without a break; we smoke cigarettes to calm our nerves or take the place of meals that we must 'skip' because of time pressures; we use various pills and potions to ensure sleep, or 'pep' ourselves up; we eat 'comfort' foods, particularly sugars and fats with low or poor nutritional value. These forms of coping render us less fit to cope with the demands of change and in the long term actually become the source of stress, when the addiction exacerbates the problem.

Studies of employee response to organizational restructuring have emphasized the negative effects that might be manifest, and these include, 'worry', 'uncertainty', 'job insecurity', 'decreased job satisfaction, organizational commitment, trust in the company' and 'intention to remain' (Schweiger and DeNisi, 1991). Nevertheless, 'change is here to stay' is the old adage whose truth permeates all our lives (Cooper, Cooper and Eaker, 1988). Thus, it would appear that exposure to 'change' as a source of stress is an inevitable part of modern day living and working. Unless we effectively manage this form of workplace stress, it can result in adverse and costly outcomes for employees and the organization. In the Chapter 4 we will examine the ways that 'change' permeates organizational life to become a source of stress.

4 Understanding the Nature of Stress: Organizational Hot Spots

The interactive model of stress described in Chapter 3 specifies that we need to identify, measure and understand three separate issues, including:

1. sources of stress (that is, the stressors) that exist in the environment;
2. the moderators or mediators of the stress response (that is, those individual differences which shape our response to stress);
3. outcomes or the manifestations of exposure to a source of stress.

Outcomes, or symptoms of exposure to stress have already been discussed in Chapters 1 and 2. These can be either individual or organizational outcomes. The issue of moderators and mediators of the stress response are considered in Chapter 6, which describes the process of conducting a stress audit, or risk assessment. Therefore, in this chapter we review potential sources of stress, or 'stressors', in terms of the 'hot spot' issues identified by us while working in contemporary organizations. Since an understanding of the nature of stress is a vital part of an organizational approach to stress management, it is necessary to identify and measure the main sources of stress in the workplace.

The model of stress proposed by Cooper and Marshall (1978) suggests that we can classify sources of stress in terms of six different stressor categories (see Figure 4.1). We will use this framework to present 'stress hot spots' within the workplace. These include:

- *Stress in the job itself:* these stressors intrinsic to the job include workload conditions, the physical work environment, hours of working, decision making latitude, and so on.
- *Role-based stress* that includes stressors such as role conflict, role ambiguity and job responsibility.

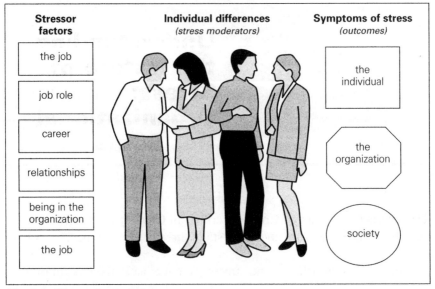

Fig. 4.1   Dimensions of stress

- *Stress due to the changing nature of relationships with other people at work:* these extend to include relationships with managers, supervisors, subordinates and co-workers.
- *Career stress:* this is associated with the lack of opportunity for career development and promotion and job insecurity.
- *Stress associated with the organizational structure and climate:* this includes the stressful nature of the culture and politics of the organization, the restrictions imposed on behaviour, and no sense of belonging. Essentially it is about, 'simply being in the organization'.
- *Stressors associated with the home and work interface:* this includes conflicts of loyalty; the spill-over of demands from one environment to another; life events and life crises.

Hot Spots: Stress in the Job Itself

Without a doubt, the key 'hot spot' stressors in the work environment are the issues of 'work overload', the need to work long hours, changing patterns of employment and the rapid development of computer technology (this is discussed in Chapter 5). These sources of pressure exist within a work environment that exerts physical demands and the potential for distress caused by noise, vibration, extremes of temperature, inappropriate lighting levels and poor hygiene. In the following sections, the stressor 'hot spots' in contemporary organizations are considered first, and then the physical demands of the work environment are discussed.

Stress and work load

Before we examine the issue of work overload further it is necessary to acknowledge that both overload and underload are potential sources of stress in the workplace. According to Hans Selye, a certain level of arousal (a stimulus) is needed for optimal performance. In this 'optimal' state we are likely to feel creative, calm and highly motivated to do the job well. When a level of arousal exceeds our ability to meet the demand placed upon us we experience feelings of 'burnout', exhaustion and, ultimately will collapse. This phenomenon can be explained in terms of a simple 'underload/overload inverted 'U' illustration (see Figure 4.2). If we do not feel challenged or stimulated by the job, or do not believe that our contribution is valued, it is possible that we will experience feelings of apathy, boredom, poor morale, and a lack of self worth. Ultimately, such individuals may 'vote with their feet' and stay away from work, whilst complaining that they are 'sick of the job' rather than feeling physically not well.

An additional distinction must be made at this point in that 'qualitative' load differs from 'quantitative' load. Quantitative overload or underload

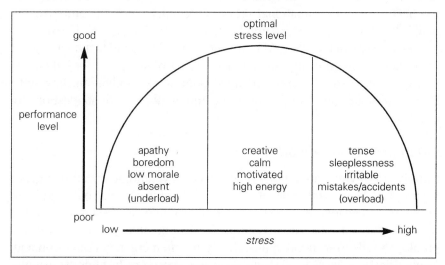

Fig. 4.2 Optimising stress: the relationship between work overload/underload, performance and health

occurs when the employee is given too many or too few tasks to complete in a specified period of time. Qualitative overload or underload occurs when the individual does feel capable of doing the prescribed task, or the task does not utilize the skills, ability or potential of the worker (French and Caplan, 1973). Work overload and underload can result from an irregular flow of work that is outside the control of the employee. This problem is not confined to paced assembly line workers since many occupations face these restrictions that are caused by climatic conditions, seasonal variation and market fluctuation. Certain occupations such as air traffic controllers, fire fighters, the ambulance service, and pilots must deal with periods of inactivity and the need to spring into action on demand or when a crisis happens.

Quantitative overload

Various studies have shown that both physical and mental overloads are potent sources of stress in the workplace. Working under time pressures in order to meet deadlines is also an independent source of stress and stress levels begin to rise as these deadlines draw near. French and Caplan (1973) observed an association between objective, quantitative overload and cigarette smoking, a risk factor for coronary heart disease and certain cancers. Among British tax inspectors, both quantitative and qualitative overloads predicted levels of anxiety and depression (Cooper and Roden, 1985). Many blue-collar workers feel overloaded because the pace of work is too high. Rate of working has been shown to be a significant factor in the health of this occupational group, especially when the employee is unable to control the pace (Frankenhauser and Johansson, 1986). In a national survey in the USA, Margolis *et al,,* (1974) found that quantitative overload was significantly related to a number of symptoms or indicators of exposure to stress. These included poor work motivation, low self-esteem, absenteeism, escapist drinking and an absence of suggestions to employers.

Quantitative underload

Simply not having enough to do may affect psychological well-being. As Figure 4.2 shows, this type of underload, known as 'rust out', leads to boredom and apathy. Boredom in the daily routine, as a result of too little to do, may result in inattentiveness. This is potentially dangerous if the employee fails to respond appropriately in an emergency (Davidson and Veno, 1980). This lack of stimulation may be more hazardous at night when the individual must adjust to the change in sleep pattern but does not have enough work to do to keep alert (Poulton, 1978). Work underload was identified as a significant source of stress among crane operators. Boredom and a lack of challenge were both significant predictors of job dissatisfaction, anxiety and depression among this group (Cooper and Kelly, 1984).

Qualitative overload

There is evidence to suggest that qualitative overload as a source of stress is linked to low levels of self-esteem among white collar workers. However, it is also likely that qualitative overload may be experienced by blue collar workers who are promoted into supervisory positions on the grounds of superior performance, but who have no past experience in the supervision of other people. This, good, reliable employee is rewarded with a promotion but faces considerable stress because the skills to do the new job are lacking. Many individuals in this type of situation describe the need to take disciplinary action against a previous co-worker as a particularly stressful experience.

Qualitative underload

This appears to be more commonly reported than an overload condition and is damaging because the individual is not given an opportunity to use acquired skills and abilities, or to develop potential. The individual is likely to feel that she/he is not getting anywhere and is powerless to show their talent. Thus, a 'rust out' condition will exist. However, it is important to remember that this situation will only be perceived as stressful if the needs and expectations of the individual are not met. For example, research evidence suggests that new graduate recruits are likely to suffer from qualitative underload when starting their first full time job after leaving university life. They enter the world of work with high expectations that are not realized and this form of stress becomes manifest as job dissatisfaction and poor job motivation (Hall, 1976). Many individuals in this situation will quickly move on to another organization that appears to be offering what they are seeking from a job. Unrealistic job previews are the major cause of this type of stress. It is very costly to organizations in terms of recruitment and initial training costs and the individual is scarred by a bad experience at the beginning of his or her career.

Udris (1981, cited ILO, 1986) suggests that qualitative overload is associated with job dissatisfaction, tension and low self-esteem, whereas qualitative underload is linked to dissatisfaction, depression, irritation and psychosomatic complaints. Lack of stimulation, under-utilisation of skills, and boredom characterize many blue-collar occupations. Benyon and Blackburn (1972) reported the feelings of tension resulting from boredom among workers on a packing line system. The workers said that their jobs did not provide any sense of achievement or satisfaction. Job stress associated with passive, low skill demands, lack of variety, repetitiveness, and low decision latitude factory work, also spills over into leisure time. This negatively affects life outside of the workplace (Gardell, 1976, cited ILO 1986) and a lack of stimulation that can be dangerous. For example, Cheliout *et al.*, (1979) found a high incidence of deactivation episodes among electronic assembly workers (monitored by continuous electro-encephalography, over the entire day). The theta rhythm pattern observed, referred to as micro-sleep, is indicative of the boredom and tedium experienced by these employees. They were, in fact, 'sleeping with their eyes open'.

New technology that leads to the increasing automation of industry can lead to the simplification of work. The repetitive, simple, short cycle jobs that are the outcome of automation can cause qualitative underload at work (this is discussed further in Chapter 5 on the impact of 'new technology'). Although a hectic pace at work is stressful, work that is dull and monotonous is equally detrimental to the individual's physical and psychological well-being (Kornhauser, 1965). Research has shown a high incidence of angina pectoris among industrial workers employed on a conveyor line system. However, the results from research into this type of workplace stress are equivocal. For example, O'Brien *et al.*, (1979) found that the heart-rate of medical nurses was sensitive to emotional stress, whereas the response among truck assembly line workers (also 'wired' to unobtrusive monitoring of heart rate and blood pressure) was a function of the physical work and activity. However, Salvendy and Knight (1983) used on-line monitoring of blood pressure to demonstrate that industrial workers in machine-paced tasks did not display any greater stress-response risk than those workers in self-paced tasks.

Work overload

Therefore, it is apparent that a significant change for many of us at work is in the *volume of workload* and the level demand placed upon each of us. It usually means having too much rather too little work to do, although, as we have noted, both of these are potential sources of strain. Aided by rapid technological development, many organizations have, 'streamlined, downsized, or rightsized' in order to continue to meet increasing competition from home and foreign markets. Therefore, it is likely that there are now fewer employees, but engaged in more work. Thus, a high level of demand appears to be a common problem for many people working in contemporary organizations.

Simply having too much to do in the time allowed, unrealistic time and deadline pressures that lead to long hours of working; ever increasing production demands and responsibilities; the fast pace of work which is often controlled by others or machines; the level of difficulty of work; the lack, or uneven distribution, of resources available; and fluctuations in the form of peaks and troughs in work demand also create uncertainty that can also be stressful.

Siegrist (1997) suggests that a theoretical concept is needed to identify the 'toxic' components of stressful experiences at work. To understand response to stress we need to apply an interactive model of stress and consider the interaction between work characteristics and the individual. For example, the demand-control model of work stress proposed by Karasek and Theorell (1990) suggests that we can understand response to job demands only if we also take into account the individual's perceptions of 'control' in the workplace. According to this model, the combined effect of high job demand and of low job control (low decision latitude at work; low skill discretion) create recurrent negative emotions and associated physiological stress reactions that, in the long term adversely affect health, including the cardiovascular system (Siegrist, 1997). Social support from both work colleagues and supervisors will also moderate the impact of job demand and job control.

The effort-reward imbalance model proposed by Siegrist (1997) offers another model to explain how an individual copes with the demands of work. This concept claims that the same types of tasks may produce quite different psychological and physiological reactions depending on the person's way of coping with a demand. Two sources of high effort are defined. Extrinsic effort refers to demands and obligations, and intrinsic effort refers to the motivations of the individual. Siegrist states,

> Stressful experience associated with high effort results from the absence of an appropriate reward, either in terms of esteem, money, career opportunities and job security. Having a demanding but unstable job, achieving at a high level without being offered promotion prospects, or receiving an inadequate wage in comparison to one's efforts or qualifications, are examples of 'toxic' psychosocial experience at work which adversely affects cardiovascular health.

Siegrist suggests that jobs can now be defined by 'psychomental' rather than physical demands. Psychomental overload and underload, work pressure due to rationalization, job insecurity, and forced mobility are now commonplace sources of stress at work.

Long hours of work

The move towards downsizing, fuelled by new technology and global market pressures have spurred a need for more flexibility in the labour market. This has created new patterns of employment that are a potential source of stress in themselves, in addition to creating work overload conditions and the need to work longer hours. A variety of reforms were introduced in order to free the labour market from legal and other constraints, supposedly to encourage employers to hire labour and create the flexible employment practices needed in a competitive economy. Whilst such practices did result in some falls in unemployment, one impact has been on working hours. Simpson (1998) suggests that the increase in working hours can be partly explained by the emphasis in the UK on numerical flexibility, whereby employers are able to vary hours worked and numbers employed in response to changing demand conditions. According to Beatson (1995) this contributed to the development of a dual labour market. Typically, this is characterized by a small 'core' of permanent and increasingly overworked employees, and an outer layer of 'peripheral' workers, employed on a variety of short term, project-based, casual contracts. These individuals have little security of tenure whilst those with a 'permanent' job face the pressures of work overload and fear of job loss! The need to work longer hours is one of the consequences of work overload.

Simply having too much to do (quantitative load) in the normal working day can result in a need to work overtime. This can be either paid or non-paid work. Also, the employee who struggles to do a job that is too difficult (qualitative load) is likely to end up working long hours because he or she will take more time to complete the task to a satisfactory standard. Work overload resulting in longer hours of work has been linked with stress (Cooper *et al*., 1982), indefinite complaints (McCall, 1988), and fatigue (Ono, 1991). In addition, the need to work long hours has been associated with poor lifestyle habits such as heavy smkoing, inadequate diet, and lack of exercise (Maruyama *et al*., 1995). These behaviours, themselves, can lead to health problems. Thus, establishing links and the issue of causation, between long hours of working and ill health, remains a controversial and much debated topic. The following studies show some of these findings:

1. A relationship between the number of hours worked and death from coronary heart disease (CHD) was been reported by Breslow and Buell (1960). Their study of light industry workers in the USA found that subjects of under 45 years of age, but working more than 48 hours per week, had twice the risk of death from CHD, compared to similar individuals working 40 hours or fewer a week.

2. Russek and Zohman (1958) studied 100 young coronary patients and showed that 25 per cent of them had been working at two jobs and an additional 40 per cent had worked for more than sixty hours or more, on average, a week.

3. Uehata (1991) investigated long working hours and occupational stress-related cardiovascular attacks among middle-aged workers in Japan. The subjects were the families of 203 Japanese karoshi (that is, fatal attacks due to work overload). Of these, 196 were men and seven were women. Their ages ranged from 21 to 67 years. Causes of death comprised 123 strokes, 50 acute cardiac failures, 27 myocardial infarctions and four aortic ruptures. Uehata found that two-thirds of the subjects worked for long hours. Among the white collar subjects this also included the need to take excessive business trips and changes of workplaces. Eighty-eight of these subjects (white- and blue-collar employees) had experienced work-related emotional anxiety or excitement, rapid increase in workload, unexpected work troubles, or environmental changes, 24 hours before the fatal attack.

4. Waldfogel, and Cobb (1954), conducted a psychosomatic study of 46 young men with coronary artery disease. Both questionnaire and interview methods were used to compare differences between 46 coronary patients and 49 members of a control group. It was found that 50 per cent of the patients, as opposed to 12 per cent of the control group, reported working long hours, with few holidays, and under considerable strain before falling victim to heart disease.

5. Talbot, Cooper and Barrow (1992) investigated the relationship between creative climate and perceived stress among 202, mostly male respondents working in one organization, at all levels, including management. They found that as stress levels increased the creative climate worsened. That is, high levels of stress intrinsic to the job (which included long hours of working and time pressures) were associated with a decrease in 'idea time' (that is, the amount of time people used for elaborating new ideas) and promptness of response to arising opportunities.

6. Sutherland and Davidson (1993) found that long hours of working were part of the culture for 561 onsite managers in the UK construction industry. It was clear that certain peer group pressures operated to encourage the managers to arrive early and stay late. It was commonly believed that promotion prospects and assignment to the more lucrative contracts were contingent on being highly visible at work and demonstrating a strong commitment to the company by working very long hours. However, this pattern of behaviour was observed to have an adverse impact on the workforce. Managers who had worked in excess of 20 hours overtime in the month prior to taking part in a health and stress audit screening were significantly worse off in terms of poorer psychological health (depression) and job dissatisfaction. They also perceived more stress and strain at work and at home. They reported significantly higher levels of stress for 'role ambiguity, work-overload, manpower problems, home-work interface and boundary relationships', when compared to managers who had worked fewer than 21 hours of overtime that month. Overall, this occupational group tended to work 10.3 hours on average per day, and only 20 per cent of them said that they never worked at weekends.

There was a toll on the health of this occupational group and a high level of sickness absence was reported. Although sickness absence data for those in managerial occupations tends to be rare, 46 per cent of this group of construction site managers indicated absence due to illness in the previous year; 43 per cent had been absent on two occasions and 17 per cent on three occasions. A total of 1702 days' sickness-absence was lost, ranging from 1–90 days (average 6.7 days). Comparisons with another ongoing research project was possible. This was among managers employed in a large retail organization. In this company we observed a 59 per cent absence rate during the previous years, with a total 1815 days lost; the average number of days lost was 8.4.

The need to work long hours has other negative consequences in that the individual consequently spends less time in social relationships. It means that the benefits of social support as a buffer in a stressful job are reduced. It may also cause strain in his or her relationship with a spouse or partner, thereby creating work-to-home overspill stress.

7. Cooper and Sutherland (1991) found that senior and top executives (CEOs) across Europe also experienced 'work spill-over' problems that adversely affected their home and social lives. This survey of 118 chief executives found that two thirds worked nearly 12 hours each day; some up to 16 hours a day. Almost all of them worked at the weekends, thus

restricting time spent with the family. The top sources of stress were work overload, time pressures and deadlines, work-related travel and working long hours. Many of these senior executives seemed to realize the potentially damaging consequences of their lifestyle. Twenty-five per cent of them believed that they were at substantial risk of job burnout (physical and emotional exhaustion). More than a quarter of the executives responding to the survey perceived themselves to be at high risk from heart disease (especially the younger CEOs). From the results of this survey it was clear that these individuals were questioning their lifestyle, and many were actively thinking about quitting `life at the top'.

8. A recent quantitative and qualitative review of 21 study samples into the effects of working hours on health concluded that there was a small, but significant association between overall health symptoms, physiological and psychological health symptoms and hours of work (Sparks, *et al.*, 1997). Quantitative analysis of 12 further studies supported these findings. However, the type of job will moderate these health outcomes. For example, the impact of long hours of work may be greater for jobs that require attention (for example, driving), or repetitive work. It also seems that a certain amount of physical activity at work can protect the individual from coronary heart disease, although excessive physical demands can lead to exhaustion, injuries and poor health.

Nevertheless, it should be acknowledged that some individuals regard work and working long hours as a psychological haven and a way of escape from the pressures of home and family or an unsatisfactory personal relationship. Distress only exists when demand exceeds or fails to satisfy abilities or expectations (real or perceived). Also, we may decide to accept a stressful situation for a given period of time because the 'pay off' is highly desired. Unfortunately, we often fail to balance the true costs and the gains and thus become a casualty of exposure to mismanaged stress at work.

Long working hours and the effects on health are still unresolved issues. Many of the studies have focused on the impact of shift working, long hours and health, and much of the focus has been on health outcomes such as cardiovascular disease. There is still a need to consider the impact on long hours of working on performance, safety and mental ill health. Limited empirical evidence suggests that these deleterious effects of working an excessive number of hours should be a cause for concern in organizations where employees regularly work long hours (Spurgeon *et al.*, 1997).

Many countries in Europe have introduced reduced working times. However, the UK is the only member state where the number of hours worked each week has increased over the past decade. Britain works on average 44.7 hours a week, the highest in Europe (Rubery *et al*., 1995), compared to between 30 and 40 hours a week in the other European countries. A European Directive on the organization of working time is now in effect (Council Directive 93/104/EC). The core provisions of the Directive include a minimum daily rest period of 11 consecutive hours in 24, an average eight hours in 24 for night workers, one 35-hour period off every seven days (that is, 24 hours off plus 11 hours), four weeks paid annual leave a year and maximum working of 48 hours per week. An employee is entitled to refuse to work over 48 hours a week but can agree to do so. Many are still not happy with the restriction on working hours prescribed by the EC Directive. However, it seems that we must accept that these limitations are probably appropriate at the present time.

Work overload among managers

Some of the studies reported above illustrate the adverse impact of working long hours at work and it appears that this takes its toll on those employed as managers in the workplace. Whilst all employees have suffered the impact of change in employment patterns, Wood (1989) suggests that managers have acquired a 'dual status'. Thus, in theory they are likely to have a permanent contract and access to an internal labour market of promotional opportunities, but in practice they often face redundancy or limited career prospects in their organizations. Their 'dual status' of being part of the reduced 'core' of workers, creates a double burden, which is exacerbated by the long hours of working (Simpson, 1998). Hours of working seem to have increased for two main reasons:

1. First, in the face of restructuring, new technology and the loss of key personnel, their workload is considerably increased. Studies of personnel in managerial positions suggest that many of these individuals, at all levels of the management structure, are increasingly exposed to working longer hours (Institute of Management, 1996; Wheatley, 1992), a heavy volume of work, time pressures, difficult and demanding deadline pressures and a lack of, or uneven, distribution of resources. The Institute of Management Services survey found that 47 per cent of a sample of 1100 managers reported that their workload had increased greatly in the past year (1995–6), Nearly six in ten respondents claimed that they always worked in excess of their official working week. Half of the respondents took work

home and over four in ten always worked at weekends. Only half of these managerial personnel actually looked forward to going to work and 65 per cent felt that their professional and personal lives were not in balance. Unreasonable deadlines and office politics were identified as key sources of pressure (IMS: Charlesworth, 1996). Similarly, Scase and Goffee (1989) found that the majority of managers in their survey worked an average week in excess of 50 hours. Those working in the National Health Service worked an average of 56 hours per week (IHSM Consultants, 1994). The survey by Wajcman (1996) of five multinational companies reported that over 60 per cent of managers worked on average 50 hours, and 16 per cent worked more than 60 hours, a week. McKay (1995) also observed a strong link between restructuring, increased workload, hours worked, plus an increase in hours worked following large-scale redundancies. For example, the proportion of British Telecom employees working more than 46 hours a week, increased from 39 per cent in 1991 to 51 per cent in 1995, following a major restructuring exercise (Newell and Dopson, 1996).

2. Since employers are unwilling to promise job security, many managers (and their subordinates) react to the insecurity and fear of redundancy by staying at the desk or workplace for longer periods of time. This is viewed as an attempt to demonstrate visible commitment to the organization and the job itself (Goffee and Scase, 1992). Brockner *et al.*, 1993 described this behaviour as part of a 'survivor' syndrome that affects many managers who have experienced restructuring and downsizing of their organization. Characteristics of the survivor syndrome include heightened anxiety, decreased morale. According to Clarke (1994) this fear of being in line for redundancy, drives the individual to work harder, and to be seen at work for longer periods of time. This means that they tend to arrive very early and stay very late into the evening. It is the work ethic of making sure that you are never first to leave the workplace! We are able to cite one group of managers who actually produced a 'breakfast club' tie that could be purchased by 'members' who regularly arrived at work by 0700 hours. This dysfunctional outcome is more commonly known as' 'presenteeism'(Cooper 1996, p. 15). It means, 'being at work when you should be at home either because you are ill or because you are working such long hours that you are no longer effective'. The survey reported by recruitment consultants Austin Knight (1994) supported these notions. They found that more than 50 per cent of respondents felt pressurized by a prevailing culture of presenteeism. Also, 20 per cent worked long hours either because they feared job loss or because they felt under direct line-manager pressure.

Among a sample of managers who attended business schools, Simpson (1998) observed that long hours were worked for three reasons:

- The job demanded it; for example, sudden deadlines imposed one-off necessity, or, a temporary phenomenon while new skills or procedures were being learnt;
- Restructuring had led to higher workloads because of loss of staff or because of the demands of continual job changes;
- Managers who had been through restructuring were made to feel that they could only retain their position by working long hours as a way of demonstrating visible commitment to the job. Simpson also found that this was more likely to be a feature of male behaviour, but they were more likely than the female managers to deny working longer hours than necessary.

Whilst personnel in managerial positions are under stress due to long hours of working, the blue collar and shop floor employees face the need to work long hours and a shift pattern that is imposed rather than chosen.

Shift work

The need to work for long hours is not restricted to personnel in management jobs in the organization. In order for companies to respond to demands for faster service and products, the need to operate a 24- hour a day operation is a reality for many organizations. Therefore, many employees in non-management jobs face the need to work shifts, including evening and night shifts, in addition to working extra hours and overtime in the downsized workplace. This is to facilitate the needs of industry to maximize the useful life of expensive technology and increase profitability. Other companies are required to remain open around the clock because of the nature of their business. Increasingly, the world of business and industry resembles 'the sleepless gorgon' described by Toffler (1970) in *Future Shock*.

A great number of different shift patterns has been identified. Singer (1985) reported 487 different shift-work systems operating in Europe, including permanent, continuous and rotating patterns, some which require night-shift working. Shift work, described as 'continuous', requires the employee to work at weekends, whereas, 'discontinuous' rosters normally require the individual to work a variety of shifts from Monday to Friday only. Whilst some individuals work a permanent shift, for example, 'permanent nights', the most common pattern of shift work is to rotate the hours of working. Indeed, Mitler (1992) reported that one-third of the US labour market worked a rotating work schedule. A plethora of research evidence indicates that the consequences of shift working include physiological, psychological and performance-related outcomes. Nevertheless, it seems that the trend is towards working shifts of longer duration.

Many organizations, for example, manufacturing industry, oil exploration and production industries, and hospital and ambulance services, have introduced the 12-hour shift. This extends shift duration, with a concomitant decrease in the number of days worked. It is known as working a 'compressed working week' or the '4/40 work week'. Typically, ten or 12-hour shift rosters are the norm, and organizations work a four- or five-shift roster to facilitate this process. Overall, the number of annual hours worked remains the same, or even slightly fewer. Those who favour this work pattern enjoy the extra leisure time, long weekends, or 'ten-day breaks' and appear to be more satisfied with their job and work schedules. Also, Williamson *et al.*, 1994 found improvements to the health of computer operators following a change from eight-hour irregular, to 12-hour, regular shift working.

However, it means that many employees are required to work for, perhaps, 12 hours at a time, often engaged in work that is physically or mentally demanding. Thus, there is some evidence to suggest that the 12-hour compressed schedule can lead to lower performance. For example, Rosa *et al.*, 1989 found performance decrements or increased errors of 187 per cent, for workers on a 12-hour schedule, compared to the same workers who had previously been on an eight-hour roster, even after seven months of adjustment time to the new shift pattern. Older employees, who are more susceptible to fatigue appear to suffer most from these compressed work schedules and appear to be less enthusiastic about this way of working. The impact of the 12-hour compressed working week is not truly understood. Research results are mixed; some indicate improved performance and productivity, some show no change and other indicate decline. In certain instances, safety performance levels improve (Daus *et al.*, 1998).

Some individuals prefer the compressed working week, while others loathe it! In order for compressed schedules to work, both management and shop floor employees must support the concept. However, it seems, that for certain individuals, the need to engage in shift work of any kind, is unacceptable. For example, in a study of 880 nurses in Austria (Kundi *et al.*, 1995), 44 per cent of nurses working the 12-hour shift were dissatisfied with their work schedule. However, 47 per cent of the eight-hour shift workers were also dissatisfied! Whilst the impact on work strain was less among the nurses working the eight-hour shift, some of those working the 12-hour shift pattern rated this as superior with respect to the 'potential value of free time'. However, neither shift pattern was very appealing to the nurses.

In comparison with eight-hour shifts, 12-hour shifts may be associated with increased fatigue and decreased performance; however, not all studies have observed these effects (Duchon and Smith, 1992). In our experience, the extended break (ten or 12 days) away from work, necessary for rest and to catch up on sleep, is often used by employees to engage in 'second jobs'. These are often in a self-employed capacity, or moonlighting in the black economy. Whilst the extent of these activities is not documented, it appears not to be uncommon. For obvious reasons workers do not wish to admit to these extracurricular activities. Thus, the fatigue effects observed in some studies might not be caused solely by the impact of the main, or legitimate job. Some workers find additional work because they need the income, others complain of the boredom and loneliness of the ten- or 12-day work breaks. Their children are in school and their partners work during the day. Yet, the ability to plan up to one year ahead for time off is one of the acknowledged benefits because shift rosters are usually produced annually. This means that it is likely that workers can exchange shifts with a colleague to avoid missing an important family or social gathering. So, subjectively, the picture is not totally bleak, although the need for longitudinal, well-controlled research on the impact of 12-hour shift working is evident.

Nevertheless, evidence suggests that the need to work shifts can be a potent source of stress. Individuals are required to engage in work activity at a time of day when they should be sleeping. Conversely, they must try to sleep at the time of day when normally they would be active and alert. Normally, sleep, metabolism, temperature and the production of many hormones follow a 24-hour cycle, or circadian rhythm. It is controlled by our biological clock. This is an endogenous 'pacemaker'(Daus, Sanders and Campbell, 1998). It works in combination with exogenous environmental cues (known as 'zeitgebers'; for example the day-night light cycle) to keep our bodies synchronized to a 24-hour cycle. When we reverse these natural tendencies, by engaging in night shift work, the circadian system becomes disrupted and rhythms move out of phase. Thus, shift working has a biological and an emotional impact on the individual due to circadian rhythm disturbances to the sleep/wake cycle, body temperature and adrenaline excretion rhythm. It can affect neurophysical rhythms such as blood temperature, blood sugar levels, metabolic rate and mental efficiency (Monk and Tepas, 1985). For example, Cobb and Rose (1973) found that air traffic controllers had four times the prevalence of hypertension, more mild diabetes and peptic ulcers than a non-shift working control group of US Air Force personnel.

The disturbance of nocturnal sleep leads to daytime fatigue and sleepiness impairs motivation and vigilance, thereby affecting the performance level and safety of the individual (Hellesøy, 1985; Moore-Ede, 1993). It is known that the neural processes controlling alertness and sleep produce an increased sleep tendency and reduced capacity to function during early morning hours. This occurs, approximately, between 0200 and 0700 hours, regardless of whether one has slept or not (Mitler, 1992). Studies indicate that night-shift employees tend to have a great number of performance failures, lower productivity and efficiency (Scott, 1994). It is suggested that a decline in capacity for work, in the magnitude of 5 to 10 per cent, should be expected during nocturnal work periods, compared to daytime work (Bonnet, 1990). This will dissipate if the workers maintain a consistent sleep-wake routine.

In one survey of industrial workers, Lavie *et al.*, 1982 found that employees who complained about 'sleep', had significantly more work accidents, repeated work accidents, and more sick days per work accident than their non-complaining work colleagues. Their complaint about day-time sleepiness was related to multiple work accidents, irrespective of the age of the employee and the physical effort required in the job. Whilst it is acknowledged that daytime sleepiness can be symptomatic of breathing disorders or narcolepsy, this behaviour may also be a response to stress and a symptom of depression or somatic anxiety. Whilst psychological problems such as depression and mood disturbances might be observed among those individuals working normal hours, it suggests that personnel engaged in shift working might experience these effects to a greater degree (Moore-Ede, 1993). Sutherland and Cooper (1991) found that personnel in the offshore oil and gas industry, who worked longer 'tours' (that is the number of consecutive days spent offshore), of 14 rather than seven days, were more likely to report job dissatisfaction and a poorer level of mental well-being than their counterparts who only worked for seven days offshore at a time.

Since individuals engaged in night working or rotating shifts have reported lower levels of alertness, concentration and vigour, and higher levels of confusion and fatigue, it is not only the individual who is at risk. Customers and clients serviced by shift workers may also suffer negative consequences in terms of poor performance and mistakes. At risk are those individuals who must respond to monitors as part of the job. For example, these include intensive care nurses and nuclear power plant operators; or those who need a high level of concentration at critical times, such as paramedics, and operators in process plants when potentially hazardous materials and chemicals are being used.

Monk and Folkard (1983) stated that there are three factors that must be considered for successful coping with shift work, namely, sleep, social and family life, and circadian rhythms. Since these are all interrelated, problems with one can negate the positive effects of success achieved in the others. Ultimately roster designs must aim to maximize the positive effects and minimize the negative impact of shift work. It would appear that certain individuals might adapt to shift working more effectively than others. For example, individuals with steeper adrenaline curves than normal tolerate shift work best. This 'steeper' rhythm is less vulnerable to distortion and the rationale is that non-adaptation is better than partial adaptation. A study of railroad workers supports this hypothesis. These employees worked three weeks of day work, followed by three weeks of night work. Very little adjustment in the pattern of adrenaline excretion was observed after three shifts of night work, with adrenaline remaining high during the day when the employees should have been sleeping. Even after three weeks of night work, no significant adjustment was observed. Akerstedt (1977) suggested that high day-time adrenaline levels were the source of the disrupted sleep pattern. Both the duration and quality of day-time sleep differ from nocturnal sleep (Smith *et al.*, 1995). This means that the sleep is more fragile and unstable. Many night shift workers report that they are able to take catnaps to help them catch up on sleep loss. However, a 'sleep debt' can accumulate over a seven-day period, to the extent that the employee effectively loses the equivalent of at least one night's sleep. In fact, Mitler (1992) found that over 55 per cent of a sample of 1500 shift workers admitted to falling asleep on the job during a given week. Akerstedt (1988) reported that 11 per cent of locomotive engineers 'dozed off' on most trips, while 59 per cent admitted to falling asleep at least once.

In a recent study of tolerance to shift work, personality variables such as 'neuroticism', 'eveningness', 'hard-driving and competitiveness' were not found to be useful predictor variables of health outcomes. However, 'rigidity of sleeping habits' consistently and reliability predicted poor health, respiratory complaints and psychosomatic-digestive complaints scores, after one and three years of shift work experience in the oil-refinery business (Kaliterna *et al.*, 1995).

Selye (1976) suggested that individuals do habituate to shift working and it becomes physically less stressful with time. However, it would seem that alternate work schedules do not achieve their expressed objectives.

The original intention was to design work schedules to reduce absenteeism, tardiness, turnover and withdrawal behaviours. Research evidence suggests that this is not the reality of shift working. For example, Jamal and Baba (1992) report an increase in sickness absence, tardiness and turnover among nurses working a rotating shift compared to employees on non-rotating shifts. In our experience we have found that night shift personnel admit that they will call in sick to avoid this disliked shift; also paramedics will take holiday entitlement in order to avoid their 12-hour night shift. Again, not all research supports this view. Absence rates among shift workers are sometimes lower than for their non-shift work counterparts. The degree to which the individual can volunteer for shift work is obviously a factor in influencing these findings.

However, since many employees do not have any choice about the pattern of their hours of working, Knauth and Rutenfranz (1982) suggest that rapidly rotating shift systems, with few night shifts in succession, may be the best strategy for the individual. Also, individuals need to understand the importance of sleep hygiene. These recommendations include maintaining regular sleep times, a proper sleeping environment, taking regular exercise, regular and balanced meals, avoidance of alcohol and caffeine prior to sleep, avoidance of time-in-bed worrying, and using the bedroom for only sleep and sexual activity (Nicholson and Marks, 1983). Shift workers are more likely to complain of fatigue and gastrointestinal problems than day workers and the disruption to eating habits caused by shift working is the most likely explanation of these digestive tract disorders. Mitler (1992) suggests that approximately 20 per cent of shift workers experience gastrointestinal disorders. However, increased alcohol, caffeine and sleeping pill usage, are some of the possible consequences of shift working (Mitler, 1992) and these behaviours could explain some of the observed consequences of shift working. For example, high levels of caffeine can have an adverse effect on the digestive tract.

In another study of shift workers, Sigman found that over 80 per cent of respondents reported serious sleep disruption, leading to drowsiness at work and insomnia. Workers felt that this adversely affected the quality of their lives and productivity levels at work. Sigman (1993) suggests that workers on night shift are more irritable, restless, less alert, quicker to make mistakes and more lethargic at home than day workers. Smith *et al.*, 1995 found that whilst workload remained stable, night shift workers in the nuclear power industry had lower levels of alertness and poorer performance in terms of 'response time' and accuracy, compared to day and evening shift employees. However, in some components of performance on the 12-hour night shift, a demonstrated improvement was observed, during what could be considered a critical time. It was suggested that these reactor operators recognized that it was a long and tiring shift, which potentially could have a more serious impact upon performance. Thus, they invested more effort to function effectively at this time.

Working the night shift can also have a negative impact on social relationship. Shift workers have trouble maintaining friendships and relationships with friends who do not share their work pattern. Some shift workers report that their unsociable working hours, and the fatigue experienced, causes problems in socializing with friends and family. This can lead to feelings of isolation and often the pursuit of lone activities (Prossin, 1983; Sutherland and Cooper, 1991). They do not have the energy or motivation to socialize with non-shift working individuals. Furthermore, the need to engage in shift work can cause strains within the family. It interferes with family time, and can have negative impact on relationships with spouse or children. The quality of a marriage or relationship might suffer when issues of jealousy and infidelity are a concern. However, not all shift workers complain about disruptions to family life or domestic problems (Barton and Folkard, 1991). Many report that they spend more time with their children and find it easier to attend school and family gatherings. They are also able to plan childcare in a more desirable and cost-effective way because one parent is usually at home (Skipper *et al.*, 1990).

Despite considerable research efforts into shift working it is still not possible to make generalizations regarding 'optimal' shift systems. There are numerous variations and combinations but an 'ideal' shift system still has not been identified. Current wisdom suggests that shift schedules should:

- have a shift rotation that is predominately fast, where there are only few consecutive shifts of the same form
- the blocks of working days are short and there are always days off between different shift blocks
- only two to four consecutive night shifts are worked
- ideally, free evenings from Monday to Friday appear in almost most weeks.

In addition to the pressures of adapting to the changes associated with increased volume of work, shift working and long hours of working, patterns of employment are being altered. This may be an additional source of stress in the work environment.

New patterns of employment

The global restructuring of production, the resulting shift of focus from manufacturing industries to the services sector, and the recessionary climate, have caused the loss of jobs for many. Others face job insecurity. The advent of the 'contingent worker' has led to changes in the nature of employment. The associated strains and pressures exist for individuals directly and indirectly employed, although differences will exist between 'core' and 'periphery' workers. Organizations now 'contract out' many services and staff are given fixed term contracts. Many employees work on a part time or temporary contract basis, and more and more women are now in the workplace. The power and the role of trade unions are also diminished. Hartley (1995) provides a comprehensive review of this, but the following offers a flavour of these changes in the patterns of employment.

- 15.5 per cent of the work-force were part time employees in 1971; this increased to 26 per cent by 1991 and is estimated at 32.3 per cent by the year 2001 (TUC, 1994). Many organizations now refer to these employees as 'keytime' workers rather than 'part time', in order to signify the importance of this form of employment to their businesses (Hartley, 1995).
- In 1994 there were 157000 temporary employees in the UK and this represented a 10 per cent increase over the previous year.
- Women are more likely to occupy part time jobs than men and ultimately are more likely to be employed than men if the trend towards part time working continues.
- Legislative changes have decreased the influence and scope of trade unions and membership has declined; since women are less likely than men to join trade unions, this decline will continue if action is not taken to rectify the situation.

Contingent employment, suggests Christensen (1995), is a cost framework in which the worker is perceived as a commodity rather than an investment. As such it creates a divisive workforce where one group is perceived as a cost whilst the other, 'core' worker group is seen as 'the investment'.

Such changes, described as intrinsic to the job, will combine with existing pressures. This means that many of us will remain in a high state of stress-induced arousal for much of the working day, without any natural release of the normally protective 'fight' or 'flight' responses against exposure to stress. Many of us have now have mainly sedentary jobs, and those in fulltime employment are working very long hours. This means that it is unlikely we will have the opportunity, or the inclination to engage in much needed physical activities outside work. Either we have no time, or feel burned out, psychologically exhausted, depressed or anxious, because we are not coping with the job. Thus, the problem will become compounded and the vicious downward spiral of stress begins.

Stress and the physical work environment

In addition to the task demands of the job as a source of stress, it is important to consider the stress associated with the physical nature of the environment at work. These include the distress caused by noise and vibration, extremes of temperature, lighting, and hygiene factors. Many of these potential sources of stress were the focus of attention for early researchers who investigated the links between the physical conditions of the workplace and productivity levels (Munsterberg, 1913; Roethlisberger and Dickson, 1939). The significance of the relationships between emotional and social factors, performance and health was identified in these early studies. However, the work of Roethlisberger and Dickson, 1939, in the famous 'Hawthorne Studies', identified the significance and importance of 'subjective reactivity' as a response in these conditions. They correctly identified the weakness of using only objective measures of these factors and forced subsequent researchers to acknowledge that, 'stress is in the eye of the beholder'. Whilst the early studies of stress at work attempted to identify the work conditions that were optimal for performance and productivity, Kornhauser (1965) found that unpleasant work conditions, the necessity to work at a fast pace, expend a lot of physical effort, and work excessive and inconvenient hours were associated with poor mental health. More recent research suggests that there is still a need to consider poor physical environment a source of strain in the workplace. Piotrkowski, Cohen and Coray (1992) conducted a survey for the National Institute for Occupational Safety and Health in the USA (NIOSH). This was a comprehensive study on the relationship of working conditions to health and well-being among women office workers, in the context of women's dual roles as employees and family members. Data was collected from 625 respondents in this study of both the public and private sectors in the USA. The results from questionnaire, interview and ergonomic data indicate that poor organizational climate, lack of job control, excessive workload, interpersonal tension AND a poor physical environment were related to greater strain. The European Foundation for the Improvement of Living and Working Conditions (EFILWC) survey of 1996, found that stressful physical environments, characterized by noise, polluted air, heat, cold and vibration, carrying heavy loads and working in painful or tiring positions were just as prevalent in 1996 as in 1991. Of the 15 800 people surveyed within the fifteen member states, almost one third of employees indicated that they were still exposed to intense noise, or required to handle heavy loads. More than half had no personal control over comfort factors at their workplace (lighting, temperature and ventilation, and so on).

In the next sections, issues of noise, vibration, temperature (heat, cold ventilation), hygiene and exposure to danger and hazard, are considered as potential sources of stress at work.

Noise

Whilst language and communication enrich human culture, 'acoustic noise' defined as 'unwanted sound'(Jones, 1983) can be a source of stress. Two health hazards are linked with exposure to noise in the environment. First, the risk of occupational deafness, and secondly, that as a source of stress, noise increases a person's level of arousal and might cause some psychological imbalance. Exposure to noise can also impede hearing ability and cause a situation to become dangerous if a 'wanted' sound is not heard. For example, an accident can occur if warning sounds are not heard (Poulton, 1978). The extent to which noise, as a source of stress, can cause an increased level of arousal and a psychological imbalance, is still debated. Ivancevich and Matteson (1980) suggest that excessive noise, of approximately 80 decibels, on a recurring, prolonged basis, can cause stress. The noise from a pneumatic chipper is measured at around 130 decibels. Our pain threshold is 140 decibels (Oborne, 1994), whereas 70 decibels is normal conversational speech and a bedroom at night is measured at 30 decibels. However, noise operates less as a stressor in situations where it is excessive but expected, rather than in those circumstances where it is unpredictable or unexpected. Both continuous noise and intermittent noise, are therefore, potentially stressful. Nemecek and Granjean (1973) studied noise in landscaped offices and found that the noise of conversation was the most annoying. In this survey, 46 per cent of employees were disturbed and annoyed by the noise of conversation (and referred to the content of the conversation rather than the loudness of it). Only 25 per cent disliked the noise of the office machinery and 19 per cent complained about the noise of telephones.

However, it also appears that personality characteristics mediate the response to noise as a source of stress. Lader (1971) suggests that those at risk from noise are those who habituate more slowly than normal and who are often characterized by anxiety. Although noise can be expressed in objective, physical terms according to its intensity, variability, frequency, predictability and control, reaction to noise is ultimately a subjective experience. Exposure to noise is associated with reported fatigue, headaches, irritability and poor concentration. Behavioural consequences include reduced performance, lowered productivity levels and accident occurrence. It is also possible that there is some adverse impact on our social behaviour. Exposure to noise can reduce our willingness to help other people and increase levels of hostility and overt aggression towards those people around us. Thus, when exposed to noise, we exhibit a more extreme or negative attitude towards other people (Jones, 1983). This will lead to poor relationships in the workplace as a consequence of imposed isolation due to excessive noise, or the need to wear hearing protection. Poor interpersonal interactions will result from an accumulation of physical frustration and tension (Keenan and Kerr, 1951).

Nevertheless, the main psychosocial impact of 'noise' and other physical environmental demands, is to reduce worker tolerance to other stressors and to adversely affect the level of worker motivation (Smith *et al.*, 1978). These forms of stress in the workplace are known as 'noise factors', since they take up the attentional capacity of the individual and limit capacity to attend to task-relevant information (Hockey, 1970). Therefore, their impact is usually additive, not primary. However, noise as a harmful source of stress is reported by many groups of blue-collar workers. For example, those in the UK steel industry (Kelly and Cooper, 1981) and personnel working on offshore drilling rigs and platforms, report noise as a potent source of stress (Hellesøy, 1985; Sutherland and Cooper, 1986, 1989). Indeed, unpleasant working conditions due to noise was associated with job dissatisfaction among offshore workers. Other studies have investigated the relationship between exposure to noisy work conditions, productivity and rate of error (Broadbent and Little, 1960). Kerr (1950) found that noise levels were associated with accident frequency but not accident severity. Also, Cohen (1974, 1976) observed an increased rate of accidents in noisy working areas, particularly among the younger and the less experienced employees. The introduction of hearing protection among these employees produced a significant reduction in the frequency of accident occurrence.

In summary, therefore, the impact of noise is a cause for concern because of the following:

- A narrowed focus of attention which has detrimental effects on performance of complex tasks.
- Noise that is unpredictable and uncontrollable reduces one's overall perception of control over the environment. This is often accompanied by a depressed mood and a decrease on motivation to initiate new response. This is described as 'learned helplessness'.
- Research evidence suggests that performance remains impaired after exposure to noise, which reduces tolerance to everyday frustrations.
- Physiological arousal to noise includes increased blood pressure and other stress related hormones (adrenalin and cortisol).
- Exposure to noise levels of 85 decibels (or greater) at work for three to five years is associated with an increased prevalence of a variety of specific non-auditory diseases, such as cardiovascular disorders, gastrointestinal complaints, and infectious diseases. Disease prevalence seems to be greater when the noise is unpredictable or intermittent (Welch,1979).
- Exposure to noise is associated with a variety of negative, behavioural outcomes including a reduction in helping behaviour, and a more extreme or negative attitude towards other people. Thus, there are implications for impoverished relationships and team working in a noisy work environment.

Vibration

Sound at the low end of the range is felt as vibration. Noise below 16Hz is described as infrasound as this can be produced by any pulsating or throbbing piece of equipment such as ventilation systems. The experience of driving on rough ground (for example, tractor drivers) can cause vibration levels that might lead to structural damage to the body over time (Rosegger and Roseggger, 1960). The drivers in this survey, exposed to the vibration of vehicle driving over a long period of time, complained of spinal disorders to the lumber and thoracic regions of the body and stomach complaints.

The health hazards of exposure to 'vibration' at the high frequency end of the range include loss of balance and fatigue, numbness or clumsiness of the fingers, and possible damage to bones, muscles and joints, and the condition known as 'white finger'. It is acknowledged as a source of stress that results in elevated catecholamine levels and alterations to psychological and neurological functioning (Wilkinson, 1969; Selye, 1976). The vibration of rotary or impacting machines (for example, road drills and chain saws) that cause vibrations to transfer from physical objects to the body may lead to performance deterioration. In addition, the 'annoyance' factor may also contribute to some psychological imbalance. Personnel working in the steel casting industry (Kelly and Cooper, 1981) and the offshore oil and gas industries (Sutherland and Cooper, 1986, 1989) are exposed to vibration as a source of stress. Although these individuals claim, 'you get used to it', unpleasant working conditions due to vibration and disturbance in the living quarters were rated as significant stressors in the offshore working environment. The long term impact of this exposure to vibration is not known. The European Foundation for the Improvement of Living and Working Conditions survey of 1996 found that 11 per cent of the 15 800 workers were permanently exposed to vibration in their job. An additional 24 per cent experienced 'vibration' as part of their job for more than one quarter of work time (1996).

Temperature, ventilation and lighting

Inadequate illumination is an obvious contributory factor in accident occurrence. Thus, the aims of a good lighting system are to facilitate performance of the job, to ensure that the work can be carried out safely, and to assist in creating a pleasant environment (McKenna, 1994). Poor lighting, the flicker of fluorescent lights, or glare, lead to eye strain, damaged vision, visual fatigue, headache, tension and frustration. Also, the job is likely to be more difficult and time consuming to complete (Poulton, 1978). However, the findings from the Hawthorn Studies (Roethlisberger and Dickson, 1939) indicate that creating a pleasant environment, that facilitates performance and promotes safety, is not a simple matter of the objective measurement of lighting levels in the workplace. Architects have tried to combat the problems of illumination and 'glare' by designing the 'windowless' workplace and rely on artificial lighting. However, in one study of a windowless office environment, whilst there were very few complaints about the quality of the artificial lighting, 90 per cent of employees who worked on their own expressed dissatisfaction about the absence of windows. They complained about the lack of a view, daylight, poor ventilation, and a lack of awareness about the state of the weather (Ruys, 1970).

Ramsey (1983) states that physiological response to thermal conditions varies greatly between workers and within the same individual from one occasion to the next. Attitudinal and physical problems arise because the factory environment is characterized and described by workers as too hot, too cold, too stuffy and too draughty, and so on (Smith *et al.*, 1978). Manual dexterity can be reduced in a cold environment. This may be a factor in accident causation, due most likely to reduced sensitivity, slowed movement and interference from protective clothing, rather than from the loss of impaired cognitive ability (Surry, 1968). However, work that requires critical decision making, fine discrimination and performance needing fast or skilled actions may also be adversely affected by exposure to thermal stress. Thus, the subjective perception of thermal comfort is all important. It seems, also, that an inability to personally control one's physical work environment could also be a key factor in the perception of thermal discomfort. For example, Ramsey (1983) observed an association between 'comfort' and an individual's performance on perceptual motor tasks.

Noise, fumes and the heat were the most commonly reported problems for casters in the steel industry (Kelly and Cooper, 1981). In the Norwegian offshore oil and gas environment draughts, uncomfortable temperatures and the dry humid air were perceived as sources of environmental stress (Hellesøy, 1985). However, it was also noted that workers were more likely to complain about overheated work conditions (25 per cent of respondents) than the cold (12 per cent of respondents). The general effect of working in overheated conditions is a negative reaction to one's surroundings, and this may result in a lowered tolerance to other stressors and lead to a reduction in worker motivation.

Hygiene

A clean and orderly place of work is important for both hygiene and safety reasons, and it is acknowledged that as housekeeping standards in the workplace improve, the level of accidents is likely to decrease. Poor hygiene standards are likely to cause poor health or disease and have an adverse impact on the level of morale of the workforce. Shostack (1980) reports blue-collar grievances about the often neglected working conditions and the double standards that exist in industry. The all glass, lavish 'front offices' and headquarters accommodation are compared to the noise, lack of windows and air conditioning in dirty and poorly maintained factories and workshops. Likewise, workers in the steel industry described their dirty, dusty conditions, the poor accommodation provided for rest periods and the lack of lavatory facilities nearby (Kelly and Cooper, 1981). These features of the physical work environment were rated as key sources of stress among steel casting crews. In a dirty work environment it is more likely that employees are exposed to the inhalation of dust and vapours from inefficiently stored chemical-based products. In addition to good housekeeping standards, employees must also be provided with the correct protective clothing and apparatus, but also actively encouraged to use them.

Exposure to danger and hazard

Various occupational groups are exposed to physical dangers at work. Whilst police officers, prison service personnel, fire fighters, mine workers and military personnel face obvious physical dangers and potential harm as part of the job, other workers are also exposed to physical hazards at work. These include a variety of customer service and clerical workers, who by virtue of their job, have to face and deal with aggressive and sometime violent clients, customers and criminal offenders. Thus, many building societies and housing departments now offer training in dealing with physical assault and abuse incidents. Others provide a counselling service for those who have become victims of these frightening situations and who suffer psychological trauma as a result (see also Hot Spots: Changes in the Nature of Relationships at Work, below, on violence at work).

The risks and hazards to blue-collar workers tend to be different in that the hazard arises from exposure to the dangers of plant, machinery, chemicals and so on. Inhalations of certain vapours, gases and dust are potential hazards in the workplace. Although strict controls are in place, incidents leading to injury do occur, and businesses continue to be prosecuted by the Health and Safety Executive for breach of the rules and regulations.

For example, in 1998 the Post Office and a contractor were fined £17 000 for failing to take proper precautions when dealing with asbestos, while refurbishing a central sorting office in Birmingham. It was decided that the Post Office suspected the presence of asbestos, but failed to make proper checks or advise the contractors about the potential hazards. The contractor also failed to make checks before the work commenced, causing the release of asbestos fibres into the atmosphere, and putting employees of both organizations at risk. The contractors also failed to use workers who had been properly trained in dealing with asbestos, neither did they provide these employees with the protective equipment necessary to work safely with asbestos (Health and Safety Bulletin, 1998, p. 7). Indeed, in this same news bulletin, it was announced that Mr Bryan Ward, aged 48, was awarded £749 795 for an asbestos-related illness. These damages are the largest ever awarded for this type in injury. Mr Ward was exposed to asbestos between 1967 and 1976 and developed bilateral diffuse pleural thickening, a progressive lung disease, which severely restricts physical activity and will reduce his life expectancy. The Court of Appeal ruled that he is also entitled to return for further damages if he develops mesothelioma or lung cancer (HSE, 1998, p. 7).

Failure to protect workers from potentially hazardous machinery, or to provide safe systems of work also leads to prosecution. Each month the HSE provides a bulletin report on these incidents and the fines imposed. Clearly it indicates that the work environment for the blue-collar employee still poses dangers, hazards and risk to life. For example, organizations are still being fined for inadequate guarding of machinery and equipment. One company was recently fined £3 000 with £823 in costs after an employee injured his arm when it was drawn into the in-running nip between a moving belt and the pulley of a feeder belt on a mobile screening conveyor. In this instance the company failed to prevent access to dangerous parts of machinery and the employee was able to clean the roller and belt with the machinery still moving. He managed to stop the machine before he was drawn further into it. Had this happened, he could have been killed because he was working alone. In fact, the HSE figures for the ten years to 1993 show that 11 per cent of quarrying fatalities occurred on in-running nips between moving belts and pulleys on conveyors (HSE, 1998, p. 9). The HSE also report on a maintenance company fined £30 000 after it was found guilty of failing to observe a safe system of work while working on a railway line, indirectly resulting in the death of an employee. In 1996, this London-based company carried out maintenance on an overhead electrified line, but failed to follow railway rules and safe systems of work on track. The company was fined £8 000 for failing to ensure the safety of its employees and ordered to pay £22 000 costs (HSE, 1998, p. 8).

Hot Spots: Changes to Job Role

Changes to job role structure are common as companies continually re-invent themselves and, as we have described, change itself can be stressful, especially if we try to resist it. Nevertheless, the impact of changes in the workplace can alter the nature of one's job role, causing role ambiguity or role conflict.

Role conflict

Role conflict exists when an employee feels confused by opposing demands or incompatible goals surrounding the tasks connected with the job. Having to do tasks that are not perceived to be part of one's job role will also lead to stress associated with role conflict. For example, having to deal with the demands of meeting high and perhaps unrealistic production targets whilst satisfying product quality demand, or meeting production demands without compromising safety standards, can lead to stress caused by role conflict. Role conflict has been associated with absenteeism (Breaugh, 1981); job dissatisfaction, abnormal blood chemistry and elevated blood pressure (Ivancevich and Matteson, 1980). Miles and Perreault (1976) identified four types of role conflict.

- Person-role conflict. The individual would like to do a task differently from that suggested by the job description.
- Intrasender conflict. This happens when a supervisor or manager communicates expectations that are incompatible; for example, the employee is given an assignment but without sufficient resources to complete the task.
- Intersender conflict. When an individual is asked to behave in such a manner that one person will be pleased with the results whilst another will not be satisfied, intersender role conflict occurs.
- Role overload. When the employee is assigned more work than can be effectively handled, the stress associated with role overload is experienced (see Hot Spots: Stress in the Job Itself above).

Role conflict is a potential problem for personnel working at organizational boundaries (Cooper and Marshall, 1978). It happens when job demands take the individual into contact with people external to the organization, or across functions or department within the company. Thus, for example, trade union, and health and safety supervisors or representatives can experience conflict because they work at a boundary role in an organization. Trade union representatives pledge to help employees receive all the rights that they are entitled to, and ensure the organization provides work conditions that adhere to the standards set by safety and health agencies. At the same time they are required to meet their own job description demands and the goals and objectives of the business. These interests are not always compatible.

Some supervisors or managers perform boundary-spanning roles that are more typically described as being 'piggy in the middle'. Margolis *et al.*, 1974 found that personnel occupying this type of job were seven times more likely than shopfloor workers to develop ulcers. Personnel in managerial positions can experience the stress associated with role conflict when required to satisfy the policy demands of the company, in the knowledge that the actions required are not in the best interests of his or her staff. Studies have shown that certain personality types are likely to react to role conflict situations in a more extreme manner. For example,

Warr and Wall (1975) found that individuals described as 'rigid' in their style of behaviour were more prone to adverse reaction from role conflict situations, than those individuals who could be described as having a 'flexible' style of behaviour.

Role ambiguity

Role ambiguity refers to the lack of clarity about one's role or task demands at work. It occurs when an employee does not understand, or realize the expectations and demands of the job, or the scope of the role. A lack of training or inadequate information can lead to role ambiguity. Research evidence has shown that role ambiguity at work has been associated with tension and fatigue, intention to quit or actually leaving a job, and high levels of anxiety, physical and psychological strain, and absenteeism. The stress arising from unclear objectives or goals can lead to job dissatisfaction, a lack of self confidence, a lowered sense of self esteem, depression and low work motivation, increased blood pressure and pulse rate, and intention to leave the job (Kahn *et al.*, 1965; French and Caplan, 1970; Margolis *et al.*, 1974)

A wide range of work situations can cause role ambiguity. For example, being in one's first job, promotion to a new position, a location transfer, having a new boss, or changes to the work structure or systems, can all create ambiguous work conditions (Ivancevich and Matteson, 1980). Some of these role changes are made by necessity, in response to organizational change, and not of choice. A move to a new type of industry or business exposes the individual to the unique technical language, colloquialism, jargon and workplace culture. Unless adequate job previews and induction training are provided an employee is likely to be exposed to role ambiguity and perhaps is more vulnerable to error or accidents at work.

Role conflict and role ambiguity situations are exacerbated when employees perceive a lack of managerial or supervisory support at work. Significant downsizing of a workforce also impact upon management grade personnel. They experience high workload demands, long hours of working, plus the realization that they might not be available to their employees when a need arises. These individuals may experience conflict between different role sets, such as the conflicting demands of the job and the home or social environments. Nevertheless, feeling unable to fulfil others' expectations of one's job role is now a commonly cited source of pressure experienced by personnel with responsibility for other people.

However, it is also commercially essential to run many business operations on a continuous basis, and work a twenty-four hour shift system for both blue collar and service workers. Managerial staff still tend to work mainly day shifts with only a skeleton staff available for night-shift duties. This compounds the problems associated with the lack of availability of one's supervisor or manager when needed. So, in addition to the problems associated with role conflict and role ambiguity, having 'responsibility' is a potential source of stress at work.

Responsibility

Being responsible for other people's work and performance demands that more time is spent interacting with others. Thus, responsibility for people is acknowledged as more stressful than responsibility for 'things', that is equipment or budgets and so on (French and Caplan, 1970). Wardwell, Hyman and Bahson (1964) found that spending time interacting with others, attending meetings and having to meet deadlines were associated with increased risk of coronary heart disease (CHD), such as elevated serum cholesterol levels and high diastolic blood pressure. Pincherle (1972) also found that the level of one's responsibility in the organization was a predictor of CHD risk factors among 1200 managers in the UK. Also, responsibility for people's safety and lives was a key factor in predicting risk of heart disease among air traffic controllers (Crump *et al.*, 1980). This potential source of stress is not confined to managerial or professional occupations. Cooper and Kelly (1984) found that crane drivers onshore, and offshore (Sutherland and Cooper, 1986) are aware of the risk of serious injury or a death to one of their colleagues if they make a mistake while working. Thus, they are responsible for the safety of others.

It is suggested that one of the impacts of rapidly developing new technology is to facilitate the ability to push responsibility for decision making lower down the organization. This means that a potential stressor problem will exist if the employee is untrained or lacks the experience to deal with the situation. Indeed, a move to change the culture of the organization by empowering the work force, and giving them more responsibility for decision making about their jobs is a mixed blessing. Having more control and a say about the things that affect us at work is recognized as a way of reducing stress at work, if the process is managed effectively. However, if the organization tries to make these changes towards an empowered model of working, in a way that is too fast, or poorly managed, employees are likely to resist their newly ascribed level of responsibility. It is unrealistic to expect employees, used to a 'dependency' culture of 'tell me what to do', to transfer quickly and successfully to a, 'let us together decide what to do' culture, without full debate and adequate training. It is important that managers are also trained to delegate responsibility and manage effectively through an open process. These are important if the change in culture to an empowered work force is to be successful. In our experience, shop floor employees are most likely to describe lack of trust as the strongest barrier in moving towards an empowered or interdependent culture and climate at work. As many shop floor employees have told us, 'They tell us we are empowered, but they still don't trust us to get on with the job!'.

Hot Spots: Changes in the Nature of Relationships at Work

Good relationships between work colleagues are considered a central factor in individual and organization health. A study of workers in the offshore oil and gas industry found that 'teamwork' was rated as the most important quality in the job (Livy and Vant, 1979). Feelings of security and confidence were generated by the sense of belonging to a stable work crew. However, some of us are required to work with 'difficult' or abrasive personalities (Levinson, 1978), who simply fail to see a need to 'oil the wheels' of amicable social exchange in the workplace. These achievement oriented individuals might be stubborn, tactless, critical of the efforts of others or condescending about ideas. They need to be in control and tend to dominate meetings; they are self-opinionated, impatient with the efforts of others, confrontational, or distant and cold. Some abrasive people are only preoccupied with symbols of power and status and so drive themselves hard. Other people are simply regarded as rivals. In the extreme the inconsiderate colleague can become an intellectual bully or even physically violent.

A recessionary climate, characterized by job insecurity and the use of contingent workers is not likely to be conducive to good relationships at work. These circumstances often lead to divisiveness, rivalry and unhealthy competition for jobs, and poor interpersonal relations at work, which are low in trust and supportiveness. Research has shown that mistrust is positively related to high role ambiguity, inadequate interpersonal communication between individuals and psychological strain in the form of low job satisfaction and decreased well-being (French and

Caplan, 1973). These researchers found that supportive relationships at work mediated the effects of job strain on cortisone levels, blood pressure, glucose levels and the number of cigarettes smoked. Conversely, having to live and work with others can be one of the most stressful aspects of life.

The lack of supportive relationships or poor relationships with peers, colleagues and the boss, are potential sources of stress, leading to low trust and low interest in problem solving. For example, perception of the quality of supervisory relationship among nurses was found to impact on performance. It buffered the impact of role ambiguity on global satisfaction levels and intention to quit among the nurses. As we have already observed, a lack of managerial or supervisory support in the workplace might occur if significant downsizing of the workforce has included managerial personnel. Likewise, the level of social support perceived by managers working in the food retail industry was also found to be an important factor during a period of organizational restructuring, whereas work demand was most closely linked to mental health (Moyle, 1998). Perceptions of managerial support, role clarity and job satisfaction declined during a period of business process-re-engineering. Job satisfaction levels could be predicted from a combination of high managerial support, high control and low ambiguity. As Callan (1993) suggests, managerial support might of particular benefit during organizational change.

Whilst many of us suffer stress because of the behaviour and actions of other people at work, it would appear that computerization has taken over many jobs. Therefore, certain individuals now work in relative isolation, with limited opportunities to socialize with their co-workers (Cohen, 1984). People seem to expect more from their job than income and appear to need companionship and social interaction. Sometimes the isolation is due to the massive downsizing of the workforce. The individual is relatively alone, working in computer-controlled operations for much of an eight- or 12-hour shift. At other times the use of computers has reduced the need for us to move around in the workplace and so opportunities for social interactions are reduced. It means that channels of communication with other people are restricted and the opportunity to develop strong social support networks may be denied if the employee is restricted to a workstation. Although the use of closed-circuit television and video-phone links for isolated employees may ultimately help to overcome the problems of isolation, a fear that 'big brother is watching' does seem to exist. This seems likely to sustain while a culture and climate of mistrust pervade the organization. Cohen (1984) suggests that some of the problems associated with social isolation in the workplace might be reduced by improving social support networks. This includes the provision of places for work breaks and meals where employees can meet and take breaks together. Start of shift meetings, digital information boards, and sports and social clubs also help to reduce the impact of social isolation at work.

The quality of interpersonal relationships at work is important in that supportive relationships are less likely to create the pressures associated with rivalry, petty bickering and rumour mongering. It is also acknowledged that social support in the form of group cohesion, interpersonal trust and a liking for one's supervisor appear to contribute significantly to feelings about job stress and health. McLean, (1979) found that inconsiderate behaviour on the part of a boss contributes to feelings of job pressure. Thus the nature of the superior-subordinate relationship is potentially stressful. A leadership style that is, inappropriately, authoritarian can be a potential source of stress. This type of leader is less likely to engage in a participative style of leadership, or appreciate that feedback about performance and recognition and praise for effort are beneficial to the boss-subordinate relationship, and effective in reducing levels of stress at work. Also, a boss with a technical or scientific background may be more oriented towards 'things' rather than 'people' (Cooper and Marshall, 1978). This means that he or she might view consideration for working relationships as trivial, mollycoddling, time consuming and an impediment to doing the job well. Reaction to the authoritarian or inconsiderate boss varies. In some instances such tensions may be repressed. The outward calm and passive response from the workforce may hide the seething intention of, 'Don't get mad, get even!'. Usually, this type of boss will only be told what they want to hear. They are likely to be shielded from information that is needed, but likely to cause an unwanted reaction directed towards his or her staff. Repression of the arousal-response and internalization of anger is, in the long term, harmful and can result in elevated blood pressure. In this type of work climate, levels of morale are likely to be low and staff feel a sense of helplessness. From their perspective, the boss appears to be getting away with unacceptable behaviour and even being rewarded by the organization, in the form of a promotion. Buck (1972) found that managers and workers who felt most under pressure reported that their supervisor always ruled with an iron hand and rarely allowed participation in decision making or trying out new ideas.

Sometimes feelings towards an authoritarian or abrasive boss are expressed outwards and an overt display of aggression is observed. Indeed, levels of violence in the workplace appear to be on the increase thus creating another dimension to stress in the workplace (Bulatao and Vanden Bos 1996; Cox and Leather, 1994). Whilst this includes violence between staff and towards members of staff from people on the outside of the organization, incidents of violence towards managers and supervisors themselves appear to be on the increase. For example, the 1996 study conducted by the European Union reveals that, in the EU, 6 million workers were subjected to physical violence, and 12 million workers were subjected to intimidation and psychological violence.

Fear of occupational violence and exposure to crime is known to be a serious and widespread source of anxiety and worry, capable of having a negative impact on health (Nasar and Jones, 1997). It is not only physical assault that is damaging in its consequences because some form of post-trauma reaction, for example, can occur without any physical injury being sustained (Flannery, 1996). This can include simply being a witness to violent circumstances in the workplace. Nevertheless, in a study of urban bus drivers, Duffy and McGoldrick (1990) found that the actual experience of a physical assault was a better predictor of poor psychological health than was concern about potential occurrences. However, Leather *et al.*, 1997, in a study of public house licensees, observed that as the severity of violence increased, fear of becoming a victim, and self-reported symptoms of impaired well-being increased. Job satisfaction levels and organizational commitment decreased. Thus work-related violence was a potent source of stress in the lives of the pub licensee's work environment. In fact, any specific episode of actual or threatened violence would be described as an acute stressor, while the ongoing potential for violence would be considered a 'chronic' source of stress. This means that the individual does not have to be the specific target of a violent incident. Thus the impact of exposure to the stressor can be both direct or vicarious (Barling, 1996; Wynne *et al.*, 1995). Research evidence suggests that fear of workplace violence is associated with anxiety, thoughts about leaving the organization and active search for alternative employment. The results of studies into exposure to crime and fear of crime, have led to the suggestion (Dickson *et al.*, 1994) that fear appraisal should be one element of a tripartite system of intervention that addresses prevention, reaction and rehabilitation. This neatly fits the model of stress management that we propose in Chapter 7.

Hot Spot: Changes in the Concept of Career

In addition to the pressures associated with starting, developing and maintaining a career, a mismatch in expectations, feeling undervalued and frustration in attaining a sense of achievement are common 'career' stressors. Job dissatisfaction, burnout, poor work performance and unsatisfactory interpersonal relationships at work are associated with career stress (Ivancevich and Matteson, 1980).

The ability to use and develop our skills are significant predictors of self-esteem (Margolis *et al.*, 1974). Lack of promotion is a potential source of stress for the individual who has mastered a job, but does not gain recognition such as advancement, or a chance to develop his or her skills. Lack of stimulation and challenge will add to the stress of being passed over for promotion.

Whilst needs and expectations about career opportunities vary as a function of career stage, the structure of the organization has become a major force in shaping our career paths. The previously recognizable 'pyramid' shape of the organizational structure has become a rare exception. Many individuals now find themselves employed in a company *Org struct* with a much flatter hierarchical structure as layers and steps have been removed from the career ladder. Restricted opportunities for promotion and job insecurity, which result from changes to the organizational structure and downsizing, are potent sources of stress. This leads to the observation that perhaps the nature of 'career' has undergone a radical transformation. Also, employees are discovering that career movement (if it happens), has changed from clearly defined paths, to one based on proof of performance, efficiency and visible commitment (Simpson, 1998).

However, it is suggested that stress is experienced by some individuals because their expectations of 'career' have not kept up with the pace of change in industry. It no longer matches the reality of work life in the new millennium. For example, Hellesøy *et al.*, 1985 identified 'limited career opportunity' as a source of stress among offshore platform workers in Norway; however, whilst 29 per cent of respondents were dissatisfied about their chances of promotion, a third of workers were neither satisfied or dissatisfied with their promotion prospects. This suggests that these workers had no expectation regarding upward career movement in the organization. It is an important observation, since under promotion will only be a source of stress when expectations are not met. Nevertheless, disruptive behaviour, poor morale and poor interpersonal relationships are associated with the stress arising from disparity between actual status within the organization and our expectations. Threat of job loss is a potent source of stress linked to several serious health problems, including ulcers, colitis, alopecia and increased muscular and emotional complaints.

Certain occupational groups might be at increased risk from career stress. For example, Hall (1976) found that for graduates entering a managerial career often did not meet their expectations. Also, women managers (Davidson and Cooper, 1981), who were most likely to be clustered at the lower levels of an organization, were likely to report 'career stress'. Clearly contemporary employment relations are in transition. The demise of loyalty and the need for employees to take care of themselves are viewed as a sign of the times (Hirsch, 1989). Thus it might be said that the nature of 'career' will continue to change.

Hot Spots: Changes to the Organizational Structure and Climate

We have already begun to describe the changing nature of industry and the structure and climate of the organization as potential sources of stress at work. It is difficult to avoid some overlap between stressor categories since stressors rarely exist in isolation. Thus the interactive and dynamic nature of stress must be acknowledged. Nevertheless, it is accepted that simply 'being in the organization' (Cooper and Marshall, 1978) brings with it concerns about the way the organization treats its people. It concerns the perception of culture and custom and, for example, can describe the sense of not belonging or the pressure of workplace politics. 'Being in the organization' can impose a threat to freedom and autonomy. Many of us also feel that we are not consulted adequately about the decisions that affect our working lives. Poor communication and a lack of decision making opportunities can be a part of 'being in the organization' and potent sources of stress.

The structure and climate of the organization determine the way it treats its people, and exposure to these sources of stress is associated with negative psychological mood, escapist drinking and heavy smoking. Increased control and opportunity to participate have recognized benefits in terms of improved performance, lower staff turnover, improved levels of mental and physical well-being and accident reduction (Sutherland and Cooper 1991). However, employees will often resist the offer to adopt a more participative style of working since they are sceptical that the proposed changes in working practices, to improve productivity, customer service, quality, or safety, are required to gain competitive advantage.

Levine (1990) suggests that employee support for a participative work climate is more likely to succeed when an industrial relations system is characterized by the presence of some form of profit, gain sharing or job security. Also, ways must be in place for the development of group cohesiveness and there must be some guarantee of individual rights. As we have stated, many organizations are trying to 'empower' their employees. However, they tend to encounter problems because they fail to realize that a workforce acclimatized to a dependency culture, where they are simply told what to do, and are not expected to solve problems or make decisions for themselves, cannot move easily or quickly to a condition of mutual dependence (control shared by mutual agreement), or to interdependence (characterized by flexibility, interchange of activities, joint decision making and sharing of control), which are vital for the success of the empowerment process. If management attempts to hand over control too quickly, or employees try to escape from being controlled when the authority figure will not relinquish control, the work-force will become counterdependent (Cox and Makin, 1994). In these situations there will be a 'fight back' with acts of rebellion, such as a ban on overtime, strikes, sit ins, or 'work to rule' policies. To avoid these problems it necessary to overcome the state of learned helplessness, low levels of confidence and lack of esteem that characterize the 'dependent' workforce. This is important for success in changing to an empowerment model of working (McGrath, 1994). Also, an understanding of this concept explains how changes proposed as 'stress reducers' sometimes become more damaging than the original source of strain!

An additional explanation for the resistance to change in the workplace might be the stress of job insecurity. This has been associated with a high level of stress and anxiety (Jacobson, 1987). Workers feel anxious about the lack of certainty regarding when layoffs will occur and who will be affected by these changes associated with downsizing, mergers and acquisitions. Therefore, job dissatisfaction, alternative job search and non-compliant job behaviours might be manifest as outcomes of exposure to the stress of job insecurity. These negative behaviours are costly to the organization and the individual. However, research evidence suggests that there are potential negative effects caused by the 'survivors' of cutbacks in organizations. After the axe falls, the survivors often find themselves in a high workload situation, sometimes with much curtailment of their original job, and reduced resources. Role confusion exists while the organization restructures. In the re-engineered business, employees face the likelihood of career plateauing, and interpersonal conflict as competition for the remaining jobs heightens. Temporary contract staff move in to fill gaps and workplace politics often become difficult. Erera (1992) found that under such conditions of ambiguity, a reduction in communication channels and withdrawal from others may be common responses. In this structure and climate a culture of tension exists. Levels of creativity will suffer because individuals may be too insecure to suggest radical or risky solutions to problems (Jick, 1983). The following effects of cutbacks in organizations have been documented:

- centralization: decisions are passed upward, participation decreases, control is emphasized;
- absence of long range planning: crises and short term needs drive out strategic planning;
- decrease in innovation: no experimentation, risk aversion and scepticism about non-core activities;
- scapegoating: leaders are blamed for the pain and uncertainty;
- resistance to change: conservatism and 'turf protection' lead to the rejection of new alternatives;
- increased labour turnover: the most competent leave first, causing leadership anaemia;
- lowered morale; decreased effort and commitment: few needs are met and infighting is predominant;
- no slack: uncommitted resources are used to cover operating expenses.
- fragmented pluralism: emergence of special interest groups of a 'political' nature;
- loss of credibility of senior management;
- non-prioritized cuts: attempts to ameliorate conflict lead to attempts to equalize cutbacks; across the board versus prioritized cuts;
- conflict: interpersonal conflict and 'infighting', competition for control predominates when resources are scarce.

(Cameron, Kim and Whetten, 1987)

Therefore, further changes proposed by management will be seen simply as yet another attempt to make more cutbacks in the manpower levels. Lim (1996) suggests that support from colleagues and supervisors help to buffer the individual against the effects of job insecurity, particularly for work-related outcomes such as job dissatisfaction, job search and noncompliant job behaviours. These include tardiness, absenteeism, job theft – including theft of time by leaving early, counterproductivity such as putting less effort in at work, working slowly, spending time gossiping and in idle conversation, instead of working. As Lim suggests, some individuals admitted engaging in counterproductive behaviours as a means of getting back at their organization because they were dissatisfied that the company had not ensured them of secure jobs.

Job insecurity will continue to be an issue of concern for the considerable future. Therefore, to the extent that job insecurity is shown to be detrimental to outcomes that are valued by employees as well as employers (Roskies and Louis-Guerin, 1990; Schweiger and Lee, 1993), organizations can play an important role in enhancing social support at work, to assist individuals in coping with job insecurity.

Hot Spots: the Interface Between Work and Home

It is not possible to obtain a complete stress profile by looking only at sources of stress in the workplace. Thus we must consider the interface that exists between work, home and social life. This includes the personal life events that might have an effect upon performance, efficiency, well-being and adjustment at work (Bhagat, 1983). Concerns within the family, life crises, financial difficulties, conflicting personal and company beliefs, and the conflict between organizational, family and social demands, are examples of potential stressors that might spill over into the individual's work domain. Research evidence suggests that job and life satisfactions are influenced by the demands and conflicts of home and family life. It would appear that negative life changes, such as divorce or bereavement are related to lower levels of satisfaction with supervision, pay and the work itself. Positive life changes are associated with satisfaction about promotional opportunities.

Changes in the economy and labour market have forced more workers to relocate in order to find a job or stay in employment. Blue collar workers are likely to change both career and work location as their employment in heavy industry and manufacturing is replaced by service sector employment. Some individuals are required to remain geographically mobile in order to retain a job. Other members of the family also must cope with the changes associated with job relocation. They will be required to put down new roots without the benefit and support of a work environment structure and climate. Often individuals move for short term contract employment opportunities, thus requiring the individual to work away from home and family.

Obviously, life and career stage will influence the outcome of exposure to these potential sources of stress. For example, young, single employees have the pressures of starting a new job and being alone in a strange town or city. They will need to build a new life structure without the support of a partner, family or friends. Young couples without children usually have the least constraints but the dual career couple tend to face problems when one partner is forced to relocate. Children tend to experience relocation as stressful because they need to make new friends and cope with a different school environment. However, research does suggest that these children, who are exposed to frequent new and challenging situations are likely to develop a 'hardy' personality. In the long term these individuals, in adulthood, might have a less adverse reaction to stressful situations because they can accept new situations as a challenge. They tend to feel in control and committed to meeting the challenge of change. Thus 'hardiness' is considered to keep a person healthy despite the experience of stressful life events (Kobasa, 1979). Stress resistance is expressed as commitment versus alienation, control versus powerlessness, and challenge versus threat. Challenge involves the expectation that is normal for life to change and that change stimulates personal growth. Therefore, the individual looks forward to opportunities for stimulation and personal growth with an openness of mind and a willingness to experiment. Control is defined as the tendency to behave and act as if one can influence the course of events. Therefore, even undesirable events are viewed in terms of possibilities rather than threats.

Various factors can affect the relationship between work and family, and family and work. The job itself may elicit and reinforce certain styles of behaviour (including personality traits). For example, the Type A behaviour disposition, or the need for power or position can cause conflict in the home domain. The aggressive, controlling behaviour that brings results and even promotion in the work environment may not be welcome at home! Also, the individual who feels thwarted and disillusioned because his or her promotion expectations have not been met might exhibit 'revenge' behaviour at home. Probably it is the only place in which the individual can express feelings that are, by necessity, repressed at work. Job structure can place constraints upon the amount of time spent at home with family and friends. The need for more and more people to engage in shift working can also have an adverse impact on the quality of our social relationships. Indeed, the decision to accept a job and sustain it may be affected by our family commitments. For example, it has been observed that attitudes to night shift working were influenced by whether a spouse or partner could adjust to being alone at home at night. In similar ways, exposure to stress at work might have a spillover effect and adverse impact on one's family and personal life. The impact of long working hours and overload conditions on family life can only be detrimental. The Institute of Management Survey (1996) found that two-thirds of managers felt they had not achieved a good balance between work and home. Also, 45 per cent of male respondents claimed that not seeing enough of their children was a major source of stress. In the Parents at Work Survey (Daniels, 1996), nearly three-quarters of respondents reported feeling exhausted at the end of the day. Two-thirds stated that the only saw their children for an average of two to four hours a day.

Conclusion

Clearly anything and everything can be a potential source of stress. However, the management of stress in the work environment can be successful only when we understand the source of unwanted strain or pressure. Therefore, identification of the factors that have a negative impact on performance and well-being is an essential part of a stress management programme. This is the objective of the stress audit described in Chapter 6. Before we describe the stress audit process, issues concerning stress and the rapid developments in new technology, and the process of electronic monitoring, are reviewed in Chapter 5. These have important implications for the changing face of the workplace.

Stress and New Technology

Rapid technological development in the work environment has exposed more of us to the need to work 'with' and 'for' computers at work. 'Computer phobics' are still found in the workplace, but a great majority of us are now required to work with computers, in some way. It has become a part of daily work practice. Advances in computer technology have created dramatic changes in the work environment and our conditions of work. New technologies and computer-aided technology describe the information and materials processing hardware and software that transform information and materials (Majchrzak and Borys, 1998). Such technologies are found in service and manufacturing sectors everywhere. Since people 'partner' these technologies, the potential for unique forms of stress exists in the workplace, in addition to the pressures and strains of living and working.

Typically, new technology might expose us to:

- communication tools such as email, internet and other electronic commerce such as fax machines;
- computerized decision support systems;
- computer information systems;
- computerized tools such as word-processors;
- advanced manufacturing technology (AMT);
- computer aided design (CAD);
- computer aided manufacturing (CAM);
- computer integrated manufacturing (CIM);
- computer numerically controlled machining (CNC);
- flexible machining systems (FMS);
- mechanized product systems such as conveyor belts or workstations.

(Majchrzak and Borys, 1998)

These new technologies and computer aided systems alter the ways that people perform their work. Ultimately, new technology is introduced to maximize performance potential and replace physical activity with cognitive activity. This leaves people to deal with important, unpredictable and random occurrences, while machines deal with repetitive, predictable and non-random activities. The intention is for 'machines' to take over the mundane, boring and routine tasks. However, certain questions about technologicial advances and the drive to automate the work environment need to be addressed. For example, we need to ask if:

- Automation has freed us from the drudgery of work?
- We have been released from the shackles of alienating labour?
- New technology has created a stratified society, with an élite commanding the robotocized labour of the masses?

Also,

- Who is in control – man or machine?

The answers to these questions are complex and far from being satisfactory from a humanistic perspective. Thus, it is likely that the potential for stress does exist in the workplace because we are not able to provide positive answers to these questions. The demands of new technology have created some instances where we have traded manual dexterity skills for cognitive skills, and greater levels of responsibility. Whilst some jobs have become deskilled, other have become upgraded and more complex with the need to learn the use of the new technology, and the ever evolving and developing universe of the computer. Clearly, skills have changed, but many jobs have also vanished. Some authors suggest that automation has left two main types of jobs. First there are the low skilled, operation jobs, while the others are described as, 'high skilled, planning, programming and maintenance type work'.

Indeed, in recent years, one of the most cited reasons for the need to automate has been based on the perception that traditional metal working and craft skills are in short supply. Also, the cost of training has prompted employers to develop technology to the extent that they can employ fewer skilled operators and reduce the costs of labour at the same time. However, it appears that we are moving towards a Catch-22 situation. Advanced manufacturing systems rely on skilled intervention for their operational performance. However, Bainbridge (1983) reminds us that human intervention is problematic in the monitoring and diagnosis of system error because machine 'minders' cannot develop the required skills from observing automated machinery in action. We no longer have the craftsmen to effectively engage in this type of work because it was believed that machines could do the work of these employees. Thus there is a shortage of shopfloor operators with the skills to manually control or override malfunctioning highly automated systems. In the service sectors and offices, employers also fear a white-collar labour and skills shortage, and so strive to find a way to automate systems and processes and reduce manpower requirements (and labour costs).

Whilst the changing nature of the workplace might cause skills to become obsolete, exposure to ever changing equipment or systems can be threatening for the individual. Workers must adapt to each novel situation or condition, and engage in education and training in order to cope with the new and ever changing demands. Training is vital, but the 'leaner' workforce can experience pressure when trying to find time to attend training sessions. Difficulties also arise when trying to release colleagues for training, in addition to the time off needed for holidays and to cover periods of sickness absence. All of this must be accomplished whilst trying to maintain performance and production demands and standards. When deskilling occurs (real or perceived), the employee can experience 'qualitative underload' as a source of pressure. This is because he or she believes that the job no longer is a challenge, or that the job does not offer an opportunity to use and develop their abilities. Alternately, it is possible that employees experience stress at work because they are required to become 'multi-skilled', so that maximum use is made of the costly investment in new technology (that is, in plant and equipment). Therefore, 'qualitative overload' can become a source of stress.

An additional source of stress observed in a rapidly changing work environment, related to 'overload', is having a boss or supervisor schooled in the old ways. The new employee, trained in the latest technology and methods, and probably educated to a higher level in order to compete in a competitive job market, will experience overload stress (and possibly strain in relationships at work) if the adequacy of supervision or management is questionable. Confidence and respect in the ability of those responsible for the efficient and safe operation of work are vital to good interpersonal relationships. Thus, the introduction of new technology may expose a supervisor to conflict and the experience of qualitative overload. At the same time this will threaten the subordinate with overload because the level of supervision is perceived to be poor.

In the next part of this chapter we focus on the work that is 'computer led' and the extent to which electronic monitoring can create stress at work.

Computer Based Technology

Advances in computer technology have radically changed our work environment in many ways. Manufacturing industries have witnessed the impact of technological changes due to automation for many decades. Since the Industrial Revolution, such changes have aimed to increase the amount of managerial control over production processes, reduce manpower requirements and labour costs in production jobs, and thereby reduce the cost of goods and increase profitability. Automation also aimed to reduce the level of physical and manual effort required by the work force. For example, robots do not become tired and robots do not strike! History has shown that changes towards a more automated work environment have been dramatic and turbulent, resulting in wildcat strikes, vandalism and violence, as workers resisted change and feared for the security of employment. These fears were not unfounded. Postwar manufacturing industry was characterized by a significant decrease in the number of people needed to operate machines and plant.

This trend continues as science and technology strive towards the fully automated factory of the future. Wright and Bourne (1988) suggest that advances in production engineering and computer science will result in 'peopleless production' by the year 2010. Other writers offer caution and identify the restraining forces to prevent this dream [sic] becoming a reality. Nevertheless, the introduction of computer technology into the work environment has resulted in dramatic and sweeping change in manpower requirement and the nature of work. Large manufacturing plants already appear to be characterized by one common feature – a dearth of people! The number of personnel employed on production lines is minimal, and jobs are usually confined to the activities of production operators, seated at the console of computerized control panels. Their job is to monitor the machines, make decisions, and override malfunctioning highly automated systems, while the equipment does the physical aspects of the task. Although, we can not classify all manufacturing industry in this simplistic way, it appears to be a trend. The stressful nature of this type of sedentary occupation has already been discussed in Chapter 4. However, there is another stress issue associated with automation and the use of computer technology in the work environment, namely, that of electronic or computer monitoring.

The introduction of computer technology and electronic monitoring have not been confined to the manufacturing sector. Technological advances have spurred the introduction of computer led automation into service sector and white-collar occupations. Therefore, in this chapter we focus on work that is computer controlled or monitored, and the extent to which this type of work, and performance monitoring, are likely to create stress conditions at work. While it is often assumed that the task and job demands associated with computer working are likely to result in stress, this is not necessarily so (Briner and Hockey, 1988). Obviously, there is potential for stress to exist as information overload. Indeed, feelings of boredom might result in 'rust out' or work under load conditions that can be stressful because the individual does not feel challenged or able to contribute at a cognitive level. However, these sources of stress are also found in non-computer based jobs. Thus, the view that job and task demands of computer led working are stressful is not fully supported by research evidence. In some instances, the use of computers has reduced stress levels, but there are no simple generalizations. It is might be more correct to say the demands of this type of work are 'different', and potentially stressful in certain circumstances.

This discussion focuses only on the organizational impact and work demands of computer monitored work. We do not include the ergonomic factors associated with stress and computer based work, such as the impact of working with video display units (VDU), the issues of workstation design, or systems. These are complex and fast developing areas, and beyond the remit of this publication.

Computer Based Monitoring

Technology can exert control either at the machine or the system level and it is acknowledged that certain employees are closely monitored during computer led tasks. While employees have always been monitored at work to some extent, recent technological advances have changed the nature of worker monitoring in organizations. As Aiello (1993) suggests, it is now possible to monitor employees at a level that was previously unattainable by even the most diligent of supervisors. Further, he believes that, 'Computer aided supervisory monitoring, performed in real-time or on a delayed basis, can now be constant, "unblinking" and pervasive'.

Surveillance, regulation, control, and reporting of processes, procedures and persons, can be achieved by computer monitoring. The US Congress's Office of Technology Assessment (1987) defined the process of electronic work monitoring as, 'the computerized collection, storage, analysis and reporting of information about employees' productive activities'(p. 27). Nebeker and Tatum (1993) defined electronic monitoring as the use of electronic instruments or devices such as audio, video and computer systems to collect, store, analyse, and report individual or group actions or performance. Computer monitoring is a subset of electronic monitoring. It is commonly used as a means of surveillance, but also to provide performance feedback and rewards to individual operators of video display terminals (VDT) workstations. Real-time feedback can be provided that is instantaneous and objective. Therefore, computer control systems can be used to prevent internal theft, enforce workplace rules and monitor performance levels (Susser, 1988). Systems are designed and in place to unobtrusively monitor employees' performance or behaviour. Performance measures include task completion rates, number of key strokes, or rate of errors. Computer work such as data entry, is often paid on a key stroke basis.

A system that can provide immediate feedback to the worker directly can be beneficial. For example, Nebeker and Tatum (1993) observed that computer monitoring and feedback led to increased key rate, but there was little effect of monitoring on work quality, satisfaction, or stress. In certain instances, computer based performance measures are recorded, assessed by a manager or supervisor, and then fed back to the employee concerned. Feedback is, therefore, received indirectly, although research evidence provided by Earley (1988) suggests that 'direct' feedback is more effective because the feedback source is trusted.

Koep (1986) estimated that a third of the more than 13 million US workers linked to computers are subject to some form of computer monitoring. It was believed that the number of office workers affected by electronic monitoring doubled from about 20 per cent in 1984 to about 40 per cent in 1992 (Aiello, 1993). This means that in excess of 10 million people in the USA could have been electronically monitored at work (Halpern,1992). Between 1990 and 1992, around 7000 companies spent more than $500 million in the USA on surveillance software (Blinksy 1991; Halpern, 1992).

The ethics and merits of using computers for surveillance have been the topic of much debate. In addition, the merits of computer based performance tracking has generated a certain amount of controversy, in addition to the concerns expressed about the issues of worker privacy (Earley, 1988), and the fairness of these systems (Kidwell and Bennett, 1994). However, as Nebeker and Tatum (1993) suggest, computer monitoring is not a unitary concept and can vary along certain dimensions, including:

- **Individual visibility.** This refers to the issue of monitoring of individuals versus groups of employees and the size of the group.

Clearly, the impact of monitoring and the acceptance of it as an assessment of performance will be affected by this dimension.

- **Focus.** This refers to the behavioural focus of the monitoring, for example, a focus on activities or outcomes; or a focus on processes versus products.
- **Outcome control.** This concerns the issue of results monitoring and the degree to which the results have an effect on outcomes valued by the employees and how much it influences these outcomes.
- **Privacy.** This refers to the issues associated with access to the information collected. That is, is the information made public, seen only by the employee, or by management, or both.
- **Timeliness.** This concerns the length of time between monitoring and information feedback.
- **Feedback medium.** Feedback can be given in real time, verbally in face to face communication or through computer generated reports. The medium used in feedback can be a determinant of credibility and reliability of the information received by the employee.
- **Tone.** This refers to the degree to which a monitoring system is designed to be 'positive' versus 'punitive'.

Research evidence suggests that computer monitoring has certain merits. It permits management to set reasonable productivity goals, identify problems, price products and services, and reward high achieving employees (Sherizen, 1986). In the next sections we examine the impact of computer based monitoring of work.

The negative impact of computer monitoring

Those who oppose computer based monitoring believe that it leads to an emphasis on quantity to the detriment of work quality. This results in job dissatisfaction at work and increased stress levels among the workforce (Harz, 1985; Irving *et al.*, 1986). A review by Schleifer (1990) concluded that, 'there appears to be a theoretical basis and some empirical evidence which supports the premise that electronic monitoring techniques can alter basic job dimensions (e.g., increased work load and reduced job control), thereby producing stress' (p. 6).

One of the main oppositions to computer monitoring is that it is an invasion of privacy. Research evidence indicates that other various deleterious effects may exist as low morale and poor health outcomes. Not all research evidence supports this view. For example, Nebeker and Tatum conducted an experiment to assess the impact of computer monitoring. It failed to reveal any negative consequences associated with the computerized recording, analysing and reporting of performance on database operators. Awareness of performance monitoring and performance feedback resulted in higher key rates than among a control group who were unaware of the monitoring process. This increase in productivity did not result in any reduction in work quality, job satisfaction or increased stress levels. Nebeker and Tatum could not establish whether the experimental group in this simulated study were more productive because they were aware of being observed, because they knew the supervisors had access to performance reports, or due to the fact that they personally received performance feedback. However, the results of the study should be treated with caution since it was a simulated experiment conducted over a two-week time period. The employees were 'temporary' and only worked four-hour shifts, rather than eight-hour days, on data entry tasks. They also worked in small groups rather than in isolation. Thus their work conditions were different from a real-world situation. Indeed, the results obtained are also quite different from the field survey results into the impact of computer based monitoring.

For example, evidence presented by the US Congress, Office of Technology Assessment (1987) shows that electronically monitored workers experience conflicts associated with the quantity and quality imperatives of their jobs. This research suggested that workers might not be opposed to performance monitoring in principle, but are concerned that certain aspects of their work are not taken into account. We have anecdotal evidence about the negative effects of computer monitoring and concerns about the particular elements of work that are being monitored. Such dissatisfactions were expressed by employees working in a customer telephone services department for a UK bank. These individuals were monitored and assessed in terms of the number of calls answered, and the number of callers waiting at any one time. Both of these were required to remain at a prescribed level and penalties were incurred if performance levels fell below the standards set. Therefore, it was informally acknowledged that it was 'better' for employees to disconnect a customer if the telephone discussion was becoming protracted for any reason. In this way they could be certain to achieve the performance standard for the number of calls answered since the start of the shift, and ensure that they did not fail to meet the 'number of callers waiting' criteria. While they believed that the customer would probably be annoyed by this action, they would 'ring back'; but they personally would not be penalized by engaging in this deleterious behaviour. However, these employees did complain that the organizational performance standards took little or no account of the quality of the service given to the customer. Difficulties occurred only when a complaint from a customer was received. Usually, these telephone operators could explain (blame) their behaviour in terms of faulty equipment or faulty telephone lines, and so no real problems were encountered as a result of their negative actions. Nevertheless, they were dissatisfied with this work arrangement.

Aiello (1993) observed a similar pattern of behaviour. He found that 25 per cent of directory assistance operators surveyed admitted to cheating so as to be able to reach their computer-monitor-based 22-second-per-call standard. They did this by disconnecting customers when the transaction might have taken longer than the allotted time. For example, a call from a customer with a strong accent or a hearing problem would be disconnected in order for the operator to reach the performance target, and receive praise from the supervisor. This behaviour created poor relationships at work because those who did not cheat resented those who did. As Aiello observed, conscientious operators enjoyed being helpful to customers and were very unhappy that stringent standards prevented them from providing a high quality service.

Clearly, one the main effects of computer monitoring is to instil in the workforce a perception that 'quantity' is the most important factor in the job, rather than 'quality' of performance (Grant *et al.*, 1988). Such findings have also been reported by Irving *et al.*, 1986. These authors, interviewed 'monitored' employees from two organizations that had adopted computerized monitoring systems in the two years prior to their study. They compared these responses to those of non monitored workers. It was observed that close monitoring caused workers to feel constrained and under pressure. The monitored respondents experienced increased stress, decreased job satisfaction, and a decline in the quality of relationships with their peers, supervisors and senior management, attributed to the perceived added control, gained through the monitoring system. This led to an increase in stress-related illness. Monitored workers also believed that managers were placing a greater emphasis on quantity of work than on quality. It was believed that productivity levels had increased, but that they were now working harder for the same pay. Nevertheless, these employees reported that they felt a closer tie between their organization's reward and evaluation systems as a result of the computer based performance monitoring.

An adverse impact on team working, and reductions in employees' contact with co-workers and line managers are the potentially negative effects of computer monitoring. VDT users complain that they are more lonely at work and have less opportunity to develop social support networks. Performance monitoring, and the high level of information available to them at the workstation terminal, reduces opportunities to move around the workplace in order to collect this material, and at the same time engage in social contact (Aiello, 1993). The benefits of social support as a moderator of the impact of stress in the work environment, and as a direct benefit in reducing the perception of stress and pressure at work, are well documented. Therefore, the observed higher incidence of stress-related illnesses might be linked to this decrease in social contact and social support in the work environment.

A variety of ill-health symptoms have been reported following the introduction of workplace monitoring. For example, Aeillo (1993) found that VDT workers were not as satisfied with their jobs as they had been, and described a greater number of physical symptoms, including eyestrain, headaches and musculoskeletal discomfort. In addition, they felt more irritable, anxious, and depressed. Monitored workers can experience an increased amount of control over their activities and a lack of discretion in the job. As we have already observed, a lack of autonomy and discretion in a high demand work condition defines a job as a 'strain' job, according to Karasek (1979), and is associated with reduced psychological and physical well-being. The organizational costs of this can be high if the 'controlled' employee responds by behaving in undesirable ways such as sabotage, withdrawal and diminished citizenship behaviour (Kidwell and Bennett, 1994).

Chalykoff and Kochan (1989) suggest that the introduction of computer based monitoring can lead to a dramatic increase in supervisory workload because of the amount of information generated. While the perception exists that employees now have an 'electronic supervisor', experience indicates that line managers can feel overwhelmed by the feedback task and the pressure to provide more and more information (Aiello, 1993). Clearly, a supervisor who is expected to electronically monitor employees, and 'look in' on their computer based work activities, is no longer able to spend so much time being visible on the shop floor or 'at the sharp end'. Thus, opportunities for personal contact with employees are further reduced.

The benefits of computer monitoring

Empirical evidence indicates that observing the performance of workers and providing feedback to them can result in impressive productivity increases of around 20 to 40 per cent (Locke, *et al.*, 1980). Therefore, it is not surprising that one of the benefits of computer monitoring is an increase in organizational profitability. In addition to providing an employer with improved productivity, greater control and more effective resource management, the feedback gained from computer monitoring can be used by managers to plan workloads, design training programmes and provide more flexibility in work locations and work hours. Thus, employees can benefit from having more flexibility in work arrangements, or by becoming a 'teleworker' or 'telecommuter'.

It is also suggested that computer based work monitoring provides a more accurate and less subjective assessment of performance and so is more fair towards employees. Computers are acknowledged by employees as 'proper monitoring devices' and so are accepted because they provide a credible assessment of performance (Grant *et al.*, 1988). This is regarded as more accurate (Irving *et al.*, 1986) and fair than a performance evaluation provided in the more traditional way, by a supervisor.

Electronic monitoring can enhance the quality of an organization's work if it is integrated in the operation and collects information that aids employees in performing their jobs, rather than collecting private information about employee behaviour (Griffith, 1993).

Factors influencing the acceptance of computer monitoring

Rapid development in plant, machines and office technology was originally thought to be stressful because it was associated with the de-skilling of jobs. These fears seem to be mostly unfounded and it would appear that the method of introduction of the new technology is more significant as a potential source of pressure. Stress is more likely to occur as a result of the manner in which the new technology is introduced and applied in the organization (Daus, 1991), or when the individual fails to adapt to the changes brought about by the introduction of computer led jobs. These circumstances and conditions also apply to the introduction of computer based performance monitoring in the work place. Research evidence has highlighted a number of other factors that exist to influence the acceptance and success of computer based work monitoring.

1. Managers should communicate the role and purpose of the computer monitoring system to employees in an explicit way. Employees need to understand who will be monitored, why, what information is to be collected, and the purpose for which it is to be used. DeTienne (1994)

found that employees' reactions to computer monitoring could be positive when used correctly and accompanied by effective management communication. However, high levels of stress were associated with job dissatisfaction, lack of personal control, lack of commitment to the organization, and feelings about the appropriateness of the way in which managers used the information gathered by monitoring.

2. Technological changes are often introduced without effective consultation with the workforce. Sometimes a new system or method is actually not fit for the purpose. It might fail to do the task or job expected of it, or employees do not receive adequate or timely training in the use of the new system, plant or machinery. Ultimately, it means that the employee is exposed to a new and unfamiliar work routine and this can create a potentially stressful situation. The same will apply to the introduction of computer based monitoring. It is suggested that resistance to such a system will be lower, and acceptance is likely to be more positive, when employees are given the opportunity to take part in the design, setting up and implementation of computer based performance monitoring (Aiello, 1993). Acceptance of, and satisfaction with, new technology is related to 'a sense of achievement'(Kaye and Sutton, 1985), and 'autonomy and control'(Mankin *et al.*, 1984). Therefore, it is suggested that decisions about performance levels should be set in consultation with workers and in a flexible way (Long, 1984). This is key to the acceptance of new technology and change, and enhancing the quality of employees' work lives. This, of course, makes the assumption that employees actually know that they are being monitored. Clearly, some organizations use surveillance devices without the knowledge or consent of the work force! (Blinsky, 1991).

3. Increasing the perception of job control helps to minimize the impact of high job demands and reduce levels of stress. Creating a sense of ownership and personal control over a computer based monitoring system and process would reduce the stress associated with the introduction of this type of management control system. Job control can be exercized at three levels (Sainfort 1990).

  • instrumental level – that is, feedback and control over pace, which corresponds to the task being performed by the employee;
  • conceptual level – that is decision latitude, control over how tasks are carried out and work is scheduled, which involves conceptualization and cognitive processes;

- organizational level – that is, participation in decision making and employee involvement.

Carayon (1993) suggests that computer based monitoring systems have the potential to increase or decrease employee job control. For example, a monitoring system might be used to provide feedback to help workers gain instrumental control over a task. However, systems also have the potential to decrease levels of autonomy and decision making (conceptual control), so must be handled properly to ensure that this lack of perceived control does not lead to negative outcomes and rejection of the monitoring system.

4. Perceived fairness of the system is a factor that plays a large part in determining affective reactions to workplace control (Kidwell and Bennett, 1994). Fairness judgements affect employee attitudes such as satisfaction as well as supervisor evaluation (Alexander and Ruderman, 1987; Lind and Tyler, 1988). However, it is necessary to make a distinction between 'procedural justice' and 'distributive justice'. Procedural justice is concerned with perceived fairness of establishing outcomes, rather than what those outcomes are (distributive justice). Perception of procedural justice is important because it can predict how employees will react to other workplace controls such as performance decision making, participatory decision making, dispute resolution systems, job applicant interviewing methods and pay system (refer to Kidwell and Bennett, 1994 for a review). Indeed, a monitoring system must be seen to be objective and 'look fair'. Procedural justice is more closely related to global computer monitoring evaluations, whereas distributive justice is related to evaluations of specific outcomes (such as pay) and personally relevant outcomes.

5. The nature of the tasks being measured; frequency of measurement, constancy and appropriateness of the measures, are factors that affect employee acceptance of a monitoring system (Grant and Higgins, 1991). For example, it is important that a system does not collect information that is unrelated to job performance. Employees must feel that their most important and appropriate tasks are being measured fairly, and that comparison of their performance with reasonable standards is being made (Aiello, 1993). If surveillance is made of non-work activities, such as bathroom trips, problems are likely because employees will feel that this is an invasion of their privacy. Therefore, a monitoring system should be consistent across:

- individuals and time,

- the potential bias of the system,
- the accuracy of information obtained,
- the flexibility of the system to correct mistakes,
- the compatibility of the system with employee moral and ethical values,
- the voice employees have in setting up the system.

(Kidwell and Bennett, 1994).

6. How the results are derived and used will effect the degree to which computer monitoring is accepted. As we have stated, monitoring can be used for performance feedback or performance control. Chalykoff and Kochan (1989) found that computer monitoring systems used for the purpose of providing performance feedback information and training employees can be beneficial. It can have a positive impact on employee attitudes, compared to when it is used for the purpose of performance control. In the latter, Chalykoff and Cotton found computer aided monitoring to be directly related to job dissatisfaction and labour turnover. Studies of 'excellent' companies by Peters and Waterman (1982) indicated that non-punitive monitoring systems contributed to high performance and satisfaction. Also, these companies permitted their employees to work towards 'moderately easy' rather than difficult goals. Thus, they allowed these individuals to be 'winners' by letting them succeed, and rewarding them for performance above standard. This strategy provided an opportunity for employees to experience a 'sense of achievement'(described in 2). This is a necessary dimension in the acceptance of new technology and work monitoring.

   It also includes consideration of who actually sees the results of computer monitoring. Reactions of employees will vary, depending on whether only the individual concerned sees the results, or they are made available publicly. If an employee believes that results are influenced by factors other than their own performance, such as computer downtime, or they are unable to correct any inaccuracies, they are likely to be more negative about the experience of being monitored (Aiello, 1993).

7. Earley (1988) suggests that computer based feedback will have a greater impact on an individual's performance if he or she receives it directly from the computer system than if it is provided by a supervisor. The effective introduction of a computer tracked performance feedback system may also be strengthened if the individual's perceived trust in the source of the information is high. In addition, specific rather than

general feedback appears to be more effective in influencing performance in a positive way because it facilitates and stimulates task planning by directing the individual's attention to the task.

8. Share the rewards. If employees feel that they have something to gain by the increases in productivity and organizational profitability as a result of computer based performance monitoring, they are more likely to react in a positive way and accept the new initiative. As Aiello (1993) warns, fewer than a quarter of US workers are unionized. Therefore, the perceived tilting of the balance of power between employees and employer could 'open the door' to increased union activity, as workers seek protection from this perceived threat to the quality of their working life. This response is not unique to workers in the USA. European workers are likely to return to the protection of unions if they believe that monitoring leads to profit gains, as a result of their hard work, and they are not receiving any reward.

9. Certain dimensions of the organizational structure and climate are likely to adversely affect employee acceptance, and the success of a computer based monitoring system. For example, a work climate that is typical of a 'theory X' environment and already heavily control-orientated will be further intensified if a monitoring system is imposed on the workforce and resisted by them. A climate of openness and trust would be more conducive to the acceptance of a monitoring system. The implications of this for leadership and supervisory style are important in the successful acceptance of a monitoring system. If employees do not trust the source of feedback, or perceive the boss to be instrumental in manipulating the results of a performance monitoring system, co-operation will be low and negative reactions are likely to be manifest.

In summary, Carayon (1993) suggests that a framework, consisting of three main processes, can be used to identify potential stress when setting the parameters of a computer based performance monitoring system. This framework should be used to evaluate and determine the potential for these dimensions to influence worker stress and negative affect. Each of the following major dimensions can be characterized as positive or negative, along a continuum.

A Determine the characteristics of the information gathered by the system in terms of:

Relevance: is the technique relevant to purpose?

Completeness: does it include all the necessary performance parameters?
Unit of measure: does it measure individual or group performance?
Intensiveness: the amount of detail monitored

B Determine the method for gathering information:

Frequency: how often?
Continuousness: how constant is the monitoring in terms of duration and intervals?
Regularity: how predictable are the intervals between monitoring?

C Determine use of the information gathered:

Visibility: does the system provide feedback to the employee or supervisor?
Comparison of workers: does the system make comparisons among workers?
Relevance of measure of performance: does the system emphasise quantity at the expense of quality of work performance?
Performance standard: is the information used to gather performance standards?
Incentive pay system: Is the information used to develop an incentive pay structure?

Carayon (1993) says,

a system that collects data only on outcome quantity (completeness) or that overemphasises quantity at the expense of quality (change in relevant measure of performance) can be more stressful than a system that measures group performance as opposed to individual performance (unit of measure). A system that gathers a lot of detailed information on worker performance (intensiveness) can be more stressful than one that collects performance data infrequently (frequency) or continuously (continuousness) at predictable intervals (regularity) (p. 388).

Some authors believe that if computer monitoring is managed and handled properly it will not create the problems feared by its opponents. As Eisermann (1986) found, workers did not report concerns for a monitoring initiative because they had adapted to it, and had learned to minimize any of the possible negative effects of performance monitoring. Also, the perception existed that they were buffered from it by their supervisors. Nebeker and Taum believe that organizations need to concern themselves with three main issues in the introduction and implementation of computer based monitoring in the work environment. These include issues about the quality of work life, such as stress and health; the political rights of employees, such as rights of privacy, individual due process and legislative action; and economics, concerning the debate over monitoring and productivity. Therefore, we must ask if 'quantity' at any cost is truly our objective. Decisions need to be made about the role of 'quality of work', 'worker satisfaction', and the costs of stress in the work environment. We need to accept that these are important factors to be included in the calculation of the 'real bottom line' in business profitability.

Conducting a
Stress Audit

We have argued for an organizational approach to the management of stress, but also acknowledge that a successful stress management package will need to operate from more than one level. Indeed, a number of stress researchers have pointed out that stress control can be successful only if it is tackled at the level of the individual *and* the organization (DeFrank and Cooper, 1987; Hart, 1987). Therefore,

- We should operate at an organizational level to prevent or limit stress where this is a possible and reasonably practicable solution (Elkin and Rosch, 1990).
- We can work with individuals, teams or groups, to educate and train employees to cope more effectively with sources of stress that can not be removed from the job. However, we need to ensure that the weaknesses of this approach are overcome.
- We must also have in place strategies to deal with employees who 'fall through the net' to become victims of exposure to stress, since no organizational intervention is likely to be perfect or foolproof. Individuals are complex and unique and so they vary in their response to stress. Therefore, a stress management solution for one individual will not suit all employees or occupational groups.

This holistic, organizational approach to stress management is discussed fully in Chapter 7. At this point we must ask how we choose the best course of action. Many options are available for the management of stress. Some of these initiatives are complex, time-consuming to implement, potentially disruptive and sometimes costly. Few organizations would be prepared to commit themselves to change, and an extensive organizational developmental programme, without justification of its necessity, and a means of evaluating the effectiveness of the initiative. Likewise, the provision of, for example, counselling services or an exercise fitness facility, without consulting first with employees on the need for these particular methods of stress control, an assessment of the potential usefulness of them, and the perceived benefits to be gained, might otherwise be a waste of organizational resources. In order to identify a course of action we need to ask

1. If a potential problem exists.

2. If we can we identify the cause of the problem – is it stress related?

3. Who is affected by the situation?

4. What do employees need in place to overcome the problem or potential problem?

In order to understand the nature of stress and to design an appropriate stress management programme, we suggest that it is necessary to conduct a stress audit or psychological risk assessment.

In order to successfully implement an effective stress control programme, it is necessary to identify and measure the sources of stress that exist in the workplace. This should include the sources of stress that spill over from home and family life, to act as barriers to performance effectiveness and well-being. This process is known as 'conducting a stress audit'. It can also be referred to as 'a psychological risk assessment'. Human resources personnel and health and safety managers are familiar with the system and practice of conducting risk assessments since this is a legal workplace requirement. A psychological risk assessment is quite similar in many ways but some of the tools and methods are somewhat different.

Until we can identify sources of stress, known as 'stressors', it is unlikely that our stress management activities will be focused or successful. Clarification of the term stress, an understanding of the potential sources of stress in our environment, and recognition of our response to stress, are all vital steps in the effective management of stress. Since it is likely that different groups will experience different problems, and research findings are variant, it is important that a stress audit identifies specific problems and high risk, vulnerable workers. We need to ask why some individuals handle difficult situations and thrive in a demanding environment while others clearly do not prosper or even survive. Research evidence suggests that this 'tailored' approach, which aims to increase our understanding of human behaviour in the workplace, has many potential benefits for the organization. Improved productivity, good health, and safety performance are just some of these benefits. The ultimate advantage can be an important determinant of business success in a highly competitive business climate.

The Stress Audit Process

Under the terms of our definition of stress any situation or condition is potentially stressful and so it is necessary to distinguish between positive and negative pressures in the workplace. To identify the action to be taken is it vital to accurately diagnose the problem. Therefore, we must ask, what, who, where, why, when and how. This is the essential function of the stress audit. However, it must be conducted in a systematic and objective way.

Benefits of a stress audit

The benefits of a stress audit are described below:

1. As a diagnostic instrument it is thus a proactive rather than a reactive approach to the management of stress at work.

2. A stress audit aims to identify organizational and individual strengths and weaknesses in a similar manner to that of an appraisal or a training and development needs analysis. Therefore, it helps the organization to target scarce budgetary and time resources.

3. The audit enables us to identify both target and strategy for stress management actions. These can be classified under three headings. First, primary prevention, which is a stressor directed strategy that aims to either eliminate or minimize the source of stress. Next is the classification known as secondary prevention. This is a response directed strategy that aims to help the individual or group respond to the source of stress in an appropriate and effective manner. Finally, the tertiary stress management strategies are 'symptom directed' initiatives that are intended to cure victims of exposure to mismanaged stress.

4. A diagnostic stress audit provides a baseline measure from which to evaluate subsequent interventions.

5. The action of conducting a stress audit helps to make 'stress' a respectable topic for discussion in the workplace. By using a stress audit to understand workplace stress problems and the perceptions of employees to both problems and possible solutions, it is likely that

resistance to change, associated with the subsequent introduction of stress management interventions, will be reduced. Employee participation and involvement in a well-conducted stress audit will help to reduce any threat or fear associated with potentially sensitive stress related issues in the workplace. It is important that feedback of the results of the stress audit is provided to employees. The mechanism for this and the scope of the feedback should be decided and mutually agreed by all parties involved before the process begins. This includes management, the employees taking part and those conducting the audit.

Components of a stress audit: What should be measured?

Essentially there are five key components in the stress audit process. This is consistent with the occupational stress model proposed by Cooper and Marshall (1978) which is described in Chapter 4.

1. **Sources of Stress.** First we need to identify and measure the sources of stress that exist. In research terms these are called, 'independent variables'. The Cooper and Marshall (1978) model conceptualizes stress within six main categories, described as 'factors intrinsic to the job'; 'role in the organization'; 'relationships with other people'; 'career development and achievement'; organizational structure and climate' and 'the home-work interface'

2. **Stressor Outcomes**. Measures of stress outcomes include performance indicators such as quality or customer complaints. Measures such as sickness absence levels, physical symptoms of ill health, accident rates, job satisfaction levels, labour turnover rates, levels of anxiety or depression are also 'outcome' measures. In effect, these are the 'symptoms' of exposure to the experience of stress and in research terms they are described as 'dependent variables'. For example, we might be interested in understanding the impact of hours of work (the potential source of stress) on levels of depression or job satisfaction (this is, the outcome or 'dependent variable').

3. **Individual Differences.** Identify and measure the individual differences that can moderate or mediators in the stress response. These include a wide variety of individual differences that act to shape our response to exposure to stress, such as:

   - Physical condition such as levels of fitness and health, life stage, diet and eating habits, exercise activity, sleep patterns, relaxation activities, hobbies or interests.

- Biographic and demographic differences such as age, gender, race, occupation, education level, and socio-economic status.
- Personality traits and behavioural characteristics, for example, extroversion, neuroticism, need for achievement or power, internality versus externality (perceived degree of control), tolerance for ambiguity, Type A Coronary Prone behaviour pattern, needs, values. This list is not exhaustive and many more examples could be included. However, it begins to explain the diversity of individual differences as outcomes and symptoms observed in response to the experience of stress. It helps us to understand why people respond in such varied ways to a common source of stress. Indeed, we can say, 'one man's meat is another man's poison'. This, of course, makes it difficult for the decision makers in an organization to plan a holistic stress management strategy. Nevertheless, it is possible to identify the key stressors that appear to act to have a negative impact on the majority of the group, team or department. Then an informed decision on the most viable and acceptable method for stress control can be made.

4. **Predictors of Stress.** Identify stressor predictors of the outcome measures, that is, the dependent variables. In simple terms this means that we use a technique (known as regression analysis) that will identify the factors most strongly associated with a given outcome measure. For example, in stress audit conducted among General Practitioners in the United Kingdom (Sutherland, 1995) it was observed that the strongest predictors of levels of depression were:

- The high level of demand in the job itself and the patient expectations of the doctors.
- The stress associated with trying to balance work and home life demands.
- Low use of social support as a strategy for coping with the experience of stressful situation and conditions.

Thus the strategies recommended for stress control among General Practitioners were to:

- Initiate a campaign to educate the general public about the role of the General Practitioner, particularly with respect to night calls and locum duties.
- Increase levels of social support by having regular meetings after surgery hours and extending these sessions into a social gathering that included partners and spouses.

Both of these recommendations were successfully implemented to great effect by one large general practice group in the South-West of England. They included General Practitioners, the practice managers, nurses and administrative staff in these sessions. The meetings were used to solve problems and plan future strategies. Opportunity for resolving role conflict situations, which were previously rife, were especially welcomed by the group and the initiative was deemed to be a great success.

5. **Ascertain and measure staff attitudes** to the options available for the management of stress. That is, to acknowledge and understand what employees need and want in place in order to remove the stressor barriers to their effectiveness, productivity, health and satisfaction at work. In this part of the audit process it is important to ensure that employee expectations remain realistic about the options and potential for the management of a stressful situation. If unrealistic expectations are raised and not realised it is likely that the stressor problem can become exacerbated. This appears to be one area that most threatens the human resources manager and group and deters them from embarking on a stress audit. It is often referred to as, 'opening a can of worms' but finding that 'you can do nothing about the situation'. Again, much of this problem can be avoided before the audit process begins. Clear and consistent communications about the remit and scope of the audit are essential. One large pharmaceutical company avoided potential problems by setting up multilevel teams to discuss the audit findings and identify potential solutions. Possible methods of controlling a source of stress were considered by using a SWOT analysis (Ansoff, 1969). Thus, the strengths, weaknesses, opportunities and threats that faced the group and organization were listed and used in the decision making process.

Stress audit instruments

A wide variety of techniques and measures are available for use when conducting a stress audit. These include arranging focus group discussion sessions, conducting one-to-one or group interviews, the completion of stress logs or diaries, the use of critical incident techniques, and the administration of questionnaires. Certain standardized measures are available and these have the advantage of providing normative data comparisons. The use of computerized testing has simplified this procedure considerably although care must still be taken to ensure that the assessment tool has been developed in accordance with recognized test procedures.

One extensively used instrument is the Occupational Stress Indicator, known as the OSI, and devised by Cooper, Sloan and Williams (1988). This provides a comprehensive tool for use in a stress audit and is based upon the model of stress proposed by Cooper and Marshall (1978). It includes measures of:

1. Sources of pressure at work with respect to the job itself, job role, interpersonal relationships, career and achievement, organizational structure and climate and the home-work interface.

2. Individual characteristics, including biographical and demographic factors and personality measure of locus of control (that is, levels of perceived control in the workplace) and Type A Coronary Prone behaviour.

3. An assessment of certain coping strategies in response to stress. That is, the degree of social support, time management, logic, task strategies, home and work relationships, and 'involvement' used as coping strategies in response to the experience of stress and pressure.

4. Measures of individual effects of stress, that is, self report measures of physical and mental health states and job satisfaction.

The OSI is available in both paper and pencil and a computer administration format. It has an extensive data base that allows normative comparisons. It is also possible to obtain a version for use with blue-collar workers. Respondents are required to rate their responses on 'Likert' type, six point scales. This means that the OSI can be scored to produce both individual and group stress profiles that can be used in feedback sessions. This facility is very useful in helping individuals and groups to develop an action plan for the management of stress. Whilst this questionnaire has established reliability and validity data (Cooper and Bramwell, 1992; Cooper, Sloan and Williams, 1988; Rees and Cooper, 1991; Robertson and Cooper, 1990), it is important to acknowledge the issue of the high 'face validity' of the OSI. In our experience we have found that questionnaire respondents seem to be able to relate to their stress profile and see it as 'a true picture of their stress condition'.

By using a coding system in the administration process, the OSI can be used anonymously and the data can be collected and analysed without breaching confidences or the guarantee of confidentiality that help to ensure honesty in reporting. It is a highly effective stress audit tool, particularly when it is used in conjunction with a stressor item bank designed specifically for that occupational group. For example, in a study of occupational stress in the social services, the OSI was used as the main instrument of measurement but was supported by a stressor item bank developed through in-depth interview sessions conducted with social workers and home help staff (Bradley and Sutherland, 1995).

Other similar measures include, The Generic Job Stress Questionnaire (Hurrell and McLaney, 1988) which was developed in the USA by NIOSH (National Institute for Occupational Safety and Health). This instrument makes an assessment of different job stressors, in addition to providing measures of reactions to job strain. It is designed to be modular so that organizations can select individual scales and the package was developed from prior scales with known reliability and validity. The Occupational Stress Indicator, developed by Osipow and Spokane (1983) also measures a wide range of job stressors, employee resources for coping with stress, and mental and physical strain. The measure has demonstrated good test, re-test reliability, and occupational normative data are available for comparative purposes. It is possible to produce standardized scores that are plotted on to a stress profile to provide individual feedback information.

Whilst the questionnaires described above provide a comprehensive tool for use in the stress audit process there is a plethora of diagnostic instruments available to measure specific variables. Researchers are likely to select from an enormous battery of self-completion measures in order to design their own audit packages, whereas compact instruments, such as the OSI, are favoured by human resources personnel. The General Health Questionnaire, or GHQ, which is available in many versions and lengths (Goldberg, 1978), and the Crown Crisp Experiential Index, or CCEI (Crown and Crisp, 1979) are popular measures of psychological strain. Both have been used extensively and have normative data available for making population comparisons. The CCEI is a 48 item 'yes', 'no', 'sometimes' response questionnaire that can be scored numerically and provides six subscale measures of psychological health, namely, free floating anxiety, phobic anxiety, depression, somatic anxiety, obsessionality and hysteria. A measure of job satisfaction developed by Warr, Cook and Wall (1979) is also a popular choice of audit instrument. This measure has a satisfactory level of internal consistency and is quick and simple to administer. A huge selection of single variable measures is described in the literature for the purpose of measuring both dependent and independent variables.

O'Driscoll and Cooper (1994) recommend the use of a 'critical incident analysis' as a method of identifying stress and stress-coping processes in work settings. This technique was first described by Flanagan (1954). Essentially the process consists of asking individuals to describe stressful transactions in terms of three elements:

1. The antecedents or circumstances in which the stress occurred.
2. Their response in that situation, together with the responses of other people.
3. The consequences of both their own and other individuals' behaviour.

We also use this method in our 'stress log'(see Appendix). Individuals are asked to describe the most stressful experience of the day, what happened, what they did in the situation, the other people involved, and on reflection what they might have done differently. The critical incident technique can be used in an interview situation to ask individuals to describe the job related events that they believe to have placed demands upon them or caused them difficulties. It is important that the individual is encouraged to be specific and non emotive about the incident. For example, 'reprimanded by my supervisor for being late for work – felt angry all day' is too general a description of stress and not specific enough. 'My day was disrupted because I was reprimanded by my supervisor for arriving late for work; my alarm did not go off', is a specific and non emotive description of the event. It assists the individual in eliminating this particular source of stress in the future, either by ensuring that the alarm clock does work, or by the purchase of a new one! It is also necessary to establish how the employee coped with the reprimand and responded to this situation. Clearly, a negative reaction is one that results in an argument with the supervisor. It is not an appropriate coping behaviour. Continuing to behave in a disruptive manner for the remainder of the work shift is also likely to be equally damaging in its consequences. Therefore, in the final stage of this process, the individual is asked how they felt about the consequences of their behaviour in response to the situation. It is important that the interviewer does not try to judge or evaluate the individual's coping process until the process of stress identification is completed. When the employee has described a series of such incidents, the analysis will reveal specific stressors, behaviours and consequences, in addition to coping style trends and preferences. This technique can be used to identify key sources of stress among a particular occupational group, team or for a specific individual in the organization.

It is important for the organization to consider what information is already available from existing company records, to support the findings from self-report data obtained from questionnaire instruments, stress logs, or critical incident analysis. These might include, for example, sickness absence records, accident reports, grievance records, labour turnover figures and the cost of compensation claims.

Some companies have incorporated a psychological risk assessment into employee medical examinations. Typically, personnel from the occupational health department or an external organization will conduct this part of the programme. Whilst the employee is waiting to see a doctor or nurse, they might be required to complete a computerized version of the OSI. This offers the advantage of computer scoring and the facility of producing a stress profile immediately on completion of the questionnaire. The data are stored and used to produce in-house, company norms. These can be compared to either the general population scores or some similar occupational group. Consultants are also often employed to assist with the audit that is being managed and directed by either a personnel director or a human resources group. There are, of course pros and cons for both of these approaches.

Conducting a Stress Audit: Who does It?

An audit conducted by personnel internal to the organization gains benefit because it is carried out by those individuals who already know much about the business. Unfortunately this can also mean that the research results can be distorted. This is not deliberate, but due to the preconceived notions of the individuals involved. These perceptual distortions or errors are caused by stereotyping, the halo effect, perceptual defence and projection.

* Stereotyping is the tendency to ascribe positive or negative characteristics to a person on the basis of a general categorisation and perceived similarities. Therefore, the perception may be based on certain expectations rather than on the recognition of that person as an individual. It is a means of simplifying the process of perception and making judgements of other people. We can base our stereotypes on many factors including nationality, occupation, age, physical state, gender, education, social status or politics. For example, occupation, 'all accountants are boring'; social status, 'all unemployed people are lazy'.
* Halo effect is the process by which the perception of a person is formulated on the basis of one favourable or unfavourable trait or impression. Thus, the effect tends to shut out other relevant characteristics of the person. For example, a single trait, such as good attendance or timekeeping, may become the main emphasis for

judgement of overall competence and performance, rather than other considerations such as the quantity or quality or work.

- Perceptual defence is the tendency to screen out certain stimuli that are disturbing or threatening. Thus we select information that is supportive of our point of view and choose to ignore less favourable information.

- Projection is the tendency for people to project their own feelings, characteristics and motives to their perception of other people. Thus, judgement of other people is likely to be favourable when they have characteristics in common with the perceiver. However, it also means that projection will result in the exaggeration of undesirable traits in others that they fail to recognise in themselves.

On a practical note, we must also consider whether internally employed personnel fulfil the following requirements.

1. Do they have enough time to conducted a potentially lengthy and time consuming project? It is vital that those involved are able to overtly and actively demonstrate their commitment to the project. If the audit is not seen to be a priority activity then it is unlikely that the workforce will take it seriously and the rate of participation will be too low to provide meaningful and valid results.

2. Do they have the appropriate skills and qualifications to do the audit?

3. Can they be objective and remain discreet in order to guarantee confidentiality?

4. Is there likely to be any risk of breach of ethics?

5. Do they have the trust and respect of the staff who are being audited?

6. Is there a possibility that they might be influenced directly or indirectly by other stakeholders or 'politicians' within the company? Pressure from powerful others can result in information being withheld, omitted, or distorted, thereby corrupting the results of the audit or risk assessment.

The use of an external body to conduct the stress audit will overcome many of the concerns expressed above, particularly those associated with the issues of objectivity and confidentiality. However, these individuals will know little about the company initially. Thus, they will need to spend time becoming familiar with the culture and climate of the organization. Also, it is likely that the costs are certain to be higher. The use of computers for the administration, scoring and interpretation of audit instruments has helped many companies to be almost self-sufficient in the stress audit process. However, many still prefer to use external agencies in a nominal way in order to add credibility and objectivity to the audit exercise. Audit data analysis can be a lengthy procedure since the results should identify differences, for example, between departments, job grades, gender, age, length of service, location, and so on. This will ensure that the required stress control actions are targeted specifically to where they are needed in order to be successful and cost effective.

Integrating a Stress Audit into Current Risk Assessment Processes

We have already advised that it is important to identify data already available within the organization and to integrate this into the risk assessment process. Ideally, a stress audit should not become a 'stand-alone' exercise within the company. Indeed, it is also worth considering whether the term 'stress audit' is to be used. Sadly, use of the word 'stress' still has negative connotations in the workplace. This means that a 'stress audit' is often perceived as a threat to both managers and staff. If employees greet the audit with suspicion and suspect some other 'real' purpose, they will feel threatened. They will also feel that they are being blamed for not coping with stress and will try to overcome this by denying that any stress related problems exist. Typically, in this situation, employees will try to behave like swans, who glide serenely on the surface of a smooth lake, appearing to be calm and in control. However, just like a swan, all the frantic activity remains hidden beneath the surface! This is similar in certain respects to the problems encountered when conducting performance appraisals. Thus, it is now acknowledged, that to be effective, it is necessary to conduct separate appraisals for the purpose of employee development and training, and those intended for promotion and pay awards assessment. Ultimately, the objective of a stress audit is to optimize the performance and health (that is, the well-being and quality of life) of employees, so why not describe it as that and avoid using the word stress in such a high-profile way.

Stress Audit Case Studies

In the final stress part of this chapter we describe three different stress audits. The first of these was an audit conducted to examine the links between stress and accidents among personnel working in the offshore oil and gas industries (Sutherland and Cooper, 1991). Next, an audit used to investigate the impact of major changes among General Practitioners. This followed the introduction of a new work contract (Sutherland and Cooper, 1993). Finally, a different type of audit that was conducted to investigate 'career' stress in a white collar work environment (Sutherland and Davidson, 1996). The objectives of this audit were to maximize career potential and opportunities by identifying the barriers that existed to career development in the organization.

Stress in the offshore oil and gas industry

Since it is likely that different groups will experience different problems, and research findings are variant, it is important that any stress audit identifies specific problems and high risk, vulnerable workers. We need to ask why some individuals cope and thrive in a demanding environment, while others clearly do not prosper or even survive. The results obtained from this stress audit, conducted amongst personnel working in the offshore oil and gas industry, indicated that sources of stress varied as a function of job status, installation type, the size of the installation and where it was located. Audit objectives were to identify the relationships between stress and accident involvement offshore, and investigate individual differences and accident occurrence.

The offshore working environment is potentially stressful because the workforce live and work in one restricted location for a significant period of time without a break. Life offshore has been described as dangerous, arduous and socially isolating. The environment is characterized by constant noise and activity and personnel are often exposed to crowded living conditions in this '24-hour, unnatural society' (ILO, 1986). Indeed, they also face an uncertain future as oil and gas prices continue to rise and slump in unstable, global market conditions. Such working conditions may be optimal for accident occurrence, which are at least three to five times more costly to this industry because they are exposed to an offshore working climate. Nevertheless such situations are not necessarily, inherently stressful because many factors moderate or mediate response to stress and affect outcomes; for example health, job satisfaction and accident vulnerability (Sutherland and Cooper, 1986, 1990, 1991).

A three-part questionnaire was sent out at six monthly intervals to record sources of stress. Symptoms of stress were measured in terms of accident occurrence, job dissatisfaction and mental ill-health. Personality measures included extraversion-introversion, neuroticism and type A Coronary Prone behaviour. A variety of career and biographical details, in addition to health behaviours, such as tobacco smoking and alcohol consumption, were also collected. Type A Coronary Prone Behaviour was measured with the Framingham Type A Scale (FTAS) (Haynes, Feinleib and Kannel, 1980), and a modified version of the Bortner Scale (Bortner and Rosenman 1967).The Eysenck Personality Inventory (EPI- form A) (Eysenck, 1964) was used to measure extroversion and neuroticism. Potential sources of stress in the offshore oil and gas industry were identified by conducting one-to-one interview sessions and this information was used to design a questionnaire. The Warr, Cook and Wall (1979) scale was used to measure job satisfaction, and levels of mental well-being were assessed using the Crown Crisp Experiential Index (CCEI).

Over an 18-month survey period, 310 males (32 per cent rate of response) working on 97 offshore drilling and production installations in European waters took part in the audit. The randomly selected sample included 146 unionized personnel from 14 of the major oil companies, and 164 contract workers employed by 18 contractor suppliers. Fifty semi-structured interviews were conducted with a stratified, random sample of workers to provide a basis for the questionnaire design. This was piloted on a sample of 194 workers in a preliminary study within one offshore contractor company (Sutherland and Cooper, 1986). Nearly 45 per cent of personnel worked a '14 days on, 14 days off' tour with a mixture of day and night working, usually in 12-hour shifts. Their ages ranged from 21 to 60 years; 74 per cent of workers were married and the divorced and separated rate was 12 per cent. Questions about lifestyle habits revealed that 34 per cent of employees were tobacco smokers and 16 per cent of respondents reporting consuming more than the 21 units 'safe' level of alcohol per week, while onshore.

A very brief summary of the results is reported here in order to provide a flavour of the output from an audit of this type. For example, data analysis indicated that both job status and installation type had an impact on perceived strain and pressures in the offshore environment. In general, offshore personnel did not appear to feel valued or worthy and had a depressed attitude towards their job future prospects. Differences specific to type of installation and status indicated less security and stability on drilling rigs, whereas personnel on production platforms reported significantly lower levels of stress related to 'career prospects and reward'. 'Safety and insecurity' were significant sources of stress for personnel on installations in the central and northern sectors of the North

Sea. The stress associated with 'living conditions' was highest among the contractors on production platforms in the central and northern North Sea sectors; but in the southern sector the operator personnel were more likely to express this as a source of stress. Thus it can be seen that expectations, needs and values all had an impact on the way that stress was perceived.

These differences were also reflected in stress outcome measures. For example, it was observed that the offshore worker was significantly less job satisfied than his onshore counterpart although the operator personnel were more satisfied than the contractors. Location and size of installation were also associated with reported levels of job satisfaction. Job dissatisfaction was greatest amongst personnel working on the drilling rigs compared to production platforms, but personnel in the southern North Sea sector were more satisfied than in the central and northern North Sea locations. Job satisfaction was highest on installations where there were 60 or fewer people working at any one time. Measures of mental health also reflected differences as a function of status, installation type, location and size.

Analysis of accident statistics indicated that 29 per cent of the sample reported accident involvement leading to personal injury offshore. Contrary to expectations and popular opinion, no differences were observed between the contractor and operator personnel (accident rate, 29 and 30 per cent, respectively). Those individuals involved in an accident prior to the start of the study were more likely to be cigarette smokers and had a poorer level of psychological health (that is, they were more anxious, obsessional and depressed) than the accident free personnel. There is some evidence to suggest that this was related to accident severity (measured as a function of lost time). For example, the psychological health and well-being of individuals involved in an incident resulting in more than 22 days' lost time was much poorer than those involved in a 'no-lost-time' incident. The issue of perceived blame for an incident produced some interesting findings. Previous research suggests that those responsible for an accident suffered more psychological distress than those who were pure 'victims' of an incident (that is, it just 'happened' to them, but they were not responsible for causing it). In the offshore environment the reverse pattern was observed. Accident involvement that was perceived as completely out of the control of the individual had more impact in terms of reduced psychological well-being and job dissatisfaction after the event.

It was noted that both operator and contractor personnel who had been involved in an accident perceived their work environment to be more stressful than the accident free personnel.

The stress audit results suggested that dispositional differences and poor person-environment fit played some causal role in accident occurrence and the perception of stress. A 'type B' behaviour predisposition was observed in the offshore population (73 per cent of respondents were in either Type B3 or B4 categories). However, a higher proportion of 'Type As' was found working on drilling rigs than on the production platforms. In the total offshore sample, 29 per cent of personnel had reported accident involvement. An analysis revealed that 36 per cent of 'Type As' had been involved in an accident leading to personal injury compared to only 24 per cent of 'Type Bs'. Type A individuals were also significantly more job dissatisfied and reported significantly poorer levels of psychological well-being than their Type B counterparts.

This stress audit enabled us to better understand individual vulnerability, or risk, so that we could implement effective manpower development programmes. In the offshore oil and gas exploration and production environment the results of the stress audit indicated that sources of stress were specific to certain groups of personnel. This meant that a stress control programme would be more effective if resources were targeted to a specific problem to eliminate the stressor at source. The industry also needed to introduce methods of improving person-job fit; for example, the use of psychometric assessment in recruitment and development (that is, to identify training and development needs for personnel). Whilst it may be necessary to accept that certain high-risk styles of behaviour (that is, the Type A behaviour style) may be needed to get the job done, specific training is required to address those aspects of behaviour that seem to increase accident vulnerability and reduced psychological well-being. Use of this stress audit and subsequent follow-up studies would reveal if the environment was attracting certain types of people, or encouraging deleterious patterns of behaviour. It is costly for the industry to find this out when an unsuitable individual resigns after receiving initial training and induction, or becomes ill or involved in an accident. Indeed, a continuous assessment process is vital for self-development and career progression. It also enables us to understand what happens to people exposed to a potentially hazardous and stressful job for an extended period of time, and to evaluate any subsequent interventions introduced to manage work-related stress. A stress audit guides this process, which ultimately embraces both individual coping and organizational change and development programmes to combat the problems associated with stress at work.

Identifying stress and the predictors of ill-health and job dissatisfaction among General Practitioners

The objective of this stress audit was to identify the sources of job stress and the personality factors that were most predictive of psychological ill-health and job dissatisfaction among General Practitioners (GPs) working in the UK. This study followed enforced changes to the ways of working and contractual arrangements, which seemed to have resulted in increased pressure at work. Much of this had been caused by financial constraints, the needs of ever demanding patients, increasing practice administration duties, and an element of uncertainty (Morrell, Evans and Roland, 1983; Myerson, 1991; Porter, Howie, and Levinson, 1985, 1987; Sutherland and Cooper, 1992).

It was acknowledged that a four-phased approach was required in order to identify negative stress. First, to identify the potential stressors that existed in the unique work environment of the GP. Second, to examine the individual or person factors that are known to mediate in the stress-response process. Next, it was necessary to measure the well-being of GPs in terms of certain manifestations of exposure to stress. This included certain aspects of psychological ill health, job dissatisfaction and maladaptive coping mechanisms (for example, alcohol and drug abuse). The final phase was to identify the stressors most strongly associated with negative outcomes (that is, depression, anxiety, alcohol abuse,and so on).

Following a series of focus group discussion sessions with a geographic, stratified sample of GPs working in the UK, a questionnaire was designed for distribution to a national sample. This postal questionnaire survey aimed to identify the stressor predictors of job dissatisfaction and mental ill-health among GPs. The questionnaire pack was sent to a random, national sample of 1500 GPs and respondents were given a guarantee of confidentiality. Telephone contact was made to encourage GPs to complete and return their questionnaire pack.

In this audit, mental well-being was measured using a shortened version of the Crown Crisp Experiential Index (CCEI, 1979). This provides a self-report measure of free floating anxiety, depression and somatic anxiety. Job satisfaction levels were measured with ten items taken from the Warr, Cook and Wall (1979) scale. Details were obtained about age, gender, partnership, the practice itself, full or part time working, and numbers of surgeries the GPs worked from. Two personality styles (Type A behaviour and Locus of Control) were assessed using the Occupational Stress Indicator (the 'OSI', Cooper, Sloan and Williams, 1988). Sources of stress were measured in two ways. The 31 stressor item bank developed from interviews conducted by Cooper, Faragh and Rout (1989) was used together with the sources of job pressure scale from the OSI. Finally, six coping styles were measured using the OSI.

In total, 917 usable replies were returned for statistical analysis (61 per cent response rate). The sample was composed of 670 male doctors (73.1 per cent) and 243 female doctors (26.5 per cent). Their ages ranged from 27 to 73 years. Most GPs were working in a group practice (93 per cent), mainly working from one (69 per cent) or two (25 per cent) surgeries. Only 27 respondents worked part time. The male doctors were found to be significantly more anxious and depressed than a British normative sample of men, whereas the observed scores for the women doctors were similar to the population norms for women. Levels of somatic anxiety were significantly lower than the population norms for both groups.

The next step in the audit was to find out which of the stressor factors were most likely to be the 'cause' of the outcomes observed. It is important to acknowledge that this use of the word, 'cause' is not really accurate since we cannot be sure about cause and effect relationships by using a 'one-off' stress audit. To establish cause and effect it would require a longitudinal study and the use of control groups to be sure that other factors were not confounding the results obtained. Nevertheless, it is possible to use a statistical technique (known as multiple regression analysis) to identify the important and statistically significant 'predictors' of a particular outcome. Therefore, to investigate the relationships between the stressor outcomes of free floating anxiety, depression, somatic anxiety and job dissatisfaction, and the possible predictors of these outcomes (that is the independent variables, job demographics, Type A behaviour, locus of control, coping styles, and job stressors), stepwise multiple regression analyses were used. Table 6.1 lists the stressor factors and the component items for each of these factors.

The main predictor of job dissatisfaction among GPs was the pressure associated with the 'demands of the job and patients' expectations'. Other stressor sources predictive of job dissatisfaction included the stress of 'the organization structure and climate' and 'the home and work interface'. Low use of social support as a coping strategy was also related to reported job dissatisfaction. A significant difference in the reported use of social support as a stress coping strategy was observed between male and female doctors, and women were more likely to use this method of coping than the male GPs. Women doctors were also more likely than male doctors to use 'home and work relationships' as a way of coping with stress. That is, using support from within the home environment, hobbies and outside interests as stress coping strategies. It also emerged that GPs who practised

Table 6.1 Stress Factors and Stressors Items for General Practitioners

Factor 1. Demands of job and patients' expectations

Fear of assault during night visits
Visiting in extremely adverse weather conditions
Adverse publicity by media
Increased demand by patients and relatives for second opinion from hospital specialists
No appreciation of your work by patients
Worrying about patients' complaints
Finding a locum
Twenty-four hour responsibility for patients' lives
Taking several samples in a short time
Unrealistically high expectations by others of your role

Factor 2. Interruptions

Coping with phone calls during night and early morning
Night calls
Interruption of family life by telephone
Emergency calls during surgery hours
Home visits
Dealing with problem patients
Remaining alert when on call

Factor 3. Practice administration and routine medical

Hospital referrals and paperwork
Conducting surgery
Practice administration
Arranging admissions
Working environment (surgery set up)
Time pressure

Factor 4. Home-work interface and social life

Demands of your job on family life
Dividing time between your spouse and patients
Demands of job on social life
Lack of emotional support at home, especially from spouse

Factor 5. Dealing with death and dying

Daily contact with dying and chronically ill patients
Dealing with the terminally ill and their relatives

Factor 6. Medical responsibility for friends and relatives

Dealing with friends as patients
Dealing with relatives as patients

Source: Cooper, Rout and Faragher (1989)

from more than one surgery were most likely to be dissatisfied with the job, and job satisfaction levels decreased as the number of practice premises increased.

'Job role stress', the 'demands of the job and the high expectations of their patients, and 'the stress of practice administration and routine medical work', were identified as the main predictors of high levels of anxiety. No differences were observed between the male and female doctors. Doctors who exhibited the 'Type A' Coronary Prone style of behaviour were also more likely to exhibit higher levels of anxiety than their 'type B' colleagues (that is, GPs who did not exhibit this style of behaviour). The distribution of the Type A behaviour pattern among GPs was consistent with population norms and again no differences were observed between male and female GPs. Finally, low use of 'involvement' as a coping strategy was also related to high anxiety levels. Involvement means becoming involved and committed to the issues that cause one pressure and coping with them by being aware of the reality of the problem. Our analysis showed that GPs were significantly less likely to use 'involvement' as a coping strategy than the normative population. Again, the 'number of surgeries practised from' emerged as a predictor of anxiety levels. Doctors who operated from more than one surgery were more likely to exhibit higher levels of free floating anxiety.

Two significant stressor factors predicted levels of depression among GPs. These were, 'the demands of the job and the high expectations of their patients', and the stress of 'the home and work interface'. Low use of social support as a source of coping was also associated with high levels of depression. Levels of somatic anxiety among GPs were significantly lower than in the general population and three stressor factors emerged as the predictors of somatic anxiety. These included 'the demands of the job and the expectations of their patients', 'the stress of the home and work interface' and, 'practice administration and routine medical work'.

Conclusion and Implications

Three main stressor themes emerged from this stress audit. First, the pressures of the demands of the job and patients' expectations were highlighted. This included the increasing fear of assault during night visits, worry about complaints from patients, the high expectations of patients, and adverse publicity by the media. Doctors felt that their patients had not been fully informed about the changes necessary to fulfil the terms of the new contract and this caused unnecessary conflict between doctor and patient, especially for call out arrangements. Next, 'role stressors' appeared to be associated with poor psychological well-being among this occupational group. Not surprising, in the aftermath of so much change, these pressures were due to conflict between 'job task' and the new role demands on GPs. Role ambiguity, the implications of making mistakes, and being 'visible' were key sources of stress. General practitioners reported that they no longer felt in control of the events that affected their ways of working. Also, they did not feel that were adequately consulted about the changes made to their job and way of life as a GP. The third key source of strain could be characterized as 'being in the organization' and described the work structure and climate of the GP. These sources of stress included 'a lack of consultation and communication, having to do mundane administrative work, having insufficient resources to do the job effectively, staff shortages, lack of feedback about one's performance, and low morale'. Essentially, many GPs did not like working in large group practice environments, which by necessity were usually run by the practice manager.

In addition to the stressor predictors of psychological health, the role of social support was also a contributory factor in the well-being of the GP. This variable emerged as a significant predictor of both job satisfaction levels and depression. Since women doctors were more likely to use social support as a stress coping strategy, and exhibited a better level of psychological well-being and job satisfaction than the male doctors, this is an area worthy of more investigation as a stress management technique.

In addition to an increased awareness of individual strategies to improve personal fitness for coping with stress, such as relaxation, meditation, physical exercise, time management, or assertion training, recommendations were made for stress control at 'group' and 'organizational' levels. These recommendations included team development and team building, and interpersonal skills training as a way of helping to alleviate or eliminate stress in the 'group practice' work environment of the GP. Crucial, however, were opportunities to build support networks and to allocate work appropriately. Both partnership and staff relationship problems could be addressed by more effective team working. At the highest level in organizational terms, stress management would operate by seeking to eliminate or minimize problems identified by the GPs. This is at the level of the National Health Service (NHS), where the general practice model could be examined in consultation with those working in general practice. It was apparent that GPs believed that they needed to be more involved in the decisions and actions that affected them. The concept of team management could be used to examine models of job design, methods of working and the use of new technology. Other stress management strategies might include the provision of equipment to improve the safety of doctors on call, such as mobile phones, radio alarms and car alarms. Most importantly, it was felt that stress levels could be reduced if a message was communicated to patients, about the need for more realistic expectations of the general practice doctor. Indeed, it was suggested that changes to empower the 'customer'(that is, the patients) may have swung too far in the favour of the patient, to the detriment of effective general practice. It should be remembered, however, that such stress management interventions are likely to take time to implement. Therefore, the introduction of a counselling service or Employee Assistance Programmes should be made available to GPs who might become victims and casualties of exposure to stress at work. Some authorities already have taken this as an option and provide counselling help to GPs. However, it might also be necessary to encourage GPs to use these services. It means that a clear message should be delivered which endorses the view that stress is an acceptable and important topic for discussion. It is necessary to recognize that problems might exist, and must be dealt with in a positive and proactive manner. Ultimately, for all concerned, this is the most cost effective way forward in the management of stress.

Developing career potential of employees in a white-collar work environment

This audit was different from the other two case studies in that it focused on one particular aspect of the work environment of the employee, namely, that of career and career development. The aim of the audit was to identify the potential sources of career related stress that might act as barriers or inhibitors in the development of career potential and opportunities of employees working in a white-collar organization (Sutherland and Davidson, 1996). As such, it can also be described as an equal opportunity audit that includes all employees, irrespective of their age, gender, disability or ethnic origin.

A two-phased approach to data collection was utilized in this audit, namely the use of qualitative information in the form of in-house data and materials, and group interview sessions; and quantitative data obtained from the distribution of a large scale sample postal questionnaire. The number of returned questionnaires totalled 595, that is a 30.5 per cent rate of response. The results were analysed in terms of potential barriers associated with recruitment, promotion opportunities, training, working conditions and the development of career opportunities. The self-report responses from personnel working in various locations and employed at different grade levels were examined.

The audit aimed to identify the employees' current job positions, and their attitudes to 'career and career potential' in the organization. This was to identify any reasons for job segregation and blocks to career progression. In the UK today, women constitute 44 per cent of the work-force and both racial minorities and the disabled form an increasingly significant proportion of the economically active population (Labour Force Survey, 1994). However, despite the introduction of sex discrimination and equal pay legislation, the majority of women, racial minorities and the disabled are concentrated in low pay, low status, gender segregated jobs. Recently, a growing number of organizations in the UK and Europe have introduced equal opportunity and positive action programmes in order to provide women and other minorities with the same job opportunities as men. However, all the evidence so far suggests that equality of opportunity benefits all employees in an organization. For an employer, the cost of not achieving a full equality of opportunity policy is often very high (Chater and Chater, 1992). This was felt to be particularly important by the organization which commissioned this audit. They believed they needed to maintain a competitive advantage by reducing staffing cost and therefore needed to fully maximize the potential of the remaining staff.

An Equal Opportunity Audit involves detailed analysis of men and women's current position in the workforce and to identify the reasons for job segregation and the blocks to career progression. Organizations that have successfully initiated systematic and structured equal opportunity policies usually carry out equal opportunity audits and monitoring (Davidson, 1989). According to Chater and Chater (1992), equal opportunity audits enable:

1. an organization to provide a comprehensive picture of the pattern of employment of men and women;

2. an examination of the effect of the organization's policies and working arrangements upon the potential career development of employees;

3. an assessment of the relationship between current recruitment, training, promotion and general employment policies and practices, and the development of equal opportunities;

4. a measure of the attitudes of employers and their supervisors or managers towards the present position and any potential changes.

Audits should include an analysis of current policies and workforce biographic and demographic statistics, as well as interviews, workshop sessions and questionnaire survey with a cross-section of both males and females throughout the organization. On the basis of these results, recommendations for a continued programme of action to overcome actual and potential barriers can be proposed and periodic monitoring of progress is possible.

A two-phased approach to data collection was used. This included the use of qualitative information in the form of in-house data and materials and group interview sessions, and quantitative data from the distribution of a piloted postal questionnaire. All employees received a letter of intent to inform them about the project, in the hope of allaying any fears and insecurities about the project and to enhance commitment to the initiative. Group-interview workshop sessions were held with a representative, cross-section staff. Assurances of confidentiality and anonymity were given and experiences of, and opinions about, the following issues were explored:

- Recruitment and interview procedures
- Training and job experience opportunities
- Job satisfaction and utilization of skills
- Career opportunities, prospects and barriers
- Grading systems
- Promotion procedures
- Attitudes and behaviour of colleagues and subordinates, supervisors and managers
- Organizational culture issues
- The provisions for maternity or paternity leave, childcare, flexitime, homeworking, career breaks, part time work, job sharing, and refresher courses
- Perceptions about equality of opportunities in the organization

On the basis of this data a questionnaire was designed, piloted and refined. The final format was distributed to all staff in the ethnic minority and disabled categories, and a 50 per cent sample of all other employees (sample size 1850). A Likert type scale was utilized for each of the questions and respondents were asked to indicate the extent to which they agreed or disagreed with each statement. A request for certain demographic and biographic details was included. Some of the key results are presented below.

The results indicated that the female respondents were concentrated in the lower job grades and 78 per cent of respondents had a permanent contract. Only 10 per cent of respondents worked part time.

Recruitment

In order to ensure that the organization has access to a satisfactory number of suitably qualified candidates and recruits the best possible people available into a job, it is important to ensure that recruitment policies and practices do not restrict or inhibit applicants from any group by virtue of their age, ethnic origin, gender or physical disability. Even though an equal opportunities policy exists and a mission statement is widely distributed throughout the organization, it is possible that recruitment practices do not reflect the aims of the mission statement. In fact, the policy might be perceived as a barrier to equality of opportunity, by the members of the organization, or individuals seeking employment. In the group discussion sessions it was suggested that accessibility to jobs might not be equitable because recruitment practices were not standardized throughout the organization The survey results supported that perception.

Considering these findings, the authors recommended that there was a need to improve the consistency of application of policies. This could be achieved by ensuring that all policies are communicated effectively and by identifying the barriers to the consistent and/or fair application of such policies. This should include the introduction of a monitoring system to assess the standardization of recruitment practices.

Promotion

Career and promotion prospects and perceived equality of opportunity are an important element of an equal opportunity policy within an organization. In this section, statements were included to investigate the perceptions of career and promotional prospects, including opportunities for advancement into managerial jobs; career paths and career advancement.

Career and promotional prospects

Motivation to work, commitment and loyalty to an organization and intention to quit may be linked to one's perception of the opportunities for advancement within that organization. It is suggested that when one's expectations about career advancement are not met, or are thwarted, a state of stress is said to exist. This results in certain manifestations of stress which might include job dissatisfaction, poor physical and psychological well being (sickness and absence) or lowered performance and productivity (including poor quality, mistakes, and vulnerability to accident involvement) and ultimately, exit from the organization (Elkin and Rosch, 1990). The results of the survey indicated that 77 per cent of respondents did not agree that the best person for the job gets the job. Nearly two-thirds of the sample did not believe it would be possible for them to progress in management. More than half of the respondents felt that they did not have career or promotion opportunities. These results strongly support the implementation of an effective equal opportunity programme and monitoring system to ensure fair career progression based on merit. The authors proposed that this should incorporate career development projects and a career counselling mechanism.

Career advancement

Motivation in relation to job performance is affected by our attitude to career progression opportunities. This can act at an individual level (that is, the employee may be inhibited from seeking career advancement by virtue of the attitudes and beliefs held), or at an organizational level. Thus, the culture and climate of an organization are likely to be determined by the prevailing attitudes held by those who are seen to be the most powerful. Two issues of concern emerged from the group-interview sessions. First, the concern that stereotypical attitudes might act as a barrier to career advancement. Stereotyping is the tendency to label people with traits or qualities that appear to belong to a reference group. This can lead to the creation of images that act to discourage the individual (who appears not to fit that 'type') from striving to belong to that group, or the non-appointment of certain employee categories to higher level grades (Davidson and Cooper, 1992). The results indicated that 65 per cent of employees perceived that the existence of stereotypical attitudes hindered career advancement. Secondly, it appeared from the group-interview sessions that these employees believed that a climate existed where they could not refuse a change of job position and still look forward to a career with a future. The survey results supported this perception. Stereotyped attitudes such as the prevalent 'think manager – think (white) male' have been shown by numerous research studies to act as a career advancement barrier for those who do not fit into the stereotyped category (Schein and Davidson, 1993). These attitudes can be broken down by educating employees about the negative consequences of such stereotyping; also, by increasing the proportion of individuals into jobs and grades who do not fit the common stereotypical profile. Hence, the authors believed that the organization should adopt and advertise a policy, that refusal of job position change will not have an adverse effect on future career prospects.

Training

Training as a facilitator of career progression and advancement was a major topic in the group-interview discussion sessions. A variety of factors were seen as relevant when considering training in relation to career development and equal opportunities within an organization. These included the adequacy (level of training, content and access to training) and the organization of the training itself. Whilst two-thirds of respondents reported that they had received adequate training to perform their job responsibilities with competence, the adequacy of training for managers regarding equality of opportunity was questioned. Also many employees doubted the ability of their managers to deal with bullying, sexual harassment and grievances in the workplace. Therefore, it was proposed that management training courses should be designed and implemented, in dealing with these issues.

Working conditions

Six aspects of conditions at work in the bank were explored in this section including, knowledge and implementation of policy, work patterns and flexible working; equality of reward; health and physical work conditions, maternity or paternity leave and childcare provision, and the organizational culture and climate.

An inability to effectively develop one's career might be due to a basic lack of knowledge about the opportunities and facilities that exist and are available to help each employee in the development and optimization of their career potential. Therefore, the survey aimed to examine the degree of knowledge and clarity of understanding about certain working conditions and practices in the organization. The results showed that 62 per cent of the sample maintained they were unclear about the policy on job sharing. Approximately half of the respondents were unclear about policies on flexible working, welfare and health issues. Very few gender differences were observed in these findings, but certain regional variations were apparent, suggesting that advertising campaigns could be targeted to certain areas. On the basis of these findings, the implementation of a campaign to inform staff about the policies on job sharing, flexible working and welfare and health issues, was suggested.

Health and working conditions

Optimizing one's ability to perform successfully at work and the development of full career potential is, in part, linked to health and well being and a physical environment that facilitates effective working (Margolis *et al.*, 1974). Personnel who have concerns about their health may not function well, thus many organizations provide their staff with physical health checks (Sutherland and Davidson, 1989). Restriction of access to this benefit by virtue of age or job grade is likely to be perceived as inequitable. It was believed that access to health checks should be extended to include all staff, and not provided only to those in management positions.

Optimization of career potential is likely to depend on achieving a successful balance between work and home commitments. A reduction in the spillover of home and family problems into the work environment allows an employee to work to the best of their ability as an employee (Davidson and Cooper, 1992). Access to maternity and paternity leave arrangements might be a significant part of this, but allocation of a job on return to work will also be important for the individuals who wish to maximize their career potential and opportunities in the organization. In this survey, 60 per cent of respondents (69 per cent of males; 55 per cent of females) agreed that job allocation after maternity leave was fairly and consistently applied. The results of the audit indicated that almost two-thirds of employees believed that career opportunities were retained following maternity leave. However, men were more likely to be optimistic about this than women employees. An ability to balance the demands of work and home life for staff with child dependants is usually influenced, in part, on the ability of the employee to make satisfactory childcare arrangements. Difficulties with this can have an adverse impact on both productivity and performance, resulting in absenteeism and exit from the organization if the difficulties cannot be resolved. Both the employee and the organization suffer the costs associated with these disruptions. A variety of childcare arrangements might help to alleviate these potential problems and so attitudes to these options were assessed in the survey. Of all the options possible, the childcare information register was the most valued. The respondents agreed that the provision of this would enable the organization to make best use of the individual's abilities as an employee. Respondents to the audit indicated that 'after-school care arrangements' and on-site crèche or nursery facilities were also popular choices of childcare assistance. Not surprisingly, the female staff were more likely to agree that the provision of these facilities would enable the organization to make best use of their abilities as employees. These results substantiated the need for access to health checks to all employees. It was also proposed that the formation of a regular, updated childcare information register (by regional location) listing registered childminders be undertaken and be made available to employees. However, the results of the audit suggested that while there was a strong need for childcare provisions, it varied by region. Thus the adoption of a blanket policy might not meet the needs of all employees.

Developing Career Opportunities

Factors that might influence one's career opportunities included age, sexual orientation, gender, ethnicity and disability. The results indicated that nearly two-thirds of employees did not believe that the experience of older employees was recognized, and age barriers to career opportunities did exist. Just over half of the respondents agreed with the statement, 'the perception that disabled people cause 'problems' for the organization is one of the main reasons for the potential lack of recruitment, career advancement and provision of training for disabled people'.

Belonging to a professional group or holding membership of an informal or formal network in an organization might be regarded as a facilitator of one's career development. However, the existence of certain networks that serve to exclude nonmembers might be counterproductive in an equal opportunity organization. Therefore, an understanding of these potential barriers is relevant. In this survey, over half of the employees believed that belonging to a professional group was a major asset to their career development. No gender differences were observed, but strong regional variations and job grade differences were recorded. The above results indicated that the abolition of ageism should be incorporated as part of the equal opportunity programme. In addition to this, the introduction of positive images of disabled people and raised awareness through education and training was believed to be needed

Audit conclusion

This audit illustrates the wide scope of the issues that might be incorporated and considered in an effective equal opportunity programme. The findings also illustrated that barriers to equality of opportunity and career development in an organization might be localized to specific regions or locations, or be more acute for personnel working in certain job-grades. For this reason, adoption of a 'blanket' policy is not an effective strategy. It means that the organization can target scarce resources to specific problems. Based on the findings of this audit, the organization responded positively by formulating and disseminating a policy document and an action strategy on developing career potential and opportunities of employees. A monitoring process was also set up to provide regular feedback to the steering committee. Ultimately, the audit allowed the workforce to be heard on the perceived barriers to the development of career potential. If an organization wishes to maximize the full potential of its employees, an audit will provide a vehicle to guide and inform this process.

The Stress Audit – Summary

In the final part of this chapter we provide an outline for the steps to be taken when conducting an audit. Whilst the example used is a rather formal process, it should be remembered that an audit can also be done in an informal, small-scale manner. Whatever method is used, two key points are worth emphasis:

1. Is the audit valid?
   • Is it measuring what you want it to measure?
   • Does it have face validity among the people taking part? They will not take part in the audit if they do not have confidence in those conducting the audit, or the measures being used.

2. Is the audit reliable?
   • If you repeated the survey, would you get the same results?
   • Is the sample size large enough to provide confidence about the findings of the survey

Steps in the Stress Audit Process

The process we suggest includes:

• *DECIDING ON A TITLE FOR THE PROJECT*

   For example – 'Optimizing Employee Performance and Well-being in the Workplace'.

• *AIMS AND OBJECTIVES OF THE AUDIT*
   1. To conduct a stress audit in company 'X'-
      • To identify the levels of stress currently operating comparative to similar occupational groups
      • To identify sources of stress within the sample population and observe differences between the various groups according to job type, function and location, and so on.

- To identify individual groups at risk (that is, to examine biographic, demographic, personality and behavioural style difference in response to stress).

This would highlight potential stress problems that may exist within the organization.

2. To develop an organizational stressor item bank specific to company 'X'

3. To investigate staff attitudes to a variety of stress management interventions.

4. To make recommendations as to appropriate organizational and individual initiatives as part of a stress management strategy within the company

- *PROCEDURE*

1. Identify the sample; it must be representative of the workforce and large enough to ensure confidence about the findings of the survey.

2. Method

Phase I: Planning

A Assign a project manager or co-ordinator to liaise with the consultants. This individual (or small team of people) will be the first line contact for all queries and questions, and all matters concerning the audit logistics. For example, the sample identification, planning of workshops or focus groups, the provision of absence, accident or health records, and the like.

B Design and circulate a pre-audit letter to all staff involved and all others on a need to know basis. That is, to introduce and explain the project, and the role of the consultants, if used. This should include,

WHY?
WHO?
WHAT and HOW?
WHEN?
Answers to questions you might ask
and SO WHAT?

Phase II: Qualitative Data Collection

Stress logs or diaries; critical incident data; interviews; focus group discussions can be used to collect information. This data should be collected from a randomly selected, representative sample of the workforce. Workshop or focus groups of ten–14 people are usually halfday sessions. It is common to use a two-phased approach. That is,

- One week prior to workshop attendance, employees are required to maintain a daily stress log, to be used by the individual in the workshop discussion sessions.
- Attend a half-day focus group discussion sessions to identify sources of stress and facilitators and inhibitors of performance and productivity at work.

Outcomes

1. A stressor item bank specific to Company 'X'
2. Qualitative data to assist in the interpretation of the larger-scale questionnaire survey

Note: It is important to assure attendees that any individual information divulged by participants at this stage of data collection would remain confidential. In other words, comments would be reported but not attributed to any single individual.

Phase III: Quantitative Data Collection

- Questionnaire design is based on the findings from the qualitative data.
- The Measures – for example a questionnaire package might include:
  A cover letter with instruction for completion and return; a return envelope
  (i)   the Occupational Stress Indicator (OSI);
  (ii)   a stressor item bank relevant to Company 'X';
  (iii) biographical/career demographics data;
  (iv)   health behaviours: including sickness absence information, accidents, cigarette smoking, alcohol consumption, exercise habits and general health information;
  (v)   attitudes to stress control interventions
Time to complete – approximately 45–50 minutes.

- Questionnaire distribution and return.

  The questionnaire would be distributed to, for example, all staff; a 50 per cent sample of staff, or a randomly selected, representative sample. Many organizations usually distribute the questionnaire in their internal mail system and provide central collection points for completed documents. It is important that staff are provided with an envelope that can be sealed. Ways of maximizing the rate of return should be considered. For example, staff might be allowed to complete their questionnaire during a team briefing session. In some organizations, the occupational health personnel have organized group administration of the questionnaire.

Note: We recommend that the survey remains anonymous and so would guarantee anonymity and confidentiality in order to achieve a high response rate. If it is required to provide staff feedback, a confidential coding system could be used for the retrieval of individual or group results.

Phase IV: Statistical Analysis

Data Analysis usually involves:

- Computer analysis – possibly using SPSS (Statistical Package for the Social Sciences)
- Analysis to include:
  Descriptive statistics: Comparison of results to be made between personnel, relevant subgroups and normative data, for example, by job grade, function, location, age, gender, etc.
  Factor Analysis: to identify common patterns and stressor themes
  Multiple Regression: to identify predictors and possible causal relationships between stressors and stress outcomes
  Bivariate Analysis: To examine differences in findings between various subgroups in the work force.

Phase V: Interpretation of the results and recommendations

Preparation and presentation of report:
Feedback of results to staff.

A report should provide a psychological health profile of employees within Company 'X' comparative to normative data and relevant population comparisons where possible. Comparisons between subgroups are provided. The report should identify patterns of reported sources of stress and make recommendations for further action strategies at the individual, group and, or organizational level. The audit will also provide a base line measure from which to evaluate any subsequent intervention.

Consultants usually provide a presentation of the results to management or a 'stress management steering group'.

It is vital that feedback of the results of the audit, and the recommendations, are made available to the people who took part in the survey. This can be done either by providing access to the report, or during presentation sessions (for example, during team briefing).

Phase VI

Implementation of stress control initiatives; monitoring and evaluation.

Conclusion

The benefits of conducting a stress audit are that it enables us to understand individual vulnerability or risk. This means that we can implement effective manpower development programmes or 'change' initiatives that will remove or reduce these risks. Certain sources of stress would respond to organizational change, for example, a change to the structure such as work-shift patterns, job characteristics or team working, and these will be discussed in Chapter 7. Nevertheless, raising awareness by a thorough analysis of the work environment is a sound basis from which to inform action and evaluate effectiveness in the management of stress. This is what we mean by 'optimizing performance and health in the workplace'. Those organizations which recognize the high costs of mismanaged stress in the workplace and seek to achieve enhanced levels of effectiveness and the well-being of their employees, need to adopt an integrated approach to stress management. A stress audit guides this process.

7 Options for the Management of Stress in the Workplace: an Organizational Approach

We have now considered all the necessary issues in respect of the first two of our 'As' in our 'triple A' approach to the management of stress, namely, 'AWARENESS' and 'ANALYSIS'. To achieve this we have examined the stress process, explained its origins, provided definitions of stress, and a model of stress to guide the process of analysis. In order to complete the process of ANALYSIS, a means of identification and measurement of stress at work has been described. This is the 'stress audit'. The objective of this type of psychological risk assessment is to enable the organization to optimize the performance and health of the workforce. This is achieved by eliminating or minimizing sources of stress that are damaging in their consequences. Thereby we are acknowledging the maxim 'healthy work force – healthy organization'(Davies and Teasdale, 1994). In this instance, we use the word 'health' in its widest sense, to mean not just the absence of physical and psychological diseases, but to describe feelings of well being, happiness, and satisfaction. Indeed, it is about obtaining a 'good quality of life'. Research findings highlight the nature of stress in the workplace in terms of potential 'hot spot' issues. Thus, the steps described so far are necessary to guide and inform the ACTION phase of the stress management process. This is the final 'A' in our triple A approach to stress management. 'Action' is the subject of our final chapter.

Therefore, the objective of this chapter is to present an organizational strategy for stress management in the workplace. It acknowledges the importance of both preventive and curative approaches to the management of stress. A wide variety of options are available for the management of stress at work, and as we have seen, there is not just one problem, neither is there one solution! Increasingly, public and private sector organizations are acknowledging the unacceptable costs of stress by providing stress management programmes for employees in the attempt to combat the problem of stress. However, these stress prevention activities in Europe tend to be confined to large organizations employing more than 500 employees (Wynn and Clarkin, 1992). Thus it remains a challenge for human resource professionals and organizational psychologists to find ways of extending the scope of stress management activities into both medium and small companies. Typically this type of programme teaches the individual to cope with stress rather than tackle the problem at source (Ivancevich, 1990). Therefore, the approach is described as 'reactive' rather than 'proactive', because it seeks to cure the symptoms of exposure to stress rather than to prevent a stress problem from arising. Typically, stress management courses are often introduced into the workplace as a reaction, in response to a perceived problem or negative situation within the organization (for example, to combat a high level of absenteeism or accidents at work). Other stress management initiatives, such as the use of a counselling service or an employee assistance programme seek to 'cure' the symptoms of exposure to stress. However, this is a potentially negative and harmful situation because it supposes that distressed victims of exposure to mismanaged stress are either at work and behaving in ineffective, non-productive ways, or they are absent from their job, thereby causing extra strains and pressures on the remaining work colleagues or team. Both of these situations are undesirable and costly for the employer and employees.

This type of stress control programme, which focuses on the individual, places the onus and burden for change on the employee. Thus the message is loud and clear. It is saying, 'You do not seem to be able to handle the stress and pressure of your job or life circumstances, so we will help you to cope more effectively'. Whilst these aims might be well intentioned and honourable, the underlying message to the employee also implies that, 'We (the organization) are not going to change the way we do things around here. You must learn to cope with the situation!' Although this approach to stress control has a certain appeal and can be very effective, it has also been suggested that stress control can only be really successful if it is tackled at the level of the individual and the organization (DeFrank and Cooper, 1987).

Whilst good, well controlled evaluation studies are scare, there is evidence to indicate that this approach to the management of stress has certain weaknesses.

1. Such interventions do not appear to have a lasting effect (Ganster *et al.*, 1982; Murphy, 1988; Cooper and Sadri, 1991).

2. Organizations seem to be prepared to spend precious and limited budgets on a stress management course or stress management training

initiatives, but do not know if the course or programme is actually needed, or who should attend. This decision should be made on the basis of a training needs analysis. Usually such courses are offered on a voluntary attendance basis and those who do take part are often described as, 'the worried well'. For example, Conrad (1987) found that volunteer participants in worksite wellness programmes appear to be somewhat healthier and more concerned with fitness and health matters than non participants. Participants were also less likely to be cigarette smokers, less likely to have been in hospital in the previous five years and tended to spend more time exercising than non participants. Therefore, it is possible that those individuals who really do need to attend these type of training sessions will sometimes try to avoid taking part. This happens sometimes because they are in a state of denial about their stress related problems, or perhaps they simply prefer to choose to behave like an ostrich (for example, they simply do not want to hear any bad news about their health). As Brodsky (1987) has pointed out, individuals may not be aware that they are under stress. Often they do not wish anyone else to find out that they are not coping with a situation at work or home. Some employees actually fear that the results of their stress profile will end up on personnel records held by the company and will be used as a screening tool when the organization decides to 'down-size' once again, or to block them from any further promotion opportunities. Thus, the intended programme does not reach the employees who are deemed 'at risk' for disease and disability (Conrad, 1987).

3. Training packages and courses are offered, but rarely does the organization know if it is getting any return on its investment. Whilst training institutions tend to evaluate their courses, rarely is this done in a structured way. This is because the programmes are not evaluated beyond that of the 'reaction level' of the participants (Houtman and Kompier, 1995). Indeed, evaluation information is not always made available for the company that paid for the course. It would seems that organizations tend to accept the effectiveness of such training packages as an act of faith and so the impact is not assessed. However, research findings into, 'the transfer of training problem' (Campbell and Cheek, 1978, Fox, 1978; Baldwin and Ford, 1988; Casey, 1988, 1993) have alerted us to the weaknesses and the potential lack of effectiveness of standard training packages and courses. Too often, after course attendance, the behaviour of course attendees remains the same as before and thus the training package has little or no impact.

4. The strategy of waiting for an employee to become a victim of stress before taking action is a high risk and potentially high cost strategy for the organization from both legal and insurance perspectives (Earnshaw and Cooper, 1994).

A Tripartite Model for Stress Management

Thus, an organizational appproach to stress control has three separate levels. It means we need:

- to identify and eliminate or minimise stressful situations,
- to teach the individual to cope with stress,
- to help those individuals who have become victims of exposure to stress.

Research evidence suggests that stress-related problems are complex. Both the organization and individual employees, perhaps working in a team or work group, should be encouraged to actively manage stress in order to eliminate or minimize the stressor problem at source. Therefore, it is recommended that stress in the workplace should be addressed by adopting a tripartite approach consisting of:

- Primary level stress management
  This type of strategy or intervention is '*stressor directed*' in that it either eliminates, reduces or controls a source of stress. The aim is to prevent stress at work.
- Secondary level stress management
  These interventions are '*response directed*' in that they help individual employees or groups of workers to recognize their response to stress and the symptoms of stress. Thereby, they can respond in a way that is not harmful to themselves or to the organization. Thus, the aim is to develop stress resistance and adaptive coping strategies through education and training.
- Tertiary level stress management
  These forms of intervention are '*symptom directed*'. The objective is to assist in the cure and rehabilitation of stressed employees.

Within each of these levels it is also possible to direct the focus on either the:

- individual,
- team or work group,
- organization

Figure 7.1 illustrates this integrated model of stress management. Using an 'onion' as our metaphor, we would describe stress management in the workplace as 'peeling an onion'. The organization exists within its 'universe' and is thereby exposed to many different factors. Peel off this layer and you find the organization, exposed to changes and pressures imposed by the global economy, finance constraints, international politics, and legal requirements. All of these, and more, influence the fortunes of the business and the decisions it must make. To survive, and be successful and effective, the organization must be AWARE of the potential stress problems that might exist to adversely impact upon performance, productivity and the well being of its work force. From an ANALYSIS or diagnosis, ACTION is possible at one of the three levels described.

A description of each of the 'levels' of stress management, with examples of strategies and interventions, is provided below.

Primary Level Stress Management Interventions

A more commonly used term for this type of stress management strategy is 'organizational-level interventions' (Burke, 1993). Essentially, these 'stressor' directed strategies for the reduction or elimination of stress in the workplace can be categorized in three ways, including:

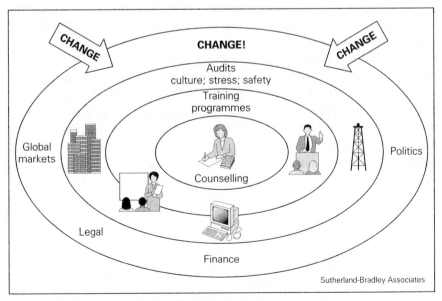

Fig. 7.1 An integrated model of stress management

1. Changes in the macro environment; that is, organizational culture and leadership, physical work conditions and workload, safety climate, career development programmes and bullying at work.
2. Change in the micro environment; that is systems and task redesign, alternative work arrangements, shift working, and communication exercises such as role negotiation.
3. Improving perceptions of worker control; increasing opportunities for decision making

Changes in the macro-environment

In this section we consider the issues of organizational culture, work overload conditions (which includes the physical work environment), safety climate, career development programmes and bullying at work.

Organizational culture

Building a supportive and open climate and culture, and ensuring that the style of management is compatible with the goals and aims of the organization, are important in the reduction of stress at work. It also means developing a culture that encourages staff to be more supportive of each other. This will facilitate team working and good interpersonal relationships in the workplace. The benefit of social support as a stress reduction strategy is well documented. It is likely to be an important stress reduction prevention mechanism since external forces prevent us from eliminating certain sources of pressure and strain in the workplace. For example, this would include the need to work shifts, especially nightshift work. An assessment of organization culture guides the process of culture change. Likewise, the use of psychometric measures to understand the appropriateness of 'management style' and its role as a source of stress in the workplace might be necessary. Thus, this type of intervention, to reduce the stress associated with poor leadership or supervision would guide us to the next level of stress management action, that is 'secondary-level' intervention. This assessment might reveal, for example, a need for management retraining or improved recruitment or selection procedures.

Literature on the impact of mergers and acquisitions suggests that more action is necessary to reduce the stress associated with this business venture. Blake and Moulton (1984) used an 'interface conflict-solving model' to facilitate the acquisition process between an American company and an acquired British organization. The top teams of both organizations engaged in meetings during which they shared perceptions about their concerns and questions. From this a successful operating model emerged. Data collected two years later indicated that this business venture had been a success and no senior personnel had left the organization. Realistic merger previews (also known as 'a communications programme') have also been used to facilitate the merger process and to reduce negative impact. Typically this means that several kinds of information are provided to employees on how the merger will affect them. This includes answers to questions concerning layoffs, transfers, promotions and demotions, changes in jobs, pay, and benefits. Schweiger and DeNisi (1994) observed the negative affects of a merger announcement in a light manufacturing plant. This included a decrease in job satisfaction, global stress, absenteeism, perceived uncertainty, a decrease in commitment and perceptions of trustworthiness, honesty and caring. Compared to the control plant, where no merger preview process was used, the negative effects of the merger were reduced in the experimental plant, both immediately and at the end of the follow-up period four months later. Thus, newsletters, access to a telephone hotline, and meetings are all needed to transmit merger preview information in order to reduce the negative impact of this type of major change in the work environment.

Work overload

It is acknowledged that work overload is a potent source of stress in contemporary organizations. A high workload leads to long hours of working, either as paid or unpaid overtime. Despite considerable research efforts it is difficult to make generalizations regarding optimal shift patterns. Clearly, the need to work shifts represents a major source of stress among blue collar workers. It is likely that individuals do habituate to shift work and it becomes physically less stressful with time, but some work patterns might prevent habituation occurring. Thus, there is a need to follow guidelines provided for minimizing the negative impact of shift-working. However, a re-analysis of staffing levels and an improved (real) costing of the impact of downsizing, or job and task redesign are also recommended to help reduce work overload stress. Some organizations have found that their enthusiasm for downsizing has been too zealous, and a subsequent cost benefit analysis has proven the reinstatement of certain jobs to be the most effective management strategy.

In a work overload condition it is important to ensure that employees are not stressed by the physical conditions of the work environment. In addition to being a source of stress in their own right, they also take up the attentional capacity of the individual, and so the employee is more vulnerable to workplace stress.

Kornhauser (1965) found that unpleasant working conditions, the necessity to work fast, to expend a lot of effort, and working excessive and inconvenient hours were related to poor mental health. The work environment must provide satisfying physical conditions and a clean and orderly place of work is important for both safety and hygiene reasons. This has implications for the morale of the workforce, especially in an environment where the work situation is acknowledged as hazardous.

Clearly, many of the opportunities for the prevention of stress associated with the physical demands of working exist at the design stage, and of course, in the provision of adequate personal protection equipment.

However, many places of work have been modified and adapted to meet the needs of industry and thus might not provide optimal conditions for the workforce. Workers complain about the lack of ventilation, or buildings that are too hot or too cold. In the modern work environment the complaints are often about the lack of personal control over physical work conditions. Whenever possible, the practice of more open discussion and debate, about the issues that directly affect working conditions, should be encouraged. This includes the arrangements made for rest and lunch breaks. The work environment should be perceived as comfortable and safe and so a high standard of hygiene and cleanliness is also desirable. Thus, the issues of safety in the workplace, danger and hazardous conditions are considered next.

Safety climate: minimizing the impact of working in dangerous or hazardous conditions

Many individuals are exposed to certain dangers and hazardous conditions at work. While a risk assessment allows us to control and minimise these dangers, some jobs still have inherent or perceived dangers. For example, the safety of helicopter travel was identified as one of the top ten sources of stress by offshore oil and gas workers (Sutherland and Cooper, 1991). It was associated with poor mental health among contractor personnel working offshore. Also, among Norwegian offshore workers, more than one third reported that they felt unsafe about the transportation of people by helicopter (Hellesøy *et al.*, 1985). Sunde (1983, cited Hellesøy, 1985) indicated that the perceived risk associated with helicopter travel was the most common reason cited for resignation from offshore employment in Norway. This action is very costly to the industry in terms of selection, recruitment and training. Nevertheless, helicopter travel is a reality that must be faced by these workers since we do not yet have any means of 'beaming people through space'. However, education about the nature of the risk and safety performance might help to overcome any irrational fears that are held. These tend to be magnified during the inevitable and intensive media coverage of a helicopter incident offshore which would probably go unreported in other industries.

Physical and psychological safety is a basic human need (Maslow, 1970) and having a predictable and non-threatening environment is fundamental to this need. Hellesøy *et al.*, (1985) suggested that a safe environment exists if:

- We are able to prevent critical situations arising.
- We are able to recognize unsafe or dangerous situations before they develop further and while the situation is still under control of the individual.
- We avoid the worst consequences of an accident if a critical situation has developed.
- We are able to reduce the consequences of an unavoidable incident by emergency training and contingency planning.

Therefore, three components of safety orientated behaviours are important. These include knowledge, behaviour (skills, routine, practice and motivation), and material and organizational support (that is, training and facilities necessary to be prepared for contingencies). As Hellesøy *et al.*, state, 'for a safety measure to be effective, it is essential that these components mutually support each other and whenever possible, they should be included as natural components in the production system itself'.

Realistic and reliable *knowledge* is needed about a work environment, the organization, technology, the job itself, and the systems and practices. Raising an awareness about work activities and helping employees to understand what is happening and why, is particularly important in potentially dangerous situations. It is necessary to understand perceptions of risk and safety in order to plan safety policies, to 'market' safety, and design safety measures and training programmes. It is important to know how safe personnel feel about potential sources of risk and to ensure that they have a realistic and 'healthy' perception of 'real' risk in their work environment. This means that we must ask if the subjective experience of risk matches the reality of the situation. A state of stress will usually exist if there is a mismatch between real and perceived expectations. Although denial is often used as a coping mechanism among people working in high risk occupations, it is vital to ensure that this does not prevent the individual from taking part in the training and drills necessary for effective working. A poor understanding about the risks of, for example, fire or explosion, and a lack of confidence about evacuation facilities may dwell on the mind of employees. This can have an adverse affect on performance, productivity and safety behaviours. Confidence in, and about the availability and effectiveness of equipment and medical help needed during these incidents are crucial to safety needs. Indeed, the perception that an organization is 'only paying lip service' to safety is likely to be a significant source of stress among shopfloor workers employed at the 'sharp end' of the business. Organizational commitment to safety, compliance with legal requirements and safety rules, and an ongoing training programme, are integral components of safety orientated behaviour because they have an effect on the attitudes and behaviours of the workforce. Training to be effective in the work environment is an important part of minimizing the deleterious impact of perceived hazard and risk to safety at work. It is also effective in reducing the stress of role ambiguity. Thus, the issue of training as a method of stress management is discussed separately in the section on 'secondary' level strategies

Career development programmes

Fear of job loss and threat of redundancy are common features of contemporary working life. Perceived or real, pay and job status inequity, lack of job security or limited potential for future career development are sources of stress. In times of instability, poor work conditions are tolerated and employees endure long hours and arduous conditions. This does not happen without personal and organizational costs. Fear of job loss and insecurity in times of high unemployment adversely affect both the individual and the organization. A keen, competitive job market can threaten the quality of coworker relationships at a time when social support is of particular importance. Indeed, the stress of insecurity that can be alleviated by supportive working relationships may be broken down if the workforce perceives that competition is necessary to retain a job. Personnel may also stay in a job that is unsuitable or disliked because no suitable alternative for change exists. This results in costs to the organization due to poor productivity or performance. Limited career opportunity can be demotivating and frustrating. This can cause negative behaviours, directed at the organization, the system of authority, colleagues at work or the family. Perceived inequity of reward or compensation can have adverse consequences for the individual and commerce. In exchange for effort, skill, tenure and education, a person expects pay, recognition and advancement (Adams,1965). Perceived inequity might lead to disruptive performance, poor morale, psychological distress, and lowered tolerance to other stressors. There is a tendency for personnel to resolve inequity by attempting to increase the magnitude of attained outcomes, for example, requesting pay raises or making demands about the environment. Although it is difficult to manage this source of pressure in the workplace when it has become ingrained in the organizational climate and culture, it is possible to take certain steps to minimize the problem, by ensuring that personnel have realistic expectations about career and reward prospects. This can be achieved in two main ways.

- Provide realistic and honest job descriptions. If terms and conditions are discussed openly at the time of selection and recruitment, the individual can make an informed choice about selecting into this situation.
- It is also possible to reduce the stress associated with uncertainty and ambiguity about the future and career potential through the mechanism of the appraisal interview. This is usually conducted on a one-to-one basis with an immediate boss or supervisor. However, this type of appraisal interview, which is used to discuss career opportunities and training and development needs, should be kept quite separate from any pay review discussions. An individual is unlikely to reveal any weaknesses and training needs if he or she perceives that it will detrimentally affect a pending pay award.

Often, employees will need to accept that a change the direction of their career is inevitable. Organizations should be willing and prepared to facilitate this process by:

- providing career development appraisal, including the use of self-assessment tools and psychological testing,
- offering individual counselling by internal staff or external services,
- providing retraining opportunities,
- providing assistance in job search and training in skills, such as producing a curriculum vitae and interviewing,
- offering access to job placement services, such as 'outplacement'.

This process is important because the stress of the job-loss situation will be exacerbated when the individual realises that the termination of long-term employment requires adjustment to a major life-events change. This might happen at a time when learning something new seems to take longer, energy is more scarce, opportunities are fewer, and the threat of competition from younger job applicants is daunting. Thus, the individual is most vulnerable at a time when they may face rejection and fear of rejection. Both circumstances are damaging to morale, self esteem and confidence.

Bullying at work

Recent reports suggest that the incidents of bullying in the workplace may be increasing. However, we can not be sure if this is now the reality of work life in the 1990s, or due to the fact that people are more willing to report that they are being bullied. Nevertheless, there is an acknowledgement that oppressive behaviour has a negative effect in terms of reduced well being, morale, motivation and contribution to the job (Douglas, 1996). It is suggested that bullies are 'stress carriers' within the organization. Usually they do not personally suffer from the effects of stress, but their behaviour causes a great deal of stress for subordinates and colleagues alike. Whilst there is no specific health and safety legislation that deals with bullying at work, employers have a general duty to protect employees' health and safety. In law, it is possible to seek redress for bullying behaviours that generate sufficient emotional distress and unhealthy physical stress (Douglas, 1996). Thus an employer must ensure that the dignity of the employee is upheld, and acknowledge that he or she has a right to be treated with respect.

Bullying is described as 'persistent, offensive, abusive, intimidating, malicious or insulting behaviour, abuse of power, unfair penal sanctions, which make the recipient feel upset, threatened, humiliated or vulnerable, which undermine their self-confidence and which may cause them to suffer stress' (MSF, 1995). As with harassment, bullying is defined largely as the impact of the behaviour on the recipient.

Bullying can be a form of misuse of power and involves a person in authority bullying those below him or her. However, it can also occur when an individual or a group of individuals bullies, or pick on a peer or co-worker. It is suggested that bullying at work might be more evident at work because:

- of an extremely competitive work environment, job insecurity and fear for one's job,
- organizational change and uncertainty are created when organizations restructure and become 'leaner and meaner'; the accompanying insecurities often generate bullying behaviour,
- excessive workload and demand, impossible targets and deadlines cause strain and pressure.

An authoritarian culture, poor work relationships, a lack of clear codes of acceptable behaviours, are all conditions that foster a climate in which bullying is likely to occur. Bullying is often confused with strong management and so becomes condoned and part of the culture of the organization. Bullying can often be insidious and subtle and so the victim has no witnesses. If there are witnesses they are often afraid of supporting a victim. The victim is usually afraid of complaining for fear of not being believed and of the bullying getting worse.

Bullying as a form of misuse of power can take many forms such as:

- excessive supervision and criticism; monitoring every action; overruling the person's authority,
- using terror tactics, open aggression, threats, shouting and abuse,
- humiliation and ridicule; belittling efforts in front of other people,
- setting impossible objectives or changing the 'goal posts' without telling the person or consulting with them,
- withholding information which the person needs to do the job effectively; removing whole areas of work responsibility and reducing a job to routine, low skill activities,
- ostracizing and marginalizing the individual by dealing only through a third party; excluding the individual from discussions, meetings and decisions which they need to be part of to do their job,
- spreading malicious rumours,
- refusing reasonable requests for leave or training,
- blocking promotion.

One of the first steps for the organization is to raise awareness of bullying through the use of newsletters, posters and meetings. All staff must be aware of what constitutes bullying and made to understand that the organization will take action again bullying behaviour. This means that the organization must have an agreed policy on bullying, which can be part of the health and safety policy. This must state clearly what is unacceptable behaviour and the sanctions imposed if people go beyond the bounds of acceptability. The MSF Union suggests that a policy should include:

- a clear definition of bullying and the forms it takes,
- a statement that bullying is unacceptable behaviour and will not be tolerated at any level of the organization,
- a statement that bullying will be treated as a disciplinary offence.

(MSF, 1995)

Employees should also receive guidance on the steps to be taken if they are a victim of bullying. This must include a guarantee of confidentiality, and that anyone complaining of bullying will not victimized. Usually complaints are dealt with in conjunction with both counselling and mediation services. In some organizations, helpline, helpdesk, employee assistance programmes, face-to-face counselling, and the occupational health service, all play some role in dealing with bullying in the workplace. Ultimately the process will depend on whether the victim is making a formal or an informal complaint. It is useful if people are advised to keep a written record of bullying behaviour since a one-off occurrence is not likely to be treated as anything more than an outburst from another person at work. Therefore the victim should:

1. Log all incidents and include dates, times, details of the behaviour and the names of any witnesses present. It is important that the individual sticks to the facts, but, at the same time, to record his or her feelings at the time, and the response made.

2. Make sure you know exactly your responsibilities and duties to ensure that any criticism towards you is actually unjustified.

3. Keep copies of all correspondence with the bully, including any information relating to your work ability and performance, and any memos that you wrote about an incident.

4. Try to find out if you are the only 'victim' or if other colleagues are being treated similarly. It might be easier to deal with a collective complaint. Talk to your colleagues or someone in authority in the organization and actively seek support. Seek help from your union. Bullies often pick on the individual who seems to be isolated at work.

5. Avoid being alone with the bully.

6. Seek help as soon as possible; do not delay in taking action but make sure you have written facts and details to present to your organization. Keep a record of events that follow once you have made a complaint.

Informally, the bully can be confidentially counselled and advised that their behaviour is contrary to organizational policy and must comply with the required standards. This means that they should be told about the impact of the bullying behaviour and that it must stop. In addition, they are required to be advised of the consequences of failing to meet this demand and that the situation will be monitored and reviewed. The ultimate sanction for the bully must be dismissal, although steps can be taken at an early stage to avoid this costly outcome.

Recently, a social worker in Canada took his case to the Human Rights Commission, complaining that he had been harassed and discriminated against because he was gay and perceived to have AIDS. Moffat, a homosexual, kept his sexual orientation a secret, but it was the subject of speculation at work. He and his partner had recently provided a foster home for a 16-year old boy. Returning to work following a period of illness he discovered that rumours were rife about his sexual orientation, that he was stricken with AIDS and the foster-child was subject to sexual abuse. He complained to his area director and the management team that he was a victim of gossip and slander and that his human rights were violated. Management's response to this situation was, that without specific allegations tracing the rumours to a particular individual, it could and would, do nothing. The Human Rights Commission Board of Inquiry agreed that Moffat had been subjected to harassment and discrimination. The employer was held liable for allowing a poisoned work environment to flourish. It had failed to appropriately investigate and address a work-place in which Moffat was targeted by discriminatory and derogatory comments. The fact that Moffat could not identify the source of the rumours did not relieve the employer's obligation to investigate the matter and curb the gossip. By failing to take his concern seriously, the employer was responsible for Moffat feeling isolated and vulnerable as a gay person. The Commission argued that it is never appropriate for co-workers to refer directly or indirectly to the sexual orientation of another employee.

Therefore, an organization should ensure that a harassment policy prohibits any form of derogatory remarks about employees relating to any prohibited ground such as race, colour, sex, sexual orientation or creed. It is also necessary to monitor the workplace and address improper comments or rumours, and instigate a grievance procedure to identify potential problems. Action must be taken on all complaints about workplace gossip that could violate the Human Rights Code. Finally, if an employee comes forward with a complaint, that he or she is the subject of rumours, but cannot identify their source, the obligation to investigate is not reduced (Levitt, 1999).

Changes in the micro-environment

Rather than put the responsibility for stress management on the individual employee, exposure to stressful work conditions might be reduced by the redesign of work systems and practices (Gangster, 1995). It is suggested that work redesign can improve worker morale, motivation and performance.

The model proposed by Karasek (1979) indicates that attention is focused on job demands (volume of demand, pace of work, and so on) and job decision latitude (that is, the ability to make decisions and the variety of skill used by workers on the job). Thus, these areas have become the focus of attention in an attempt to reduce stress in the work environment. In this section we discuss workload issues, the use of semi-autonomous work groups, alternate work arrangements, shift working, and reducing role stress. In the next section we consider ways of improving perceptions of job control.

Although many workers complain about having too much to do, or having to work at a pace that is too fast, they also complain that the job does not provide enough variety or challenge. This can lead to boredom, apathy and low motivation to work. Thus, job redesign interventions can be used to alleviate the problem of 'rust out' in the workplace.

Work under load: understimulation and boredom

Prevention of stress associated with 'rust-out', due to boredom, and lack of stimulation in the workplace can be achieved by changing the 'micro' work environment (Karasek, cited ILO, 1993). This includes increasing workers' skills, autonomy in the job and proving more opportunities for decision making. Hackman-Oldham (1976) explained how the core nature of a job influences one's attitudes and behaviour, and how it affects both personal and work outcomes, such as motivation, job performance, job satisfaction and labour turnover. It is suggested that any job can be described according to five core dimensions and these influence certain critical psychological states. The first three core job characteristics help us to understand how meaningful we perceive our job to be. These include:

1. Skill variety means the number of different activities, skills and talents the job requires. It is suggested that the more varied the skills we use, the more meaningful the job is seen to be.

2. Task identity means the degree to which a job requires completion of a whole, identifiable piece of work; doing a job from beginning to end with a visible result.

3. Task significance describes the job's impact on the lives or work of other people whether within or outside the work environment.

   The second psychological state that is known to influence both personal and work outcomes is our perception of the level of responsibility we have for the outcomes of the work. This is influenced by the amount of autonomy we have at work or in the job.

4. Autonomy is the degree of freedom, independence and discretion in scheduling the work and in determining procedures and practices.

   Finally, knowledge of work results can have beneficial personal and work outcomes. This refers to the amount of feedback received from doing the job.

5. Task feedback means the degree to which carrying out the activities required results in direct and clear information about the effectiveness of performance.

   This includes:
   (a) Feedback from other people – that is receiving clear information about one's performance from supervisors and co-workers,
   (b) Dealing with others – this refers to the degree to which the job requires the employee to work closely with other people in carrying out work activities.

By redesigning or enriching the job, to improve the amount of skill variety, task identity, task significance, autonomy and feedback, it is possible to improve both motivation and job performance and reduce levels of stress. Decisions to carry out this type of change are usually made on the basis of a job analysis, and in workforce and job holder discussions. For example, changes might be made which increase feelings of autonomy, job variety and levels of feedback, in a variety of ways including:

1. **Job rotation.** It might be desirable for workers to be able to rotate through a set of different but similar jobs, in order to provide more variety and reduce the boredom that might exist at work. Job rotation and job share opportunities can also be provided so that no one is exposed to high stress levels for a long period of time

2. **Horizontal job enlargement.** This means that additional tasks are included within the scope of the job to increase the variety and diversity of the job. The relatively flat hierarchy of many organizations does not provide upward career progression. Therefore, job enlargement is a method of providing more variety and challenge in a job, especially for the older worker who realizes that he or she has reached a career plateau.

3. **Vertical loading.** This entails assigning more important and challenging duties into the job, for example, additional decision making responsibilities. This has potential for increasing autonomy, variety and task identity. Some managers and supervisors are reluctant to delegate

work to their subordinates, and so fail to fully utilize the potential of their staff. This leads to stress due to qualitative underload, or 'rust out'. Inability to delegate is often a problem for an individual newly appointed to management from the shopfloor. This occurs because he or she does not receive the necessary supervisory or management skills training and is often required to work within the same work group. This makes it difficult for the employee to adopt the new role. An intervention strategy to reduce role ambiguity and to improve role clarity should also be included into this type of job redesign.

4. **Semi-autonomous work groups.** Job development opportunities can be improved when levels of responsibility are increased through horizontal job enlargement or by vertical loading. The use of semi-autonomous work groups is similar to the process of vertical loading, but is introduced at the level of the team rather than the individual. A group of employees is empowered to make decisions that affect their work activities. Groups might also be established to work on specific problems, including safety or quality improvement. Multiskilled groups now operate in approximately two-thirds of organizations (CBI, 1997). The same survey found that 68 per cent of managers believed that team working helped to reduce absence. In fact, the CBI found that organizations operating teamwork experience 11 per cent less absence than those organizations that did not. In a European survey, Paoli (1997) found that a substantial number of workers appeared to be involved in team-based work with the possibility of rotating tasks with colleagues. However, many workers still describe the lack of opportunity and ability to use their skills. This is acknowledged as potentially detrimental to well being, productivity and performance. As one electrician, working in the offshore oil and gas industry said, 'When you become bored you do not do a good job; you start getting stale, complacent and upset: The longer you continue like this, the more of a safety hazard you are, to everyone'.

The stress prevention initiatives described above will help to alleviate the problems associated with boredom, job dissatisfaction and low work motivation. However, it is important to note that this type of job redesign rarely occurs in the absence of other changes, such as pay rates and staffing (Wall, 1984, cited Murchinsky, 1993). There is also a need to remember that the effects of such change are not discrete and limited only to the job holder. For example, the nature of supervisory and managerial roles will be altered when the workforce is given more autonomy. Organizational change, therefore, is not simple. The process needs to be regarded in totality when changes are planned. Nevertheless, job enrichment intervention strategies can increase job satisfaction, improve production, and reduce job absence and turnover (Smith and Zehel, cited ILO,1992).

Alternative work arrangements

In order to meet challenges from consumers, governments and unions, and the internal pressures associated with the management of a more diverse workforce, organizations are now required to find ways of being flexible and responsive to rapidly changing economic and societal norms. As the proportion of dual-earner families, single parent families and female-headed families has increased, it has become necessary for organizations to ensure a 'family friendly' work environment in order to retain staff (Lewis and Cooper, 1995). Therefore, policies and programmes have been introduced to provide employees with flexibility in time and place of work, dependent care, financial aid and/or information on outside services (Lobel and Kosseck, 1996). Friedman (1991) suggests that this type of programme is a critical component of strategies that improve a company's bottom line.

Alternative work arrangements that offer staff flexibility have been found to be popular with employees and beneficial to organizations. It helps to build employee commitment. Employees are more attached to organizations with family friendly policies, regardless of the extent to which they might personally benefit, because offering assistance to employees in need, symbolizes a concern for employees (Grover and Crooker, 1995).

Specific types of alternative work arrangements include part time work; job share; leave of absence, telecommuting and other work-at-home arrangements; and flexitime. The provision of more flexible work patterns can eliminate the problems associated with travel to and from work during peak times and facilitate coping with dependant care or parenting demands. Flexibility in working arrangements or hours provides employees with time during the normal working day to attend to domestic or family issues and crises. Therefore, the introduction of flexitime and flexible scheduling aims to meet the diverse needs of the 1990s work-force. Typically, the organization defines a 'core time' and employees are permitted to arrive and leave work between certain band hours outside of the core period. They are also required to work a minimum number of hours each week, or month and are allowed take extra hours worked off with the approval of a supervisor.

Indeed, in our experience the greatest pressures reported by parents are the problems of childcare for older children, before and after school hours, and during school holidays. Flexitime would help to minimize the impact of this strain on working parents. Many companies also provide crèche facilities, afterschool clubs, school holiday activity centres, or vouchers to contribute towards the costs of childcare, to help employees cope with the demands of parenting. Together with flexible hours of working, such strategies help to reduce the strains of parenting and enable the individual to gain greater control over their work and family lives. This, in turn, leads to lower levels of work-family conflict and high levels of job satisfaction (Thomas and Ganster, 1995).

Whilst the individual effects of flexitime can be positive in terms of job satisfaction, job control, increased autonomy and improved family relationships, research findings on the impact of flexitime on the profitability of organization are mixed. Some evidence of a direct impact on productivity and performance is available. Other studies indicate decreases in sickness absence, tardiness, overtime and turnover and these can also have positive effects on an organization's profitability (Pierce *et al.*, 1989; Dalton and Mesch, 1990). In its 1997 survey of over 300 organizations, the Industrial Society found that organizations operating policies of flexible annual leave, flexible working hours and arrangements whereby employees could work from the home occasionally, all had absence rates below the average experienced by the sample of respondents as a whole. The benefits of flexitime need to be balanced against the extra organizational costs of administration and management.

For example, Powell and Mainero (1999) observed that alternative work arrangements (AWA) are unlikely to be successful unless they are supported by firstline managers. Their investigation found that the potential for work disruption was a major factor in the managers' decision making processes. Not surprisingly, they tended to focus on their own short term self-interest. Thus they were more likely to refuse requests for an AWA if it was perceived to be disruptive to work. Firstline managers were most strongly against granting requests for unpaid leave,or requests from subordinates who were working on critical tasks and possessed critical skills. This approach and focus on short term, narrow perspectives are unlikely to foster commitment to the organization from the critical personnel that the strategy of AWA was intended. Whilst organizations are advised to offer AWA to their key employees to ensure that they remain (Grover and Crooker, 1995), it would appear that firstline managers are resisting this innovative policy prescribed by senior management. They appear to be failing to recognize the long term benefits for the organization in favour of their own immediate objectives. Powell and Mainiero (1999) suggest that organizations will not reap the benefits of

AWAs until firstline managers are actively encouraged to support these company-sponsored programmes.

Clearly this strategy will not suit all types of business nor all employees. Careful evaluation of the potential need and benefits are vital before embarking on this, or other forms of stress management activity. Again, the vital need for a stress audit that incorporates the attitudes and opinions of employees is emphasized.

Reducing the stress of shift work

We have acknowledged that demands for efficiency and productivity and the rapidly escalating pace of new technology can have a deleterious impact on the working population. The need to engage in shift work and work long hours affects many people at work and the spillover impact also causes negative consequences and costs for the family and society itself. Thus it becomes a prudent part of a stress management strategy to minimize the impact of these potential sources of strain and distress that can not be eliminated from the world of work. These options include the design of the shift system, flexitime, selection and recruitment for shift working, stress management education, and physical interventions such as the use of light therapy and the drug, melatonin.

1. **Shift system design.** It is possible to meet the needs of a 24-hour production or service schedule, and reduce the impact on the individual, by designing schedules that follow the principles of circadian rhythms. This will alleviate the biological problems associated with shift work. Essentially this entails a shift system design that considers shift rotation, shift start times and the number of days for recovery between work periods. Research evidence indicates circadian rhythm synchronization is best when the shift schedule is rotated in a forward manner (that is, days, nights, evenings, days, and so on) rather than a backward rotation (that is, nights, evenings, days, nights) (see Daus, Sanders and Campbell, 1998 for a review). Forward rotation appears to reduce sleep difficulties (Mitler, 1992). Speed of shift rotation is also a factor for consideration. However, there is a complete split on opinion about this practice since North Americans believe a slow rotating shift pattern is less disruptive, whilst Europeans regard rapidly rotating shifts as the least harmful. Rapidly rotating shifts are considered best since temporary adjustment of the circadian rhythm is considered harmful. Therefore, none adaptation is viewed as better than partial adaptation. Thus, European employees work rapidly rotating shifts during a week, and work only a few (three

or four) night shifts in succession because this is the shift that requires the most physiological adjustment. In this way circadian disruption is minimized and the problems associated with sleep debt are avoided (Knauth, 1993). Typically, workers in the USA work a slow-rotation shift pattern, for example, three weeks of days, three weeks of evenings and three weeks of night shifts). Whilst research evidence is available to suggest that this pattern of working is optimal for the employee, many of the changes to shift patterns include other alterations, such as time off and/or direction of shift rotation. This means that causality and effect are difficult to unravel. For example, the re-design of the shift-work pattern for police officers included alterations to a forward shift rotation, the rate of rotation reduced from one week to three weeks, and the six-day week reduced to four or five work days in a row (Mitler, 1992). Nevertheless, after 11 months, a fourfold reduction in sleep problems was reported, a 25 per cent reduction in sleep episodes on the night shift was observed. Also, these police officers reported a reduction in the use sleeping pills and alcohol. Their families also appeared to be more satisfied with the new shift arrangements.

In some instances, workers prefer not to rotate their shift. For example, nurses working permanent nights appeared to have fewer health, sleep, social and domestic problems than their colleagues who worked the traditional shift rotation (Barton, 1994). However, the decision to work a permanent night shift normally is the choice of the individual. Thus the issue of self-selection into a unique work environment is a factor for consideration in the interpretation of these findings.

Shift start time is also a factor in optimizing performance for employees forced to work a shift pattern. Many organizations now start the twelve-hour shift pattern at 0700 rather than the traditional 0600. In our experience, this slight change has tremendous psychological benefits and is viewed most favourably by the workforce. In fact, Knauth (1993) has found that an early-morning start appears to be associated with increased accident and error rates. Recovery time between shift changes is also a factor for consideration since workers need time for adjustment. A day off after a night-shift work period seems to be beneficial. The redesign of a shift-work pattern for police officers reported by Mitler (1992), described above, indicates the potential benefits to be gained. Ultimately a flexible work pattern to meet the needs of the individual and satisfying the demands of the workplace is desirable, but not always easy to put into practice.

2. **Shift work – manadatory or self-selection.** Whilst it would seem to be practical to select individuals on the basis of their ability to work shifts, the current weakness of methods of selection (usually questionnaires), and laws on discrimination on the grounds of disability, tend to preclude this as a stress management option. Theoretically, organizations should be able to reduce the impact of shift working by identifying those individuals most suited to shift work. This might include, for example, the selection of employees for their ability to stay awake (Mitler, 1992), for shift tolerance (Czeisler *et al.*, 1982), or stress resistance (Cervinka, 1993). However, at the moment the problems outweigh the benefits. Thus, a more useful strategy is to allow individuals to self-select for shift work. When people are able to choose their shift pattern they can structure their work and family life to meet the needs of work and parenting demands with minimal disruption. People also vary according to their preferences on the time of day for working. Some are 'owls', others are 'larks'. Thus it makes sense to capitalize on this natural state when possible. However, companies usually report not being able to find enough employees to work the unsocial night shift and so cannot rely on a volunteer workforce.

3. **Stress management and education.** Understanding the nature of stress, individual vulnerability to potentially stressful situations, and the influence of time of day on behaviours are part of stress management education. It also includes the topics of relaxation training and cognitive restructuring. These are discussed in detail below. It is suggested that shift workers are also aware of the principles of sleep hygiene in order to minimize the impact of shift working (see Chapter 4).

4. **Physical interventions.** Two popular means of circadian rhythm adjustment are light therapy and melatonin therapy. These are normally used by night-shift workers. The purpose of these physical interventions is to readjust an individual's circadian rhythm. However, it must be remembered that the circadian rhythm will never completely adjust to a night schedule, mainly because the employee will usually revert to the normal societal 24-hour pattern during nonwork time. In fact, Daniel (1990) suggests that it takes 10 to 20 days of continuous night work to reverse the circadian rhythm, and that complete adaptation is practically impossible.

    Light therapy is used to trick the body into believing it is daytime when it is actually night-time. This overcomes the disruption to the individual's circadian rhythm caused by the body being active in the absence of light. In normal conditions, the suprachasmatic nucleus

(SCN), reacting to the presence of light, assumes a period of activity. When the individual works at night, conflicting signals cause disruption to many bodily functions. The desyncronization of circadian rhythms can cause feelings of fatigue and general malaise, described by Milter (1992) as 'occupational jet lag'. Thus, increasing the intensity of light in the work area, or the wearing a visor that focuses light on the individual's eyes, will provide simulated light to entrain the circadian rhythm via the SCN. Research evidence suggests that light therapy can reduce problems associated with sleep and alertness (Daus, *et al.*, 1998). Light therapy also suppresses melatonin secretion and is often used in conduction with the drug 'melatonin'. In its natural form, the hormone melatonin is produced mainly at night. Therefore, melatonin therapy involves the administration of low doses taken after the shift to simulate the onset of night, or lack of light and thus sleep (Daus *et al.*, 1998). Used in conjunction with light therapy, it can override the light-dark zeitgeber. Although melatonin is a natural hormone, and travellers seem happy to use it to overcome the problems of jet lag, not everyone is happy taking pills on a daily basis to alter the body's time clock. The longterm effects of this type of intervention, and concerns about drug tolerance and dependence are not well documented or understood.

Reducing role stress

The constructs of role ambiguity and role conflict are acknowledged as potent sources of stress in the work environment that are associated with a variety of negative attitudinal health and behavioural outcomes. Thus role clarification interventions can be used as stress control strategies. For example Quick, (1979) used participative goal setting to reduce role stress amongst employees in an insurance company. During the 14-month time period, 15 executive officers and their immediate staff took part in this field study. During a one-day training session three dimensions of goal setting were emphasized, including, task goal properties (difficulty and clarity), supervisory goal behaviours (the quality and quantity of feedback), and subordinate goal behaviour (participation). Measures were collected six months prior to formal training in goal setting and at the five- and eight-month post training points. Significant reductions in measures of role conflict and role ambiguity were observed. Considerable reductions in sickness absenteeism levels were recorded five months after training but this affect was not observed at the eight-month point.

A responsibility charting approach was used by Schaubroeck *et al.*, (1993) to reduce role ambiguity reported by personnel in the business services department of a university. After the management team had negotiated and clarified their own roles, they were assigned to either a 'waterfall' condition, in which they were helped by consultants to negotiate and clarify roles with each of their subordinates, or a wait-control group. This intervention was clearly successful in reduction perceptions of role ambiguity and also improved satisfaction with supervision. However, there were no measurable effects on subjective psychological strain, physical symptoms or lost time due to illness.

Dayal and Thomas (1968) used a role-clarification intervention in an engineering company to improve employee communication and manage stressful work demands. Also, supervisors working in a social services agency were trained in role emphasis, and efforts were made to reduce stress by prompting clear, consistent and positive feedback, and clarifying rules, policies and roles. This initiative was effective in reducing burnout among newly hired staff (Burke, 1987).

Role negotiation

Role negotiation as a way of reducing stress is a technique based on an idea described originally by Harrison (1972). It is a useful way of overcoming the problems that lead to ineffectiveness caused by behaviour that an individual is unwilling to change, because it would mean a loss of power or influence. Harrison believes that this method works because most people prefer a fair negotiated settlement to a state of unresolved conflict. Thus, they will be motivated to engage in some action themselves and make concessions in order to achieve this aim. In role negotiation the change effort is focused solely on the working relationships among the people involved. Likes or dislikes for one another is avoided. It is important to acknowledge that issues concerning the personal feelings of the people involved are avoided. During role negotiation an imposed structure is created to allow a controlled negotiation to take place. Each person involved discusses and agrees in writing to change certain behaviours in return for changes in behaviour by the other party. For example, each person asks for changes in the behaviour of the other party which would permit them to do their own job more effectively. This is in exchange for changing some aspect of their own behaviour, which would serve to improve the effectiveness of the other party involved. Therefore an accurate diagnosis of the problem is necessary. It is crucial to avoid generalities and be specific. That is, you would ask the other person, to stop doing 'x'; to do more of 'y'; or to do less of 'z'. In turn, these are the type of actions that the other party might ask of you. Ensuring that a diagnosis is carried out as the first step in role negotiation helps to overcome the problems of generalizing comments or resorting to personalized attacks. All requests and agreements must be in writing and each person must give something in order to get something. If one party reneges on their part of the bargain, the whole contract becomes invalid.

The technique can be used within a group, to negotiate among work group members; or between a team leader or manager, and their team. Often the use of an outside facilitator is used for optimal effectiveness. Some progress follow-up is required to determine whether the contracts are being honoured and to assess the effectiveness negotiations.

Improving perceptions of worker control

Lack of job control is acknowledged as a potent source of stress and perception of control seems to be important for job satisfaction, health and well-being. Whilst the research evidence to support the demand-control model proposed by Karasek (1979) has been inconsistent, there is sufficient evidence to suggest that a high level of work control has beneficial effects on levels of job satisfaction (Dwyer and Ganster, 1991), psychological well being (Perrewe and Ganster, 1989), and indicators of cardiovascular disease (Karasek, *et al.*, 1988). Warr *et al.* (1996) suggested that support for Karasek's model is found when a focused measure of work control is used (that is, the extent to which employees had control over specific items, and how and when they did the work related to these items – namely, method and timing control) rather than when a broad measure of control is assessed. Sargent and Terry, (1998) also report that 'type of control' is an important factor in the demand-control model. This study of administrative staff in a university found that job demands were buffered by 'task control' but not the more peripheral aspects of work control such as decision and scheduling control. Task control also buffered the negative relationship between role ambiguity and job satisfaction, and between work overload and depressive symptomology.

A variety of strategies exists to improve perceptions of worker control and increase the opportunities for decision making at work. These include building and developing semi-autonomous work groups, quality circles, safety improvement groups and health circles. Ultimately the aim is for the workforce to be empowered and involved in changes to any system or practice that induces stress at work. This is to create a better balance between the perceived levels of demand and worker control.

Wall and Clegg (1981) describe an intervention that aimed to increase worker autonomy among a group of employees with poor productivity, low morale and low motivation. This approach utilized the Hackman and Oldham 'Job Characteristics Model' and revealed low scores for 'autonomy', 'feedback' and 'task identity'. Job satisfaction and motivation levels were low and high levels of emotional distress were recorded. Subsequent work redesign increased group autonomy, group task identity and group feedback. Increases in group autonomy involved shifting responsibility and control from supervisors to the work teams. As part of this programme, supervisors adopted a support role, and work teams took control over the pace of work, the organization of rest breaks, the allocation of tasks and overtime working. At the 18-month evaluation point, the observed increases in 'autonomy' and 'task identity' were sustained, but not for 'group feedback'. Emotional distress was also significantly reduced at the six-month and 18-month follow-up periods.

Increasing worker participation in decision making

Lack of participation in decision making is a primary cause of role conflict and role ambiguity, mediated by one's perceived influence over the situation and the efficacy of communication in the organization. Feeling controlled rather than 'in control' is associated with a state of stress; individuals who feel controlled are likely to perceive their job as a 'strain' rather than a challenge and source of motivation. The use of small group discussions, or focus groups, is recommended, to examine how sources of stress might be reduced. Research has shown that increased participation in decision making has a beneficial affect by reducing role conflict and improving role clarity. Thus the individual perceives less emotional strain at work and more satisfaction with the job. Jackson (1983) described an intervention to reduce role stress, by increasing participation in decision making, amongst staff in an out-patient facility within a university hospital. All nursing supervisors attended a two-day training workshop and then employee participation was increased by requiring these supervisors to hold scheduled staff meetings at least twice a month. Measures taken after six months indicated that 'participation' had a significant impact in reducing role conflict and role ambiguity. Positive effects were observed on perceived influence, emotional strain and job satisfaction. It was clear that the number of staff meetings held was a determinant of the level of both role conflict and role ambiguity in the work unit.

1. **Health circles.** This concept has been extended into the use of 'health circles' (Kuhn, cited ILO, 1993). Employees meet to actively discuss

health problems and work related stress in an attempt to identify workplace stress and the strategies that could be used to reduce or eliminate stress. It is fundamental that the workers' realise that they are the best able people to do this task because they are directly involved and can benefit directly. However, to be effective they may need some initial help in understanding the process of stress. Kuhn has shown that participation in health circles can have noticeable positive effects on health. If the recommendations suggested are put into effect by the organization, positive effects on production are observed. The objectives of the health circle concept are:

- to expand knowledge and understanding about stress development,
- to improve personal stress management by adopting sound health-promoting behaviours,
- to create a work environment which is beneficial to health,
- to recognize and modify work conditions which lead to stress.

This approach has been effectively used by crane operators working in the steel industry, but easily could be adopted into other work environments. Health circles usually require some expert help initially. This could include the occupational health doctor or nurse, safety officer, or other experts as required (for example, from design, engineering or maintenance departments). In 'health circles' managers and workers join forces to systematically consider work stress and health.

One of the main problems associated with an increase in worker participation in job design is the threat it poses to managers and supervisors. Foreman and shop stewards have reported that both competencies and functions are threatened. Thus, the issue of increased stress among these personnel should not be overlooked when this type of organizational change is introduced. Indeed, many of the individuals who take part in a health circle, a working party, or any small-group discussion in the workplace, step outside their normal role. Therefore, they initially need help to overcome the stress associated with this situation, and to function as an effective member of the group.

2. **Self-managed teams.** Many organizations have introduced self-managed teams in response to the need for greater flexibility and improved speed of response to rapidly changing market competition and turbulent business circumstances. Peters and Waterman (1982) have suggested that the concept of 'self-managed teams' is a basic building block through which to achieve goal competition advantage. In addition, one of the

benefits of the self-managed team is in the improvement to the employee-customer interface (Griffen *et al.*, 1994). The popularity of semi-autonomous work groups has been enhanced by the advent of, and rapid developments in, computer-based management and information systems. Whilst many major corporations and multi-national organizations have embraced the concept, not all empirical evidence supports the view that self-managed teams are beneficial to the organization (Zemke, 1993). However, Chaston (1998) reported that the introduction of self-managed teams into small, service-sector firms had mixed impact. Some measurable positive impact on aspects of organizational capability has been observed. For example, Chaston found that self-managed teams were successful at developing new products, executing new skill development programmes, identifying new ways of enhancing employee productivity, using customer knowledge to define quality standards and utilizing computers to analyse key data. Conversely, the move towards self-managed teams did not impact on overall performance in terms of identifying specialist market niches, offering superior products, structuring the organization to optimize workforce effectiveness, increasing employee productivity or measuring the customers' service quality expectations. This study did not report the impact of working in a self-managed team on the employees involved. Whilst there are problems for employees, it is suggested that benefits exist in terms of job satisfaction, health and well being. The following study provides an example of the benefits of job redesign and the use of self regulating teams to reduce job stress. However, it must be kept in mind that the introduction of self-managing teams will not be the panacea to all the problems within an organization. This type of change can be rewarding, but is also time consuming to execute and complex to manage.

Terra (1995) describes an initiative aimed at the prevention of job stress, by redesigning jobs and implementing self-regulating teams in a factory environment in Holland. The goal of the work redesign exercise was to restore the balance between job demands and control capacity. Ultimately the aim was to reduce avoidable disturbances in the labour process and thereby the diminish workload. Thus, five potential disturbances were identified, namely:

- information – for example too late or of poor quality,
- materials – for example, of poor quality or not meeting specifications,
- equipment – for example, poorly designed, or of poor quality,
- employees – for example, poorly trained,
- environment – for example, ergonomically inadequate or noisy, and so on.

Employees became full partners in discussions about design methodology and the change process.

To increase control capacity, self-regulating production teams were established. The concept of self-regulating teams with as few separate positions as possible was accepted by the work force. The teams would be responsible for tasks such as detail planning, regulation of work activities, production control, mechanical maintenance, quality control, training of new employees, internal transport, and the regulation of holidays and days off. Over a five year period the results have remained positive for both management and the workers. The quality of most jobs in the production area has improved and standards for health and well being have been met. Sickness absence rates have decreased by 50 per cent, saving one million guilders per year. In addition, there are indirect savings on the costs of production losses and quality problems due to the high number of temporary or unqualified employees replacing absent workers. Workers are better qualified, informed and motivated. Productivity has increased 66 per cent, average wages have risen, and the innovative capacity of the organization has increased. This reorganization was also made without any forced layoffs. As Terra suggests, the implementation of self-regulating teams can create optimal opportunities for an integral improvement of the quality of working life and of the organization. However, although the sickness absence rate has been reduced by half over a five-year period, the diagnosis of the remaining sickness cases has not changed. Also, according to the occupational health service personnel, the rate of sickness absence due to psychological health problems has risen significantly. Terra suggests that this might be due to the intensive training programme necessary to implement the change. Also, as we have established, change itself is stressful, even though it appears to be positive and desirable.

Secondary Level Interventions

Although a growing body of evidence supports the view that organizational-level stress control and stress prevention interventions are more effective than individual-level coping strategies, because they have a more lasting effect (Ganster *et al.*, 1982), it is clear from the previous discussion that the prevention of all sources of negative stress is not possible. Therefore, it is suggested that the effects of exposure to stress could be minimized by the use of techniques aimed at improving stress coping processes by the individual. Therefore, secondary prevention is concerned with the prompt detection and management of potentially deleterious conditions by increasing self-awareness and improving stress management skills. Whilst these strategies are usually conceptualized as 'individual' level stress management options, they also embrace the view of individual employees working within a team or work-group. Newman and Beehr (1979) grouped these strategies into four categories aimed at:

1. Psychological condition
   - planning ahead, managing one's life,
   - self awareness,
   - realistic aspirations.

2. Physiological or physical conditions
   - diet,
   - sleep,
   - exercise,
   - relaxation and meditation,
   - anger management.

3. Changing behaviour
   - taking time off for leisure and holidays,
   - changing certain aspects of behaviour that are stress inducing,
   - building social support networks at home and work,
   - being more assertive.

4. Changing the environment
   - changing to a less demanding job,
   - changing to a less demanding organization.

It is commonplace for organizations to help individuals to either minimize the effects of exposure to stress, or to learn techniques to cope more effectively with stress. We classify these under two separate headings, namely 'skills training options' and 'healthy lifestyle education and management'.

Skills training

The term 'skills training options' refers to the fact that the stress management activity is in the provision of training *per se*. After training, individuals or work groups are required to put their new skills into practice by using them to deal with potentially stressful situations. Therefore, these stress management techniques tend to be classified as a 'reactive' approach to stress management in that they help the individual to cope effectively when exposed to a stressful situation. As we have stated, the objective is to improve or modify the individual's response to perceived strain to avoid a negative outcome. This includes a variety of skills training including:

- Interpersonal and social skills; leadership skills,
- Assertiveness,
- Cognitive coping techniques, for example, avoiding faulty thinking,
- Time management,
- Relaxation training, meditation, yoga, and biofeedback,
- Type A behaviour management,
- Anger management.

Before each of these is discussed the issue of training as an effective stress management strategy is discussed.

Training as method of stress reduction

Effective training is a method of reducing the adverse impact of stress at work. This type of programme should be tailored by finding out what the employee already knows and expects, what they need to know and do, and how the information should be presented and best received.

The transmission of information tends to be more effective if:

1. The message is presented in more than one medium, that is, using both sight and sound. This explains why a poster campaign or news bulletins have only limited impact, and the recent success attributed to interactive video as an instruction technique.

2. The receivers are active rather than passive during the communication of the message. A meeting that requires the workforce to be actively involved in small group, two-way discussions, rather delivered during a briefing session or lecture, is likely to have a more positive impact.

3. The message carrier should have credibility with the audience. Information from an untrustworthy or unbelievable source will not be accepted.

4. Resistance to change will be reduced by permitting the audience to participate in the planning of a programme or initiative, thus, they have ownership of the problem and the solution.

However, knowledge alone does not guarantee that it will be used when needed. In collaboration with the workforce, specific, observable and measurable *behaviours* need to be identified to enable a suitable training programme to be designed. The skills and procedures necessary to handle a critical situation should be imprinted and memorized through training and rehearsal. Thereby they become part of a routine that can be reproduced automatically when the individual is under stress. Realistic simulation exercises, drills and refresher training are vital for the maintenance of the skills and procedures necessary to maintain a safe environment and deal with emergencies when they occur. In a recessionary climate training budgets tend to be restricted and this might limit access to training or the updating of training. This will exacerbate stress levels because the workforce realize that they have not been allowed the opportunity to update their training, or may fear that the people around them will be not adequately trained. Unless the effectiveness of the training is evaluated, its true worth will not be recognized. Therefore, training departments are likely to continue to be regarded as only an organizational cost and 'step-child', rather than a cost-benefit strategy.

Research evidence suggests that older, experienced workers receive less formal training than their younger co-workers. This seems to be a short-sighted business strategy where we have an ageing population. Indeed, one of our challenges is to find ways of increasing the age at which people typically stop working, without damaging health and productivity (Griffiths, 1997). Since chronological age *per se* appears not to be a good predictor of job performance or health, training to meet job demands is one of the ways that we can extend the working life of employees. In rapidly changing jobs, lack of training may contribute to the under-performance of employees, particularly the older personnel who may be educated to a lower level than the younger co-workers. The stereotype of the older employee, held by managers, as more reliable, conscientious, better at interpersonal skills and team working, but less effective in terms of ability to grasp new ideas and adapt to change, the ability to learn quickly, to accept the introduction of new technology and interest in training, may create barriers to the development of the older worker. Therefore, a continuous learning environment is important for personnel of all ages. Critical are the implementation of a training needs analysis, and the use of training strategies that take account of the needs and anxieties of older employees. For example, exposure to computer training is more likely to provoke anxiety among those individuals who have never touched a keyboard before, compared to younger employees, who have been introduced to computer skills as part of a formal education programme. It is possible that the older employee might also need more encouragement to retrain (European Foundation, 1997) because they are anxious and less confident than the younger workers. These are issues that are likely to be identified by the stress audit process. Also, it is suggested that older employees should help to develop their own training programmes in order to overcome such problems.

Clearly, many of the sources of stress identified in a stress audit could be prevented by effective training initiatives. That is, is the training programme targeted, developed with input from the potential trainees, and delivered in a mode that addresses the needs of employees, and then assessed for effectiveness?

Evaluation of training should include:

- A measure of trainees' reaction to the programme. Kirkpatrick (1959) states that participants must rate a training session or course positively to obtain maximum benefits
- A measure of the particpants learning. Whilst participants might perceive a training programme to be favourable or useful, we can not assume that they have learned anything by attending the course. Therefore it is important to objectively determine the amount of learning, perhaps by the administration of a questionnaire.
- An 'outcome' measure. This is a measure of the change in behaviour as a result of attending the programme. That is, have the training objectives been met, and is the employee able to behave in the manner specified by the job description?

In the following sections we discuss interpersonal training skills and leadership, assertiveness, cognitive coping strategies, time management, relaxation and meditation, Type A behaviour management, and anger control.

Interpersonal and social skills training

As Gazda (1973) says,

> As a result of a person's socialization, he has already acquired some interpersonal skills. However, one's level of functioning in terms of these skills can be raised. Everyone has a vast capacity to being more understanding, respectful, warm, genuine, open, direct, and concrete in his human relationships. With a sound body of theoretical knowledge, appropriate models, and numerous opportunities for personal experiencing, the process of becoming more fully human can be greatly accelerated.

This is the essence of interpersonal skills training. It includes a range of communication skills and the need to understand the barriers to good communication. Skills such as listening, assertiveness, conflict resolution and collaborative problem solving, are part of this type of skills programme. Many of these skills are also embedded in leadership skills training programmes. Lazarus (1981), Sutherland and Cooper (1981), report that workers exposed to a manager or supervisor who is excessively demanding and insensitive, or abrasive (Levinson, 1978), are likely to experience a high level of strain at work. Indeed, in the USA, damages have already been extracted from companies on the charge that a supervisor in their employ was instrumental in the deterioration of a subordinates' health (Sand, 1990).

The Type A supervisor would seem likely to create a stressful work environment for subordinates, since they can be described as egocentric, self-centered, aggressive, and a poor listener. The hurried, impatient, driven, competitive, control orientated behaviours are likely to cause them to be inconsiderate towards their staff. They are unlikely to consult with subordinates on decision making and ultimately staff will avoid any interactions that will most probably lead to heated conflict with the Type A boss.

Thus, interpersonal skills training are usually key issues in leadership skills training. In addition to gaining an understanding of leadership roles and behavioural style, many such courses include various interpersonal skill modules, such as reflective listening, understanding body language, anger management, and recognition of the differences between assertiveness, aggression and abrasive behaviours. Heaney, *et al.*, (1995) describe the effectiveness of the use of interpersonal skills training as part of a caregiver support programme. The goals of this field experiment were to teach employees about the helping potential of support systems, to build skills in mobilizing available support from others at work, to teach employees about participatory problem-solving approaches, and using these in work team meetings. As part of the programme, participants, including managers, refined their interpersonal skills associated with exchanging social support with others, including clarifying misunderstandings, providing constructive feedback, and asking others for help. Six training sessions of approximately five hours each were held over a nine week period. A total of 785 employees took part in the full programme and responded to the post-test survey. Compared to a control group, programme participants who had attended at least five of the six training sessions exhibited enhanced mental health and job satisfaction. Individual skill training and modifications in team decision-making processes increased the amount of supportive feedback on the job, strengthened participants' perceptions of their abilities to handle disagreements and overload at work. It also enhanced the work team climate in the group homes (Heaney, *et al.*, 1995).Therefore, attendance on this programme appears to have enhanced mental health and increased the coping resources of these caregivers. It is an important finding because this occupational group is known to feel uncomfortable about seeking aid for themselves (Cherniss, 1980).

Although the topic of assertiveness is a form of interpersonal skills training, it is discussed in more detail below.

Assertiveness

Having to deal with other people as part of one's job can be one of the most stressful aspects of working life. It means that we can be exposed to difficult situations. For example,

- Having to convey a decision that you know your staff will not like.
- Having to handle an irate customer without losing valuable business or making promises that are difficult to keep.
- Being faced with unreasonable work demands or time deadlines; being asked to work extra time or at the weekend when you already have made other plans.

Assertiveness training helps us to deal with such demands without becoming angry or upset. When we are assertive we are able to negotiate or say 'No' to unreasonable demands without becoming aggressive or non-assertive. Thus it is a useful stress management technique. A failure to handle difficult situations can make us feel angry, anxious, frustrated and 'stressed'. Assertiveness training teaches us to be able to speak up and be taken seriously without damaging the rights of other people. The aim of assertive behaviour is to satisfy the needs and wants of both parties involved in a situation.

Typically, an assertiveness training course teaches the individual:

- To understand the differences between assertion, non-assertion and aggression.
- To recognize the verbal and non-verbal aspects of assertive, non-assertive and aggressive behaviours.
- To recognize and use different types of assertion, including empathy.
- To handle aggressive and non-assertive behaviours.
- To understand the concept of rights and responsibilites.
- To make and refuse requests.
- To give and receive praise; handle negative feelings and criticism; give bad news.

(Back, Back and Bates 1991; Fritchie and Melling, 1991)

Cognitive coping strategies

Occupational stress is now viewed as a transactional process whereby employees appraise and react to a potential source of stress. Cognitive style influences our appraisal of a potentially stressful situation and the coping strategy subsequently used. Research evidence also suggests that the use of certain coping strategies, such as 'avoidance coping' are associated with poor psychological well-being, whilst the use of problem-oriented coping is linked to positive mental health (Guppy and Weatherstone, 1997). Indeed, Beck (1987) suggests that individuals are instrumental in creating their own negative feelings by having irrational beliefs. These influence the individual's perception of an event, their ability to cope and the consequences of failure.

It is suggested (Beck, *et al.*, 1987) that dysfunctional attitudes produce clinical symptomology. These include:

- Vulnerability, such as, 'Whenever I take a chance or risk, I am only looking for trouble'; or, 'People will reject you if they know your weaknesses'.
- Need for approval, such as, 'I need other people's approval for me to be happy'.
- Success-perfectionism, such as, 'My life is wasted unless I am a success', and 'I must be a useful, productive or creative person or life has no meaning'.
- Imperatives, such as,' I should be happy all the time', 'I should always have complete control over my feelings' and 'I should try to impress other people if I want them to like me'.

The use of cognitive restructuring as a stress management technique aims to examine dysfunctional attitudes and irrational thoughts. The process aims to improve the balance between perceptions of a demand and our ability to cope, by examining the potentially faulty thought processes that exist when the individual is confronted with a stressful event. It involves thinking about stressful events to make them seem less threatening and the challenging of irrational thoughts. Thus, reactions to a situation are changed by the way in which the circumstances are perceived. A variety of techniques are available to help in the cognitive reappraisal of stressful situations. The individual is encouraged to examine beliefs, thoughts, feelings, actions and the consequences of these, in order to identify rational versus irrational beliefs. To understand a coping strategy used in response to a potentially stressful situation, is it necessary to examine the rationality of a belief about the situation. A rational belief is one that sits comfortably with you and your outlook on life, whilst an irrational belief is one that causes discomfort or distress.

We tend to hold distorted or irrational beliefs when we:

- **Jump to conclusions** – when there is no appropriate evidence or fact to justify a conclusion. This happens, for example, when we conclude that someone dislikes us because they fail to turn up for a meeting or an appointment. In reality, a number of other reasons could explain this action.
- **Ignore important details** – this is 'minimization' and involves focusing on one detail taken out of its context and ignoring the more important aspects of a situation. For example, feeling hopeless and a failure because you did not get a promotion, but ignoring the fact that ten other people on the promotion board were turned down also. In fact, only one person in 12 could have been promoted, and many others did not even reach the promotion board shortlist for consideration for the promotion.
- **Overgeneralize** – this means drawing conclusions from one or two isolated events and assuming that it can be applied to all situations. For example, assuming that you are hopeless at everything you do, and punishing yourself excessively and repeatedly because you found one mistake on a fifty page report.
- **Exaggerate the importance of things** – this is known as 'magnification'. It occurs when we think that a situation is vital or very significant, when in reality, it is trivial. For example, imagining that something awful is about to happen because your boss has asked to see you in her office.
- **Take things personally** – 'personalization' is the tendency to believe that things happening around us are somehow related to us in an important way, even when there is no evidence for this. For example, the boss asks everyone to take extra care in getting ready for a visit from an important customer. However, you assume that the boss is criticizing you alone, even though the request was presented to everyone at the morning staff meeting.
- **Black and white thinking** – often we may see things only in terms of two extreme ways, with no room for anything in between these points of view.

To avoid falling into such traps it is necessary to examine our thoughts and feelings, in order to detect and define the irrationalities. A five- step approach is recommended for refuting irrational ideas:

1. Write down the facts.

2. Write down your thoughts and feelings.

3. Focus on your emotional response.

4. Dispute and change the irrational thought or notion:
   - is there any support for the idea?
   - what is the evidence for the falseness of the idea?
   - does any evidence exist for the truth of the idea?
   - what is the worst thing that could happen?
   - what good things might occur if ...?

5. Substitute alternate patterns of thought.

It is also suggested that we engage in a mental monologue and convert our destructive self-talk into constructive self-talk. Flexibility in thinking about a situation is necessary in order to manage stress effectively. By taking a problem solving approach, and reappraising the situation in a rational way we avoid stress inducing situations.

Time management

As we have acknowledged, an everincreasing volume of demand and pressure to do more and more, in less time, and with fewer resources, are some of the 'hot spot' sources of stress in contemporary organizations. However, a demand situation is only defined as stressful when the perception of that level of demand exceeds the perception of one's ability to meet the demand. Richards (1987) suggests that the concept of time management potentially gives employees a way of coping with demands. For example:

- grouping them into 'key-result areas' so that they make sense,
- concentrating on priorities so that attention is focused on fewer demands,
- reducing demands through work scheduling.

Thus, the goal of time management is, 'Work smarter not harder' (Mackenzie, 1972). Time management is concerned with developing a personal sense of time, thinking about the future and setting goals; analysing where how and why you are spending your time; finding a proper balance between working life and leisure time and achieving life goal by gaining control of time. Typically, individuals attending a time-management course will be able:

- To put time management into perspective by understanding the nature of time.
- To recognize common time problems, such as, procrastination, lack of delegation, mismanaged meetings.
- To keep a time log.
- To make effective use of time by defining values, objectives, goals and priorities, and then to spend as much time as possible engaged in priority activities. The ability to produce a list of tasks and identify each in terms of 'priority'(that is, 'A' = must do; 'B' = should do'; 'C' = can wait) is a key time management skill.
- To find the time of day when one works best at certain tasks.
- To manage meetings more effectively.
- To delegate more effectively.

However, the ability to apply all of these strategies is not within the mandate of jobs that lack opportunities for autonomy and decision making, or for those confined to working a shift roster. Quite simply, much of time is not their own. Therefore, time management tends to be perceived as a stress management technique mainly for managers, white collar and administrative staff. Nevertheless, certain time management activities can be used to help shopfloor, blue-collar employees to gain control over work demands. For example, the tendency to waste time or procrastinate can be identified by simply keeping a log or diary (Drucker, 1996). Also, the re-organization of jobs or tasks is key to the eliminating or reduction of stress at work. However, in our experience, a group of employees is often exposed to a stressful situation because they are not allowed to take some time out to reorganize a system or practice that is stressful, inefficient or ineffective. They are like hamsters running in a wheel! When an opportunity is provided to meet during a focus group session, to discuss better, safer or less stressful ways of working, ideas and suggestions for change readily flow. As Adair (1988) states, 'To save time you must spend time...... It is an investment that will pay rich dividends'. Therefore, we are suggesting that organizations should give some time to employees in order to 'make time' to reduce stress at work.

Relaxation, meditation and yoga – using biofeedback

The purpose of relaxation training, meditation or yoga is to reduce the individual's arousal level when exposed to a source of stress. These techniques are also used to bring about a calmer state of affairs, both physiologically and psychologically. The effectiveness of meditation as an arousal reduction approach to stress management has been investigated and found to be effective. As a relaxation technique it is easily taught and practised. The psychological benefits of relaxation include a sense of personal control and mastery, a reduction in felt tension and anxiety, and an enhanced feeling of well-being. The physiological benefits of relaxation include:

- a decrease in blood pressure,
- slower respiration and heart rate,
- reduced muscle tension,
- less stomach acid,
- lower cholesterol in the blood,
- alpha and theta brain waves to enhance creative and cognitive processes.

By learning and using controlled breathing techniques and relaxation, an individual can reduce tension at will, and develop the ability to adapt to stressful situations at work or home. Controlled breathing helps the individual to confront a source of stress, maintain self control, and decrease the emotional impact of the stressor. The method acts at the mechanical, chemical and nervous levels. It helps the muscles to relax, which results in an immediate reduction of stress and emotional and mental tension. Relaxation allows the individual to discharge emotional tension that has built up in the body. The technique helps one to recover quickly from accumulated psychological and physical fatigue. In time, the individual develops a capacity not only to cope with, but also to resist, stress. The techniques are easily learned and have a positive psychological and physical effect on the body when practised regularly. One oil company in the UK has produced a 'Health Passport' for each employee. This health passport includes basic information about weight, nutrition, caffeine, alcohol, smoking, exercise, blood pressure, and so on, in addition to coverage on stress, relaxation techniques and breathing exercises. Relaxation training exercises are provided with the aid of a cassette tape. This type of self-help information can provide a useful start for individuals wishing to embark on a stress management régime.

Relaxation techniques vary greatly and include meditation; progressive, deep muscle relaxation techniques; or a brief period of mental and physical relaxation while sitting comfortably in a chair at work or at home. A wide variety of audio tapes is available to help this process. These need to be chosen carefully because a voice or music that is perceived to be irritating is not likely to aid the process of relaxation.

One useful routine requires the individual to tense and relax groups of muscles in turn, and in a set order. That is, to tense muscles for ten seconds, and then relax each group of muscles for two minutes, using the following order:

1. clench fists and then relax
2. bend arms to flex the biceps and then straighten: straighten arms tightly to flex triceps and then relax
3. shrug shoulders up towards the ears and then drop them to relax
4. press head back to tense the neck muscles and relax
5. purse lips and relax; press tongue against back of teeth and relax; clench teeth to tense the jaw and relax
6. squeeze eyes tightly shut, frown and then relax
7. breath in deeply and hold to tense the chest, exhale deeply and relax
8. tense stomach muscles as if preparing them for a blow and relax
9. clench buttocks together tightly and relax
10. keeping legs straight, point the toes downwards and then relax
PRACTICE EACH DAY – because it becomes easier with time.

It is possible to purchase a variety of instruments that allow the individual to monitor the physiological reactions of the body to stress. This means it is possible to monitor the state of relaxation. For example, a commercially manufactured 'stress dot' can by applied to a fleshy part of the hand between the base of the forefinger and thumb. This responds to skin temperature. When we are stressed or tense, blood supply is diverted away from the skin surface because it is needed to prepare the body for 'fight or flight'. As we relax, the blood supply will flow nearer to the skin surface for cooling purposes and the 'dot' will change colour to reflect this change. Therefore, this acts as a visual cue in the stress response. The process is known as 'biofeedback'. Other gadgets are available, including 'watches' that monitor pulse or heart rate. It is recommended that this equipment is supplied and supervized by occupational health staff. It should be recognized that levels of sophistication, reliability and cost vary greatly, but such aids can assist in the process of understanding the physiological nature of stress.

Type A behaviour management

We have already suggested that the Type A supervisor or manager might need to participate in an interpersonal skills training programme in order to become a better leader or manager of other people. The objective of this strategy is to reduce the stress that their style behaviour causes other people around them in the workplace. In this section we refer to the TAB management programmes that are available to modify the negative aspects of this style of behaviour before these harm the health and well being of the Type A prone individual.

In the late 1950s, cardiologists Friedman and Rosenman (1974), who were treating patients with heart disease, described a certain pattern of behaviour among these heart attack survivors, which they called 'Type A behaviour'. After many years of research it is now acknowledged that the Type A Coronary Prone Style of Behaviour, referred to as 'TAB' is a risk factor for heart disease, independent of heredity factors (that is, high blood pressure and levels of cholesterol), cigarette smoking, alcohol consumption and obesity. Recent research suggests that it is the hostility component of TAB that is likely to be the factor that increases the risk of a heart attack. TAB appears to be a response to a challenge in the environment. By engaging in active coping in threat situations, the Type A individual remains physiologically aroused, and this constant recurring sympathetic activity is associated with the process of atherosclerosis. Whilst some researchers have tried to claim a heritability component to the Type A behaviour style, it is more likely that it is learned. Indeed, it must be a way of coping which the Type A individual finds rewarding in some way in order for the behaviour pattern to continue. Whilst the Type A Coronary Prone Behaviour pattern is likely to be costly to an organization in the long term, the immediate outcome is one of gain from these workaholic individuals. Thus, Type As are usually tolerated and rewarded with promotion and privilege by their actions, and so their behaviour pattern is reinforced. The Type A individual has been likened to Sisyphus, King of Corinth, who was condemned to push a huge marble block up a hill. When Sisyphus reached the top, the block rolled down again, and thus his task began again. This striving against real or imagined odds, irrespective of the outcome, an inability to enjoy the satisfaction of achievement, or relax, was the way in which Wolf (1960) perceived and described the coronary prone Type A person. Type A individuals tend to deny both physical and psychological responses to strain and are often blind to the extent of their own behaviour.

Typically the Type A individual may exhibit behaviours such as:

— Devotion to work; working long hours; feeling guilty when they are not working or relaxing; tend to take work home.
— A chronic sense of time urgency; always rushed and working under impossible deadline conditions.
— A constant need to hurry is also reflected in their overt behaviour since they are likely to move, walk, and drive fast, and even eat rapidly. Indeed, Type A behaviour is known as 'the hurry disease'.

- Use of emphatic gestures such as banging the fist on a table or fist clenching and waving are typical Type A outbursts. This happens because they become frustrated with their own efforts, thwarted goals and ambitions, and with the efforts of those who work with them. Type As often feel misunderstood by their boss.
- Attempt to schedule more and more in less and less time; making few allowances for unforeseen events that might disrupt the work schedule.
- Often attempt to do two or more things at the same time. This is known as 'polyphasic activity'. For example, it is the typical Type A individual who will want to read while eating, or continue to work on a document while talking on the telephone about a completely unrelated event.
- A hate of being kept waiting, particularly in queues. They are impatient with the rate at which most events take place. For example, they will prefer to rush up stairs, three-at-a-time, rather than waiting for the lift to arrive, even though they have pressed the lift call button. They also have the habit of finishing sentences for other people, and frequently urge them to the point by interspersing the dialogue with, 'yes, yes', or repeating, 'uh huh' over and over again. Frequent sighing during questioning is a typical Type A trait.
- The actual speech pattern of the Type A individual reflects underlying aggression or hostility by their habit of explosively accentuating various keywords into ordinary speech without any real need. They usually have a strong voice, with clipped, rapid and emphatic speech. The last few words of sentences are rushed out as if to quicken the delivery of what they want to say, thereby exhibiting impatience even with themselves!
- Find it difficult to talk about anything other than work related interests and perhaps do not have any interests outside of work to discuss with others. Type As rarely take all their holiday entitlement and are likely to cut a holiday short. They really believe that the workplace can not function without their presence!
- Rarely notice things (or people) around them in the workplace that are not related to their job or to the means of getting the job done.
- They are highly competitive with themselves and everyone around them. Type A individuals continually set themselves (and other people) goals that they try to better. For example, attempting to complete a regular car journey in a faster and faster time! Since Type A individuals constantly drive themselves (and others) to meet high, often unrealistic standards, it is not surprising that they feel angry when they make a mistake. They also experience frustration and irritation in the work situation, when they fail to achieve or become dissatisfied with the efforts of their work colleagues and subordinates.

– Exhibit a strong need to be in control of events around them. A perceived lack of control over events will cause the Type A individual to become even more extreme in their time-urgent, and hasty behaviours.

Whilst the Type A individual is usually highly sociable they are also regarded as a difficult colleague or boss because of their constant need to compete and win. They tend not to listen or let you finish what you want to say, often because they believe they already have the perfect solution to the problem. Indeed, they think they are always right. As work colleagues they are unlikely to be supportive of each other, and tend to be poor team-players. Subordinates of a Type A boss are likely to feel the strain of exposure to this difficult individual because of their tendency to demand and maintain strict control over events. The Type A supervisor often finds it quicker to do a job him or herself rather than take the time to delegate the job to others. Thus they often fail to develop the potential of their staff. This, of course, puts them under even more pressure, causing their levels of irritability and hostility to escalate. The employees of the Type A supervisor can experience the stress of qualitative work underload because they feel underutilized or not trusted. Rarely is the Type A boss satisfied with the achievements of their staff. He or she constantly expects everyone around them to work to their demanding pace and schedule. The organization can also suffer the consequences of dysfunctional TAB. Sickness absence levels may increase as staff fail to report for duties in order to get away from the difficult Type A boss, who always attends work, however ill he or she feels!

Typically, training programmes to reduce Type A behaviour tendencies aim to encourage the individual to modify some of the potentially damaging aspects of their behaviour. Obviously the individual must acknowledge and accept the need to change. It is also important to encourage Type As to set realistic goals since this is a manifest TAB problem. Sadly, many Type A behaviour management programmes have become part of cardiac rehabilitation programmes because the individual has already become a victim of heart disease. Thus it is necessary to ensure that this programme is integrated into stress management activities before the individual and organization suffer the negative associated costs of this potentially deleterious style of behaviour

Advice for Type As might include:

1. Type A individuals are not good listeners; they tend to speak for others, and even finish their sentences for them. Therefore, try to restrain yourself from being the centre of attention by constantly

talking. Force yourself to listen to other people by remembering the axiom, 'we have two ears, but only one mouth – use them in these proportions!'

2. Thank your colleagues or subordinates when they have performed services for you.

3. Control your obsessional, time-directed life. Type A individuals are bad at estimating the amount of time they need to complete tasks or make journeys. They need to identify how much time is needed, and add extra time (at least ten minutes). This will help to prevent them from driving in a 'white-knuckle' manner from place to place. They must also ensure that they carry something to read, so if they arrive early for an appointment, they will not become impatient and feel they are wasting time. Ultimately the goal should be to try to sit, relax, absorb the environment, unwind and mentally prepare yourself for the meeting. This strategy can initially create too much stress for the Type A individual. Therefore, the advice is to gradually build up tolerance levels by deliberately exposing yourself to situations where this is likely to happen. Use the technique of 'self-talk' to avoid becoming impatient or angry. Distract yourself by thinking about something pleasant that is going to happen soon. Make sure that you reward yourself for controlling your time-directed life.

4. Do not try to do numerous tasks at the same time.

5. The majority of work does not require immediate action and a slower, more deliberate pace might result in better quality decisions and judgement. When you feel under pressure, ask yourself, 'Will this matter have any importance five years from now?' Or, 'must I do this right now or do I have time to think about the best way to accomplish it?' Remember, only a 'corpse' can be said to be finished.

6. Reduce workaholic tendencies by engaging in social activities outside of work. Do not engage in activities that create feelings of hostility, anger or irritation Try to find interests that encourage a feeling of calm without triggering your natural Type A tendencies. The aim is to establish a more realistic balance between professional and personal life activities and achievements.

7. Avoid setting unrealistic goals and deadlines for yourself and other people.

8. Cease trying to be an idealist because it is likely to simply end up in disappointment and hostility towards others.

9. Do not bottle up emotions or anger because this is extremely damaging. Find ways to 'vent steam'. For example, engage in some vigorous physical activity that is not goal driven. Write an angry letter, but keep it somewhere safe until you calm down and can read it again. Then choose the best course of action. Talk to trusted friends or colleagues about your thoughts, fears and anxieties.

10. Learn to say 'No' in order to protect your time. Stop trying to prove yourself!

11. Avoid working for long periods of time without taking a break since this is not an effective work strategy. Get completely away from the work area and engage in something that is not related to the task. Make sure you take work breaks and a lunch break, preferably in the company of colleagues. Type As mistakenly think that time spent in social interchange is time wasted time.

12. Monitor the number of times a week you are the first person to arrive and the last person to leave the place of work and ask yourself if this behaviour is really necessary. Try to resolve to arrive last and leave first at least twice during the week.

13. Take all holiday entitlement and ensure that your staff follow your example.

14. Take regular exercise.

15. Learn and use some form of relaxation, meditation or yoga.

16. Do not expect to completely change your TAB tendencies. This is an unrealistic and impossible goal. Trying to get a hare to move around just like a tortoise is evolutional suicide; just ask the fox!

Next we consider anger management. This is also a stress reduction technique used to control TAB tendencies. However, certain occupational groups have also found this to be an important skill in coping with unique and difficult work conditions faced on a daily basis.

Anger management

The inability to manage recurrent anger provoking situations is associated with impulsive behaviours, aggression (Hecker and Lunde, 1985) and cardiovascular disease (Rosenman, 1985). Suppressed anger is viewed as maladaptive and also associated with cardiovascular problems. Certain occupational groups, such as police, or nurses working with psychiatric or geriatric clients with mental retardation problems, may be exposed to unique anger provoking situations. Whilst stress inoculation intervention may help to reduce the stress response when the individual is exposed to these difficult conditions, it seems that anger management courses may also help to avoid undesirable behavioural outcomes. These are related to uncontrolled aggression and unresolved anger (Abernethy, 1995; Keyes, 1995).

- Anger is defined as an emotional state that includes feelings of irritation, annoyance and rage, whilst aggression is a destructive behavioural response that is directed at others. Thus anger can motivate aggression. Essentially, anger management programmes include three components. The first, described as cognitive preparation, is needed to diagnose the anger-provoking situation. For example, the individual is asked:
- To think about the difficult person who is arousing your anger:
  - diagnose why they are behaving in this way.
  - is the situation exacerbating the problem?
  - what is the trigger to the behaviour?
  - are you the cause of their behaviour?
  - how did you react in this situation?
  - is this a 'one-off' or a pattern of events with this person?
- To acknowledge your feelings:
  - why do you feel angry?
  - are your feelings justified?
  - are you being aggressive or difficult in your anger?
  - do you feel in-control or overwhelmed?
  - are you being realistic about the situation?
  - are you jumping to conclusions?

In the second phase of training the individual will learn and develop skills such as relaxation, communication techniques and cognitive control. This means that they should:

- Stay in control; remember to keep calm.
- Use relaxation techniques:
  - take a few deep breaths; breathe from the diaphragm and force your stomach muscles out, to help you breathe slowly and deeply; pause briefly and hold your breath before you exhale.
  - controlled breathing will buy you some thinking time and help you to delay your first utterance, thus, controlling what you actually say.
- Use assertion training:
  - avoid becoming aggressive or non-assertive. This involves both verbal and non-verbal aspects of behaviour. Ultimately it means that

you refuse to allow another person to control your behaviour.
– use empathetic assertion techniques. This is active listening towards the other person, to show that you have heard what they are saying, respect them, and take them seriously.

* Apply cognitive control:
  – use silent self-talk to acknowledge how you are feeling;
  – remember that some people will try to provoke you to anger because they find this situation rewarding. Acknowledging this will help you to stay in control of the situation;
  – think about what you will do next; ignore the situation or respond? It is important to remember that we do not have to either defend or prove ourselves;
  – decide what you want to get out of the situation;.
  – do you need more information before you can respond appropriately?
  – if you are going to respond, say how you are feeling; avoid the 'yes, but' approach. The other person will usually dig in their heels and defend their own position in this situation. An argument will be the most likely outcome of this tactic;
  – avoid being confrontational: aggression breeds aggression;
  – practice 'self-talk' so you will be trained to deliver the right response and cope when you anger is provoked;
  – master and over learn phrases to use in maintaining control when you feel you are becoming angry;
  – use visual imagery to imagine yourself behaving in a controlled way when provoked.

Novaco (1980) reports a decrease in anger among probation officers following this type of training programme. However, evaluation studies for are rare. An example of a one-day anger management training programme for police officers, conducted by Abernethy (1995) included:

* An overview of stress.
* Barriers to acknowledging anger.
* Defining and recognising anger.
* Managing anger; exercizing choices.
* Relaxation and meditation.
* Dysfunctional styles of adaptation.
* Alcohol, nutrition and fitness.
* Defence mechanisms.
* Anger resolution process.
* Providing feedback.
* Anger-provoking scenarios.

Whilst Abernethy reports some limited support for the effectiveness of this training module in anger management, it was suggested that a more extended programme with opportunities for practice was really needed. On the basis of the findings from this pilot programme, the module was successfully extended. In our experience, follow up sessions to monitor progress is vital. An opportunity to practise in a role-play situation is also helpful. Also, the use of closed circuit television to record and instantly analyse performance, provides useful feedback on both verbal and non-verbal aspects of behaviour.

In this section we have described skills training as a stress management option. However, skills building can be acquired in a number of diferent ways, even in apparently 'dead end' jobs. Managers can encourage the process by matching workers with people they can learn from, giving employees the chance to participate in cross-department task forces. This includes the concept of shadowing workers in other jobs, and promoting cross-functional training. A belief exists that people can best acquire new skills by being thrust into situations that stretch them beyond their comfort level. Although this can be a successful strategy, it must be used with some caution and a 'safety net' provided for employees who may experience stress and so fail to learn in this high-risk situation.

Also at the 'secondary level' in the management of stress, options are available that aim to keep the individual fit to cope with the pressures of work and living. These aim to improve employees' general health and include stress education and awarness programmes, and on site 'healthy lifestyle options, such as 'wellness' programmes, smoking cessation and exercise and fitness programmes.

Stress education and awareness raising

This type of programme, that forms the basis for many stress management activities, is designed to increase knowledge about psychosocial stress factors, to explain the physiological origins of stress, to increase awareness of links between stress, illness and personal behaviour, and improve personal stress coping skills. The premise of an educational approach is that promoting self-awareness helps an individual to take action to reduce their own stress levels. According to Kagan *et al.*, (1995) stress reduction is due to 'increased self-understanding and self awareness of cognitive and affective reactions to interpersonal events'. The aim is for the individual worker to enhance their ability to cope with occupational strain. For example, an employee learns the benefits of using adaptive coping strategies, rather than resorting to the maladaptive and damaging ways of coping with stress. However, educational programmes are not generally used as stand-alone interventions, but commonly provide an introductory element to other stress management initiatives (Bunce, 1997). Also, a variety of stress coping skills are taught and practised. Stress education and awareness raising modules are normally delivered to a group of employees at the work site, often during work hours. A combination of brief lectures, video, group discussion and role play exercises might be included in the package that includes:

- An understanding of what we mean by the word 'stress'; differences between the terms, 'stress', 'stressor' and, 'the stress response'.
- Awareness about the ways in which stress might affect us and other people at work. This includes information on the physiological nature of stress and how and why it affects us physically, emotionally and behaviourally.
- How to identify stress and recognize it in ourselves and others. This tends to require keeping a stress log or diary for one or two weeks prior to attending the session. (See Appendix for an example of a stress log.) Also, group discussions and brainstorming techniques are used to identify the stressor barriers that exist to adversely effect performance, job satisfaction and well-being at work. Standardized questionnaires can be used to produce stress profiles. This information can be fed back on an individual or group basis (for example, the Occupational Stress Indicator (OSI) can be used in this manner).
- Options for the management of stress. This includes the use of adaptive versus maladaptive coping techniques.
- Building a personal stress management action plan. This plan should identify the specific goals or target, the type of strategy to be used and the expected reward that the individual will receive for reaching the objective. Goals must be time-based so that a follow-up session can monitor progress. It is useful for employees to identify a 'buddy', preferably in the workplace, in order to meet regularly to discuss progress and problems. However, the most important function of the buddy system is to provide a supportive relationship whilst trying to achieve a change in one's behaviour or lifestyle.
- Stress management training initiatives, such as relaxation, biofeedback, exercise and cognitive reappraisal, will vary according to the needs of the group and the length of time available for the programme. Usually, employees are advised of these options and briefly counselled on the benefits so they can use the information to develop their action plan. Further skills training takes places at a later date.

Organizations which offer this form of 'awareness raising, assessment focused' approach to stress management usually offer various action initiatives in the form of a follow-up programmes. Follow-up sessions might include interpersonal skills building, relaxation training, assertiveness training, keep fit exercise programmes, healthy life-style management assistance (that is, the management of substance abuse problems or weight control, and so on). Skills training targeted at the individual level is an appealing option because it can be introduced within a short timespan and has almost immediate impact. Addressing and changing organizational stressors require longer-term initiatives that tend to take more time to produce any positive stress reduction benefits.

Therefore, this approach simply mirrors the triple A approach already described, namely, 'Awareness: Analysis: Action'. During stress management education, the individual receives information about the stress process, and takes part in some form of stress analysis. This might include psychological and physical health screening. On the basis of the results, a personal plan of action is written. We suggest that this action plan must always be produced in a written format and the document should:

1. Identify the individual's objective and goal.

2. Identify how he or she intends to realize the set objective and goal. That is, to describe the approach and method to be adopted.

3. Provide a timeframe for the proposed activity, with a defined start and finish.

4. Provide some mechanism of social support to improve the likelihood that the goal will be met. The 'buddy system' structure enables employees to share their goals with another person. The purpose of this is to provide some form of monitoring and encouragement. Commitment to a goal and realization of the target are more likely if other people are aware of the intentions of the plan.

Participation in stress management training initiatives has been linked to certain physiological changes that are implicated in the risks for cardiovascular disease, including:

- an increase in the 'good' cholesterol HDL (high density lipoprotein) and a decrease in the 'bad' cholesterol LDL (low density lipoprotein);
- a sharp decrease in triglyceride levels, not due to changes in dietary, exercise or smoking habits

(Eriksson *et al.*, 1992, cited ILO 1992).

The pharmaceutical company, ICI, Zeneca began an extensive in-house stress management programme in the UK in 1988 that has been attended by approximately 700 employees. Measures taken two- to three- months post workshop attendance have demonstrated a 15 to 20 per cent improvement in self-reported general health and a reduction in the number of referrals to psychiatric help or counselling. In a review of stress management programmes, Murphy (1988) confirms that well designed programmes can produce relatively short term changes in measures of psychological distress, including anxiety, depression and irritation. Reductions in muscle tension, blood pressure, heart rate and stress hormones have also been observed. However, there is little evidence to suggest that these changes have long term benefits unless periodic booster sessions are provided.

The main criticism of this approach is that it misattributes the responsibility for stress management (Ganster *et al.*, 1982). Thus the responsibility for managing stress is placed on the individual, who is expected to develop a better tolerance to potentially stressful work conditions. Organizations are becoming aware of the flaws inherent in using this approach. Therefore workplace stress management programmes tend to be used in conjunction with other organizational change initiatives. Arroba and James (1990) suggest that indirect benefits may arise from this willingness of the organization to openly address the issue of work stress by offering stress management training. Employees can be reluctant to admit to strain or feelings of not coping because of fears about job loss threat or barriers to further career development. The offer of stress management training can make a statement that the organization cares about the welfare of its employees. Therefore, stress management training remains popular as a means of protecting employees from the deleterious effects of unavoidable work site stressors. Clearly there is a role for this type of intervention, which aims to help the individual employee or a task team cope with stress at work.

Healthy lifestyle options for the management of stress

In addition to stress management training, many companies have adopted health promotion programmes that attempt to keep employees healthy and to lower health risks. These include weight control and dietary advice, smoking and alcohol cessation programmes, hypertension reduction, drug clinics and exercise programmes. A generic term often used or this approach is 'a wellness programme'.

Wellness programmes

Evidence based on the experience of Néstlé UK suggests that health screening and wellness programmes are well supported by employees although their effectiveness as a means of stress reduction is less rigorously evaluated (Cooper and Williams, 1994). Nevertheless, the CBI's 1988 survey indicates that the provision of occupational health services is a key factor in reducing absence, and it was observed that absence was 20 per cent lower in organizations which provided occupational health services. A reduction in sickness absence is just one of the potential benefits to be gained from this type of initiative.

For example, the mission of a wellnesss programme, in an award-winning hospital-based project in the US, was described by Ballard (1988), as the creation of an environment that encourages employees to enhance their physical, emotional and spiritual well-being. This is to enable staff to work productively, compassionately and with purpose, in support of the institution's commitment to quality patient care. Whilst many organizations have adopted a form of wellness programme, an example of excellence is provided by the Mount Sinai Medical Centre in East Harlem, New York. This programme is now in its 12th year and is working beyond the 12000 staff, to their families and communities, with a rolling programme of wellness initiatives to attract year round participation. This 'on-site wellness programme' combines core health-promotion activities, such as breast screening and cardiovascular health, with a rolling programme of courses, lectures, events and activities. The aim is to consider the health of the whole person, not just at primary healthcare, but also psychosocial, environmental, spiritual and inter-personal well being. In addition to staff salaries, and the use of in-house expertize on a no cost basis, the programme has an operating budget of approximately £18000. The core programmes include general health screening; a four-week stress management programme that includes skill development in, for example, visualization, controlled breathing and muscle relaxation; breast health; and walking for fitness. Other 'calendar' events are aimed at lifestyle enhancement. These include a four-week nutrition programme, weight control, smoking cessation, a 12-week exercise and fitness programme, relaxation, massage, yoga, personal taxation, house buying, defensive driving, coping with sick dependants and learning to live with disability. Ilene Masser, director of the programme believes that they have learned many lessons in the past 11 years. However, they still acknowledge a need to attract more than the 'worried well', and reach out to those at high risk and those with chronic illness. This appears to be one of the weaknesses inherent in this approach to stress management. It appears to be a consistently reported problem for organizations offering stress management courses and wellness programmes to a volunteer work force.

From the above example it can be seen that many programmes extend beyond the original, and simple health screening concept of a wellness programme. This includes the STAYWELL programme, developed by the Control Data Corporation, and where stress management training and education have been combined with a physical health model. This programme provided extensive evaluation data on the benefits of a 'wellness' programme combined with stress management training options.

STAYWELL was provided for 22 000 employees and their partners, and included stress management courses, cardiovascular fitness sessions, and clinics on smoking cessation and weight control. Dramatic economic savings and productivity benefits were reported, in addition to the improved well-being of employees. For example, health costs for employees who quit smoking were 20 per cent less than for smokers, and those who engaged in exercise training had 30 per cent fewer health-care claims than the non-exercizers. Personnel who did not take part in this programme were twice as likely to absent due to sickness and were less productive than the programme participants (Cooper, 1988).

A similar but more extensive programme, developed by Johnson and Johnson, known as 'LIVE FOR LIFE' was introduced to reduce cardiovascular risk factors. They offered 40 different topics in their stress management initiative. An evaluation study indicated that this programme cost the organization between US$200 and 300 per employee, but the saving per employee, per year, was estimated at $378. The Beth Israel Hospital in Boston introduced a programme in 1990 that offered stress basics; communication and relationship management; job organization and time management; anger management; relaxation techniques; and lifestyle management. Over a three year period, nearly 600 employees participated at a cost of £50 per employee. Subjectively, employees perceived themselves to be more in control over stress in the workplace. During a five-year period, staff turnover was reduced by 50; psychiatric claims dropped 20 per cent in one year.

The scope of this type of programme appears to be expanding. For example, in Canada, The Halifax Regional School Board report that they want to focus on developing a safe and healthy work environment, not just super-fit staff. As they note, 'employees can be physically fit but still be unhappy at work'(VanSant, cited Rogers, 1998). Stress, environmental health and financial planning will become part of the broad concept of 'wellness'. The intention is to include 'reduced stress' as the fourth 'R' in their wellness programme and include workshops on 'everything from nutrition to time management' (Rogers, 1998). The aim is to reduce the annual CAN $5 million expenditure on sick leave, and the organization expects to recoup the programme costs of $150 000 in the first year.

In the UK, the company Unipart have acknowledged that healthy employees can mean healthy profits. 'The Orchard' is a headquarters on site, health promotion programme, or 'wellness' suite that includes nutrition advice, aromatherapthy, reflexology, foot massage and beauty treatments. Unipart has spent £1 million on its state-of-the-art fitness programme, known as Lean Machine, of which 'The Orchard' is only a part. Their group chief executive John Neill has stated that the purpose of the Lean Machine is not solely to reduce absenteeism. The investment is a long term initiative that aims to promote health and avoid preventable damage.

However, the investment in a wellness programme need not be huge. Redland Technologies, a UK division of a building company, runs a successful health promotion programme for 250 employees, at a cost of approximately £3000 per year. In addition to introducing No Smoking policies (see below) in all office areas and some parts of its workshops, the company has provided free evening classes for smokers who want to stop. Also, with the support of the Health Education Authority, it holds an annual health exhibition with advice on eating, drinking, smoking, weight, fitness, osteoporosis, and cancer avoidance. Its staff canteen has won a Heart Beat award for its choice of healthy eating. The number of smokers in the company has reduced from 40–55 per cent in 1991 to around 20 per cent in 1994. Sickness absence has declined from between 3 and 5 per cent in 1989 to approximately 1 per cent.

Thus, the range of wellness options continues to expand. There are claims that juggling with balls can reduce stress (Safety and Health Practitioner, December 1991). Without good empirical evaluation data it is difficult for an organization to justify the costs of introducing and supporting some of these initiatives. We would recommend that an organization begins by introducing a small scale pilot project that can be monitored and evaluated carefully before a large investment and commitment is made.

Smoking cessation

The health risks of cigarette smoking are well documented and, as we have seen from the example of 'Redland' described above, many organizations provide clinics to help employees quit or reduce their smoking habit. For example, this was part of the programmes developed by Control Data (STAYWELL) and Johnson and Johnson (LIVE FOR LIFE). The introduction of a No Smoking policy needs to be handled diplomatically. It still appears to be a sensitive issue and can bring accusations of 'Big Brother' from smokers who insist they have a right to make the decisions about their own health or illhealth.

However, there is a second dimension to consider in the decision to provide smoking cessation programmes, namely to provide a smoke free work environment for non-smoking employees.

The law requires an employer to protect the welfare of employees. This includes the provision of a work environment that is reasonably suitable for the performance of contractual duties. A smoky environment that has an adverse effect on employees' welfare breaches that duty, whether or not it poses a risk to health, according to an Employment Appeal Tribunal (EAT) in the UK. Therefore, an employer who fails in this duty of care can face legal action. For example, the EAT in *Waltons and Morse v Dorrington* (I.R.L.R. 488, 1997), found that Dorrington, the employee who complained about the poor air quality at work, was entitled to resign and complain of unfair dismissal. The firm failed to comply with its obligation to deal reasonably and promptly with Dorrington's grievance about her working conditions as a non-smoker. Changes at work resulted in her exposure to a smoky environment. The HSWA implies that an employer will provide and monitor for the employee, so far as is reasonably practicable, a working environment that is reasonably suitable for the performance by the employee of his or her contractual duties. Even if sitting in a smoke-filled atmosphere could not be proven to be a risk to her health, it certainly affected her welfare at work. Thus it was reasonably practicable for the firm to have provided a suitable working environment for her, by asking the smokers not to smoke.

Exercise and fitness programmes

Employee exercise programmes are probably the most popular and common forms of stress management activity offered to employees in the workplace. Initiatives to improve the fitness of employees were originally introduced into the USA in an attempt by employers to stem escalating healthcare costs (see the description of the STAYWELL programme above). Although European countries have government-subsidized health-care services, exercise and fitness programmes as a stress management strategy are offered to staff as a means of reducing the time lost due to sickness absence, and increasing work performance. Since 1994, employers in the UK have had an added incentive to help employees stay fit. The Statutory Sick Pay Act 1994 abolished the 80 per cent reimbursement of employers' statutory sick pay costs, thereby making provision of sick pay a direct financial cost to employers.

As our understanding of the effects of work-related stress increased, it was acknowledged that our increasing sedentary lifestyle, both at work and at home, was a contributory factor to ill-health. Clearly, it exacerbated the problems associated with exposure to stress and the stress response. For example, there is general agreement that a sedentary lifestyle is associated with increased coronary heart disease risk. Heart disease occurs almost twice as often in the inactive person as compared with the highly active (Berlin and Colditz, 1990). In fact, a sedentary lifestyle increases the risk of CHD to a similar extent as the established risk factors of high blood pressure, high levels of cholesterol and smoking.

Action to increase physical fitness and physical activity generally was initiated at a national level. Organizations were urged by governments to find ways of improving the health of their employees. Therefore, workplace exercise programmes are increasingly recommended as a means of protecting employees from the deleterious effects of unavoidable stress at work (Ivancevich *et al.*, 1990). Considerable research evidence exists to support the premise that the beneficial effects of regular exercise are mediated by cardiovascular fitness. Known as 'aerobic fitness', this includes improvement in the vascular structure of the muscles and the heart; improved glucose tolerance and insulin sensitivity; reduced levels of blood pressure, cholesterol and triglycerides; increased fibrinolytic potential; weight loss, and changes in the balance of vagal-sympathetic cardiac drive, enhancing the electrical stability of the heart (Bouchard *et al.*, 1988). It is suggested that about 40 per cent of aerobic fitness is due to genetic endowment. Research evidence also indicates that measured physical fitness, rather than physical activity per se protects against CHD, but physical activity exerts its beneficial influence through changes in aerobic fitness.

Many studies have demonstrated the links between physical activity, blood pressure and cholesterol. These are acknowledged risk factors for CHD. Whilst it is difficult to control for factors such as diet and body fat, evidence from research studies indicates that highly active individuals tend to exhibit lower level of triglycerides, and a higher level of HDL, the liproprotein that reduces CHD. Several studies have shown that stress can raise levels of cholesterol (Friedman *et al.*, 1958), but stress-related sleep disturbance is also linked to increased cholesterol levels (Mattiasson *et al.*, 1990). The incidence of CHD itself seems directly related to the way people handle stress at work (van Doornen and de Geus (1993). For example, a 6.5–year prospective study of a cohort of 416 middle aged, blue-collar workers showed that status inconsistency, job insecurity, work pressure and the psychosocial characteristic of emotional immersion (that is, 'need for control') independently predicted CHD, after adjusting for major risk factors (Siegrist *et al.*, 1990).

It is suggested that the adverse consequence of psychological stress on physical health is due to prolonged activation of the autonomic nervous system. Under normal conditions this response, known as 'fight or flight' behaviour, counters the effects of exposure to an imminent threat, thus protecting us from trauma, infection, or bleeding, and so on. However, the expression of these behaviours is inhibited at work and strenuous physical activity is often denied due to the nature work in contemporary employment. Therefore, continual disruption to bodily homeostasis may, in the long term, lead to disease. For example

- Unused energy sources released into the blood, such as free fatty acids, are converted to cholesterol (Dimsdale and Herd, 1982).
- Increased, repeated cardiac output may result in the disregulation of blood pressure (Obrist, 1981), or peripheral vascular resistance (Folklow, 1987).
- The circulation of unused adrenalin or nor-adenalin may adversely influence adrenergic receptors, and in combination with cortisol, may be toxic to the vasculature (Bauch and Hauss, 1989).

Stress causes withdrawal of vagal cardiac activity in favour of sympathetic cardiac stimulation that may predispose the individual to heart rhythm disturbances (Verrier, 1987). It is also implicated in insulin metabolism (Helz and Templeton, 1990), and may effect blood clotting/fibrinogen balance (Wing *et al.*, 1990). It is possible that exaggerated cardiovascular reactivity to stress might be an independent risk indicator for future hypertension, atherosclerosis and CHD (Scheiderman, 1983; Manuck and Krantz, 1984). Thus, it appears that physical exercise reduces reactivity to physical stress. Highly fit individuals show less catecholamine secretion, heart rate acceleration, and rise in blood pressure, in response to demanding work than unfit persons (Åstrand and Rodahl, 1986). However, whilst response to this type of physical activity and the emotional stress responses are sympathetic in origin, almost no muscular activity takes place under emotional stress. During physical activity, the energy mobilized is used up by muscles that open up to receive the increased blood supply from the heart. In contrast, increased autonomic nervous system activity in response to emotional stress remains 'unused'. Thus, we cannot say that physical activity reduces stress reactivity per se.

Also, the hormonal component of the stress response (that is, adrenalin and cortisol) does not appear to be related to fitness.

Problems with research methodology, the selective recruitment of subjects actively engaged in sport or exercise, compared to those who are not, controlling for baseline levels and circadian rhythm patterns among subjects, cause difficulties for researchers and in the interpretation of results from investigations into fitness, stress and reactivity. Whilst these concerns are still not resolved, it seems from the evidence available, that we can conclude that heart rate and blood pressure levels under stress seem to decline with increasing fitness. Also, fit subjects consistently show lower heart rate and blood pressure levels during stress (van Doornen and de Geus, 1993). Fitness does seem to be associated with a beneficial reaction to stress.

Although rigorous evaluation studies are rare, proponents of exercise fitness as a stress management strategy, believe that there are benefits for organizations participating in this type of programme. These include a decrease in absenteeism, staff turnover, and healthcare costs, and improvements to staff morale and productivity (Kizer, 1987). Although many organizations simply do not evaluate the effectiveness of their EFP, some well designed research studies are available to show that participation in an EFP can result in a significant reduction in absenteeism. Cox *et al.*, (1981) reported that total absenteeism (measured as hours lost) dropped by almost 42 per cent amongst participants with high adherence to a six-month exercise fitness programme. Absence amongst non-participants in this programme increased. Kerr and Vos (1993) reported that over a 12-month period, both regular and irregular participants, in a one-hour physical exercise per week programme, showed a decrease in total absence frequency, compared to two control groups, where the absence frequency rates increased. It is noteworthy that one of the control groups in this study was composed of employees who claimed to exercise regularly, but not as part of the EFP. In this programme, employees were assigned to the various groups on a random basis, drawn from a list of employees who expressed an interest in joining the programme. Therefore, they were all potential EFP participants, and the groups were matched for age, gender and previous absence records. In a review of similar studies, Kerr and Vos (1993) concluded that participation in an EFP is effective in reducing rates of absenteeism, but the reason for this is not clear. It can not be assumed from these investigations that attendance at an EFP 'caused' absence rates to decline. Rather, it is suggested that participation in this type of programme may positively affect attendance motivation by improving employee satisfaction with the job situation (Cox *et al.*, 1981).

Thus, reducing stress precipitates a reduction in absenteeism. In order to understand this finding, there is a need to differentiate between 'voluntary' and 'involuntary' absence. Steers and Rhodes (1978) argue that voluntary absence is related to certain aspects of attendance motivation, such as job satisfaction and stress at work. This means that the employee is absent because he or she is 'sick of work'. Involuntary absence refers to the employee's inability to attend work. Clearly, the management of absenteeism would be greatly improved if it was possible to encourage staff to report the real reason for their period of absence from work. Nevertheless, potential improvements to the physical aspects of health, through participation in an EFP, may influence employees' ability to attend (Falkenberg, 1987). Cox *et al.*, (1988) suggest that the contribution of exercise to the individual's health may be through improved physical fitness and cardiovascular health, and an improved sense of well being. This may be reflected in greater self-confidence and higher perceived levels of physical fitness.

Again, empirical evidence for positive links between well-being and objective measures of aerobic fitness or weekly physical activity is not strong (Dowall, *et al.*, 1988). However, significant associations between self-reported psychological well being and measures of perceived physical fitness and activity are in evidence. Studies have shown that attendance on an EFP can reduce levels of anxiety and depression and improve mood states (Biddle, 1995). Employees appear to feel 'better' and report fewer symptoms of stress as a result of taking part in an EFP. As Long and Flood (1993) suggest, over time, exercise provides coping resources for stressed employees.

Whatmore *et al.*, (1999) reported that a structured exercise programme, tailored for previously non-exercisers, taught on-site in the workplace, and practised at home, twice weekly for approximately 45 minutes, had positive effects on the health and well-being of the group. Comparison of measures taken pre-programme and at the three-month point, showed significant reductions on levels of anxiety and depression, and improvement to mental and physical health (measured with the Occupational Stress Indicator). Levels of job satisfaction and organizational commitment remained unchanged. Sickness absence rates were reduced from 3.59 per cent for the year prior to the start of programme to 0.78 per cent at the six-month post intervention point. Sickness absence rates increased for the control group (non volunteers) and the wait-list control (who were volunteers to this programme).

The social interaction that results from exercising in an EFP can explain some of these research findings. However, this finding was not fully supported by the investigation conducted by Whatmore *et al.*, (1999). They found no significant differences between pre- and post-training session measures among volunteers on a cognitive restructuring programme. This was part of a variety of stress management initiatives offered by the organization. The evaluation study controlled for opportunity for increased social interaction, while attending the training programme and follow-up sessions. Self-reported sickness absence rates also increased among this group refuting the suggestion that participants are likely to perceive the organization as being interested in the health and welfare of their staff because they offer stress management training.

However, research has shown that perceptions of the organization do improve when an EFP is provided. The image of the organization is changed, thereby influencing employee perceptions of the job, their ability to cope with stress that can not be eliminated, and attendance motivation (Cox and Gotts, 1988). Participation in exercise programmes can also increase self-esteem, self-concept and self-efficacy as employees gain mastery and control.

Therefore, it is not surprising that many organizations provide EFPs for their staff. These are usually provided as an 'after work hours' perk, but can also be offered as free, or 'concession access' to local leisure or recreational facilities. Some companies provide an in-house gymnasium, fitness facilities, or the offer of attendance on a scheduled, tailored programme during or after work duties. Nevertheless, Kerr and Vos (1993) suggest that an organization considering the implementation of an EFP should have a clear idea about the tangible and intangible benefits to be gained. They must calculate the return on the investment. This type of initiative must become part of a long term organizational stress management strategy. Therefore, evaluation is vital to both the development and continuation of such an initiative.

One of the key problems with secondary-level interventions is the issue of who should attend. Many organizations simply offer stress management programmes and stress management training and wait for volunteers to sign up for the sessions. Some studies have shown that there were no differences between volunteer and non volunteer employees (Whatmore *et al.*, 1999). Other studies have indicated that the volunteer subject may be one of the 'worried well' or even manifest 'better' health and well-being than the non-volunteer (Murphy, 1987; Conrad, 1987; Sutherland, 1990). Conrad suggests that participants appear to be healthier and more concerned with fitness and health matters than non-participants. The perpetual nightmare for all practitioners who offer preventive medicine is that those who really need it do not come forward for help. It is would be difficult and probably non-productive to insist that an employee attends a stress management course by assigning him or her to a programme. However, the use of a training needs analysis could be extended to identify certain weaknesses that could be addressed under the broad scope of stress management training options, such as time management or assertion training. Ultimately the best approach is to develop a culture that recognizes stress, but does not label it in negative terms or as a weakness of the individual. This means that stress management training can be introduced as part of a package for everyone, just like an induction training package, because stress in the workplace is inevitable, but distress is not. Visible commitment to this policy must be endorsed by the active involvement and participation of personnel at the most senior levels within an organization. Ultimately, it is desirable that this type of training becomes just part of a portfolio of skills offered to optimize the health, well being and performance of all employees.

Tertiary Level Interventions

This type of intervention is directed at symptoms of exposure to stress. Thus, it is primarily a curative approach to stress management for individuals who are suffering from the effects of exposure to strain and pressure. It is concerned with the rehabilitation and recovery process of those individuals who have suffered or are suffering from ill health as a result of stress. Many of the primary and secondary strategies described above take time to implement. It is likely that some form of tertiary initiative will be needed to 'catch the people who fall through the net', and become victims of exposure to stress. These initiatives include the provision of counselling services, often as an 'EAP'(Employee Assistance Provider), building social support networks, or offering a career sabbatical to stressed and burnt-out employees.

Counselling services

Counselling services typically help individual employees deal with a particular personal or work-related problem. Thereby they attempt to increase the employee's capacity to withstand the perceived stressor (Cooper *et al.*, cited ILO, 1992, pp. 246–256). Counselling is described by the British Association of Counselling as the task of giving a client an opportunity to explore, discover, and clarify ways of living more resourcefully and toward a greater well-being.

Counselling programmes, such as those introduced by Kennecott in the USA (Cooper, 1985) and the UK Post Office (Allinson, Cooper, and Reynolds 1989; Cooper and Sadri, 1991), both resulted in reductions in absenteeism of approximately 66 per cent over a one-year period. The Post Office study involved pre- and post-counselling measures of employee mental health, job satisfaction, self-esteem, organizational commitment and health behaviours. Comparisons were made with a control group and counselling was found to result in a significant improvement in the mental health and self-esteem of the participating employees. However, neither job satisfaction nor organizational commitment showed significant pre-post changes.

Firth-Cozens and Hardy (1992) described the effects of psycho-therapeutic counselling on the job attitudes of clinically depressed clients suffering from distress associated with their work. The 16-week intervention showed significant change, in measures of mental health, job competence, the effect of work on home life, intrinsic job satisfaction, and the perception of 'opportunity for control'. Whilst this study did not include measures of work performance, it was observed that as symptoms reduced, job perceptions became more positive. Guppy and Marsden (1997) reported positive changes among transportation workers with alcohol related problems, assessed at the six-month point following, on average, eight counselling sessions. There were significant improvements in their mental health and levels of sickness absence, pre- and post-counselling. Also, based on both supervisor and self-rating, improvement was recorded in work performance. However, neither job satisfaction nor job commitment levels had altered post-counselling. The perception of job stress also remained the same. The results from this study again support the view that counselling can have only a limited impact in dealing with the problems of stress in the workplace. Yet, there are distinct individual and organizational benefits to be gained from counselling employees who present with problems.

Certain problems are associated with 'in-house' counselling services that need to be addressed. This includes the issues of confidentiality, the geographical location of the service within the company, and the process of access to the service. Employees may be sent for counselling on a referral basis only. In some organizations they can 'self refer'. Certain fears about counselling seem to be associated with the actual use of the service. Employees often perceive themselves to be 'non copers' because they need to attend counselling. They also fear the impact that this might have their subsequent career progression in the company, because the organization also perceives them to be a 'non coper'. Nevertheless, there are some benefits of 'in-house' versus 'external specialist' stress counselling services. Internally provided services are already familiar with the organization. They are likely to be able to identify structures, policies and practices in the organization that might be changed to prevent stress, rather than limiting actions to the more restrictive, reactive and curative approach to stress management. However, external counselling services are available. These are known as Employee Assistance Programes (EAPs). EAPs claim to offer a preventive approach to stress management. It is suggested that a well managed 'EAP' will be able to work at a 'primary' level if the main sources of stress are reported to management in a confidential manner. Thus sources of stress identified by the counsellors can be tackled directly at an organizational level.

Employee assistance programmes

An organization contracts an EAP provider to give employees (and sometimes their immediate families) access to an external, independent, confidential advice and short-counselling service. EAPs developed in the USA during the late 1970s. The technique at the heart of an EAP is employee counselling for individuals with work related problems, relationship difficulties, illness worries, redundancy or retirement concerns, substance abuse, or financial worries, and so on. In fact, Berridge and Cooper (1994) identified over 40 potential counselling issues to be dealt with by an EAP. Nevertheless, Highley and Cooper (1998) observed that only 22 per cent of presenting problems were work related. This compared to 31 per cent emotional problems, 19 per cent family or marital issues, and 18 per cent financial or legal worries. Therefore, it can be appreciated that the content of such programmes varies greatly and a standardized EAP does not exist. Typically the function of an EAP is to assist in the identification of problems that lead to impaired job performance and constructive confrontation of the issue. Once the individual has been referred (or self refers), the EAP becomes the link between the problem employee and the management structure of the organization. Counselling in person through an EAP normally takes the form of 'brief therapy' with nine out of ten surveyed providers offering individuals a maximum of six face-to-face sessions (Highley and Cooper, 1998). Some counsellors are concerned that this limit is difficult to work within. They feel that they are only counselling the symptoms in the individuals rather than the causes in the organizations that contributed to the problems.

Ultimately the outcome of the EAP is to improve job performance in addition to:

- improving the changes of employee retention, with savings in recruitment, training costs and expertise protection,
- reduced managerial workload resulting from problem employees shared with EAP,
- disciplinary and dismissal issues treated more precisely, constructively and humanely,
- improved financial control of labour costs,
- enhanced employee morale

(Berridge and Cooper, 1994)

Whilst some services offer the traditional form of face-to-face counselling on-site, it is normal practice for the first contact to be made over the telephone in order to discuss concerns. Meetings are then arranged at an agreed location off-site at professional consulting rooms. Research evidence suggests that EAP counselling-based interventions seem to have a positive impact on employee groups presenting a range of problem types. Typically, levels of absence from the workplace decline, and there are significant improvements in measures of anxiety and depression (Cooper and Sadri, 1991; Ramanthan, 1992; Mitchie, 1966). However, in these studies no changes have been observed in measures of job satisfaction, perceived work functioning or job stress, as a result of counselling.

Nevertheless, the trend towards in-house counselling or EAP services is on the increase (Murphy, 1988, cited ILO, 1992). It is suggested that about 6 per cent of the UK workforce now has access to a programme. Benefits include:

- improved psychological health (less anxiety and depression). Highley and Cooper (1998) found that employees who had used an EAP said the counselling had allowed them to cope better. However, only 15 per cent said it helped them resolve a problem, but 85 per cent would use a service again;
- improved self esteem;
- tendency to engage in more adaptive stress coping behaviours, such as yoga, exercise, and deep breathing, rather than the maladaptive behaviours noted prior to attendance at counselling. For example, consumption of large amounts of coffee, alcohol, tobacco, and food bingeing,
- decrease in absences due to sickness.

Berridge and Cooper (1994) suggest that EAPs are seen by managers as a cost effective way of handling stress at work, as well as the non-work stressors experienced by employees, and imported by them into the job context. However, this survey of 30 EAP providers, 22 EAP counsellors and 168 companies with external or internal counselling services, sponsored by the Health and Safety Executive (Highley and Cooper, 1998), confirmed that employers tended to introduce an EAP as a 'sticking plaster' for work-related stress problems. Also, both employers and providers failed to monitor the EAP properly. This research project revealed that:

- the cost of providing an EAP ranged from £15 to £57 per employee, with an average of £23.92;
- 80 per cent of EAP users received face-to-face counselling after an initial telephone contact;
- only one in four EAP providers expected their counsellors to have previous experience of workplace counselling;
- most EAP counsellors are not routinely provided with information about their client organization.

Training supervisors and managers in basic counselling skills

Knowledge that a spouse or partner is unhappy may effect one's performance, safety or well-being. Management sometimes prefers to regard these issues as 'none of our business'. However, this view is unrealistic and shortsighted. An important part of the management process is ensuring that there is collaboration with employees in order to remove any barriers that exist to adversely impact upon performance and productivity. Distressed employees who are anxious and depressed because of worries about home or the social aspects of their lives are likely to be ineffective, potentially unsafe, and often disruptive when they are at work. By helping the individual to resolve a home-related stress problem quickly and efficiently, the manager regains an effective worker and maximizes human resources potential.

Stress associated with the home and work interface can be prevented or reduced in a variety of ways, including the training of supervisors or managers in basic counselling skills. However, there is also a need to encourage employees to discuss concerns about home and family life, that cause strain and pressure. Making stress a respectable topic for discussion in the workplace is the first step in this process, because a climate of trust and openness is necessary for the exchange of potentially sensitive information.

Therefore team leaders, supervisors and managers will need training in counselling skills. These include, effective (active) listening, using empathy, and knowing when to refer a problem to more expert help. Personnel may resist these services or seeking help if they perceive that their actions will jeopardize future employment and career opportunities. In addition to basic counselling skills the organization can find ways to develop and encourage a more supportive work climate as a means of reducing levels of stress.

Social support as a stress reducer

The value of emotional support in one's social network as a protection against adverse environmental forces or negative life events is well documented (House, 1981; Losocco and Spitze, 1990; Haines *et al.*, 1991; Parkes *et al.*, 1994). House (1981) found that social support from one's fellow workers and supervisor moderated the effects of job stress more effectively than support from one's family and friends. Whilst research evidence suggests that gender differences exist, and different sources of support appear to buffer the impact of different sources of stress, there is much evidence to suggest that social support can play a significant role in enhancing the level of employee well being.

A more supportive climate could be developed or improved upon in the following ways. First, it is necessary to emphasize the importance of supportive relationships and networks during the selection process in order to promote the desired climate and culture. The culture of an organization affects the quality of working relationships, and so this supportive image needs to be encouraged, reinforced and acknowledged as criteria for selection and recruitment into the job. Since social support from a boss seems to be a very important source of support in the perception of level of strain (Ulleberg and Rundmo, 1997), affecting both job satisfaction and health, it is necessary that managers and supervisors are selected and trained for their ability to understand this need, and reflect it in their style of supervision.

The development of structures to provide support includes access to occupational health and counselling services, either provided internally or externally. Also, social networks (work and socially orientated) and self-help groups (for example, 'health circles', already described above) should be encouraged. Education about the importance of social support between work and home life is necessary, so that both employee and the spouse or partner of employees, understand the value of social support, and the damaging consequences of lack of support.

The development of social support networks plays a significant part in enhancing the level of employee well-being, particularly social support from a boss. However, self-managed work teams, or action groups, and so on, all play a part in developing social support networks, particularly for employees who work in relative isolation. Social support helps to moderate the stress-strain relationship by creating in the individual a feeling of belonging and solidarity (Rook, 1995). This can have a positive effect on the person's mood. It is also suggested that a lack of strong bonding, compounded by feelings of isolation, leads people to engage in non-compliant behaviours. This includes absenteeism, tardiness, putting in less effort at work, and engaging in idle gossip, and so on, particularly when job security is at stake (Hollinger, 1986; Lim, 1997).

Career sabbaticals

The opportunities to take a career sabbatical can help an individual recover from the effects of exposure to stress. With so many people today working to the point of exhaustion, organizations should try to encourage staff to take sabbaticals to recharge themselves. Ideally, this strategy should be used before the individual becomes a casualty of exposure to stress. The prevention of stress-related problems is both desirable, and more cost effective than waiting until a need exists to cure a victim of stress at work. However, a sabbatical can also be used to help the employee reflect on their next career steps if they have come to a career crossroads. A sabbatical as short as two months can be beneficial, though some people need up to a year to fully recharge themselves. Sabbaticals should not be tied to level of job or length of service, but should reflects people's needs to adapt to a changing and demanding work environment. Given the high cost of replacing talent and experience, this can be a highly effective strategy for keeping people who may otherwise leave the organization.

An integrated model of stress management

It is desirable that organizations will use proactive, preventive AND curative approaches to the management of stress, at the same time operating at more than one level of focus. Elkin and Rosch (1990) suggest that a multilevel approach to the management of stress might be introduced in three stages, such as:

- Level ONE – Awareness
  Introductory workshops; health fairs; lunchtime speakers; questionnaires or stress scales.

- Level TWO – Employee-directed strategies and programmes
  - Employee needs assessment
  - Relaxation skills
  - Behavioural, cognitive coping skills
  - Life and workstyle modification skills
  - Programme maintenance skills
  - Assessment of programme effectiveness
  - Introduction of reinforcement programmes

- Level THREE – Organization-directed strategies and programmes
  - Organization needs assessment
  - Identification of stress consequences
  - Identification of organizational stressors
  - Introduction of organizational change strategies
  - Assessment of programme effectiveness.

As Elkin and Rosch (1990) remind us, the best approach is one that recognizes that changing lifelong patterns, those of the individual worker or those of the organization, takes time and commitment. Therefore, it is suggested that certain issues are key to successful stress management in the workplace.

1. Have a clear idea about why you are becoming involved in a stress management programme. A stress audit will highlight problem areas and the possible ways to overcome these problems. However, it is also important to identify clear objectives and goals. For example, is your objective to reduce sickness absence or accident levels? Do you want to improve supervisor – subordinate relationships? Do you want people to take more responsibility for quality performance? Make sure you identify a real goal and work towards it, rather than live in the hope that a programme will work by 'hitting' something!

2. Once you have clear and stated objectives, and specific goals, you will be able to decide how you are going evaluate your initiative and measure the benefits. If there are benefits, share these rewards with employees to maintain and sustain a culture and climate that acknowledges the link between employee well being and business effectiveness.

3. It is imperative that you take time to understand both staff and management attitudes to your stress management policy and strategy. Ask employees for their opinions. Ask what they need to be more effective, productive and healthy as employees. Ask them to describe

the barriers that prevent them from optimizing their performance and well-being.

4. Define clearly who is to be involved in the initiative, both internally and externally. Define the project champion, and how the project will staffed. Identify who will be involved and what will you need from each employee. It is vital that a project is endorsed at the highest level to ensure that levels of commitment and support are strong.

5. Communicate your intentions in a clear manner using both verbal and visual messages; preferably, more than once.

6. Provide guarantees of confidentiality and ensure that the initiative does not breach any code of ethics or violates the rights of your employees.

7. Define how the feedback of any results of a stress audit or risk assessment will be treated and used. If a written report is to be prepared based on the results of an audit or subsequent evaluation studies, it is important that staff know what will happen to this information and who will have access to it. For example, you need to decide and communicate if staff are to be allowed to see a full report or only a brief summary of key results. Staff will be unlikely to co-operate in an audit if they perceive that information is being hidden from them. Also, plan how you intend to communicate this information. For example, do you intend to provide feedback sessions, a presentation, team briefing, a personal feedback profile, group profiles, or a newsletter?

Conclusion

It is worth remembering that stress and pressure are an inevitable part of living and working, but distress is not! Our lives continue to become more complex. Like death and taxes, organization change will continue to be a feature of life in the 21st century, and thus a potential source of stress. However, it is mismanaged stress that is damaging in it consequences. Both preventive and curative stress management strategies are essential in an organizational approach to stress control in the workplace. Increasingly, evaluation studies indicate that prevention is more effective AND cheaper than trying to cure problems and victims of exposure to stress.

Undoubtedly, stress management in the workplace must be the joint responsibility of both the organization and the individual. Both parties have a duty of care and need to exercise this obligation in order to remain healthy and free from harm. Ultimately, the effective management of potential sources of stress is about being in control of the pressures in one's life. Whilst change will continue to exert a considerable force on our working lives, it must be acknowledged that some degree of pressure is inevitable and can be spur to improved performance and motivation. Stress is a dynamic process and this means that stress management is not a one-off project. It must become an on-going process within the organization. To be successful it must become part of day-to-day management and practice, and embedded within the culture of the organization. Ultimately this is the only effective and cost-efficient strategy to avoid the unacceptable costs of distress in the workplace.

We need to understand the nature of stress at work before we can eliminate or moderate it. A stress control programme can be effective if resources are targeted to specific problems and aimed at the elimination of the source of stress. Those organizations which recognize the high costs of mismanaged stress in the workplace and seek to achieve enhanced levels of effectiveness and the well being of their work force, will adopt this integrated approach to stress management. It embraces both individual coping and organizational change to combat the problems associated with stress at work.

Appendix

Example of a Stress Log

Stress Log: Strains and Pressures

Stress may be identified or perceived as a single, dramatic incident or an accumulation of less dramatic but related incidents. It might be interpreted as pressure, strain or tension that creates anxiety, worry, anger or just mild irritation. This means that stress is in the eye of the beholder; thus a situation or event is what you perceive as stressful.

In order to begin to identify and recognize stress it is suggested that you keep this log.

1. **At the end of each working day, try to identify your most stressful incident.** It could be work or home related.

2. **Complete the responses to stress and the coping strategies sections at the end of the week, when you have had some time to reflect on how you react to stress and cope with it.**

   Do not cause yourself stress by trying to find something just to fill in the log ... however, do try and be specific if possible about the source of stress and the people involved.

3. **Bring your diary to the stress management session;** it is an important part of the course. The information will be used to generate discussion in small-group sessions. However, the material remains your confidential property. It is entirely your decision to divulge any of the information in this log. The ultimate aim is to raise self awareness and an understanding of stress and the stress process among you and your colleagues. Only by correctly identifying a source of stress or pressure can we begin to manage the situation.

Thank you

MONDAY
Incidents
Work Related

Home Related

People involved/What I did

No. of hours worked ....
What I could have done

TUESDAY
Incidents
Work Related

Home Related

People involved/What I did

No. of hours worked ....
What I could have done

WEDNESDAY
Incidents
Work Related

Home Related

People involved/What I did

No. of hours worked ....
What I could have done

THURSDAY
Incidents
Work Related

Home Related

People involved/What I did

No. of hours worked ....
What I could have done

FRIDAY

Incidents

Work Related   People involved/What I did   No. of hours worked ....
                                              What I could have done

Home Related

SATURDAY

Incidents

Work Related   People involved/What I did   No. of hours worked ....
                                              What I could have done

Home Related

SUNDAY

Incidents

Work Related   People involved/What I did   No. of hours worked ....
                                              What I could have done

Home Related

Finally, please describe:

1. How you recognize your own reactions to stress – what symptoms do you experience?

2. How you cope with stress. Describe any techniques that you rely on and/or find helpful.

NOTE: Please remember to bring your log to the stress management session.

References

Abernethy, A.D. 'The development of an anger management training program for law enforcement personnel' in L. R. Murphy; J.J. Hurrell Jr.; Sauter, S.L.; and Keita, G.P. (eds.) *Job Stress Interventions*: Washington DC: American Psychological Association, 1995, pp. 21–30).

Adair, J. *Effective Time Management*. London: Pan, 1988.

Adams, J.S., 'Inequity in social exchange' in L. Berkowitz (ed.) *Advances in Experimental Social Psychology*. New York: Academic Press, 1965, Vol. 2.

Aiello, J.R. 'Computer-based work monitoring: Electronic surveillance and its effects', *Journal of Applied Social Psychology* (1983), 23 (7), pp. 499–507.

Akerstedt, T. 'Sleepiness as a consequence of shift work', *Sleep*,(1988), 11, pp. 17–34.

Akerstedt, T. 'Invasion of the sleep-wakefulness pattern: Effects on circadian variation in psychophysiological activation', *Ergonomics* (1997), 20, pp. 459–474.

Alexander, S.; Ruderman, M. 'The role of procedural and distributive justice in organisational behaviour', *Social Justice Research* (1987), 1, pp. 177–98.

Allinson, T.; Cooper, C.L.; and Reynolds, P. 'Stress counselling in the workplace – The Post Office experience'. *The Psychologist* (1989), 384–8.

Ansoff, H.I. (ed.) *Business Strategy*. Penguin:1969.

Arroba, T.; and James, K. 'Reducing the costs of stress: An organisational model'. *Personnel Review* (1990), 19 (1), pp. 21–27.

Ashford, S.J. 'Individual strategies for coping with stress during organisational transitions', *Journal of Applied Behavioural Science*, Vol. 24(1), 1988, pp. 19–36.

Austin Knight, *The family friendly workplace*. London: Austin Knight; 1995.

Back, K.; and Back, K. *Assertiveness at work; A practical guide to handling difficult situations*. London: McGraw-Hill; 1991.

Bainbridge, L. 'Ironies of automation', *Automatica* (1983), 19, pp. 775–779.

Baldwin T. T.; Ford J. K. 'Transfer of Training: A review and directions for future research' *Personnel Psychology*, 41 (1988), pp 63–105.

Ballard, J. 'Keeping the wellness ball rolling', *Occupational Health Review* (1998), May/June, 73, pp. 10–13.

Barling, J., 'The prediction, experience, and consequences of workplace violence', in G.R. Vandenbos and E.Q. Bulatao (eds.) *Violence on the Job*. Washington, DC: American Psychological Association; 1996.

Barton, J.; 'Choosing to work at night: A moderating influence on individual tolerance to shift work', *Journal of Applied Psychology* (1994), 79(3), pp. 449–54.

Barton, J.; Folkard, S., 'The response of day and night nurses to their work schedules'. *Journal of Occupational Psychology* (1991), 65, pp. 207–18.

Bauch, H.J.; Hauss, W.H. 'The significance of plasma catecholamine levels in the pathogenesis of arteriosclerosis', *Chromatographia* (1989), 28, pp. 69–77.

Beck, A.T. 'Cognitive models of depression', *Journal of Cognitive Psychotherapy* (1987), 1, pp. 5–37.

Beck, A.T.; Brown G.; Steer, F.; Weissman, A.N. 'Factor analysis of the Dysfunctional Attitude Scale in a clinical population'. *Psychological Assessment* (1991), 3, pp. 478–83.

Beatson, M. '*Labour Market flexibility*'. Employment Department Research. 1995, Series No. 48.

Beehr, T.A; Newman, J.E. 'Job stress, employee health and organisational effectiveness: A facet analysis model and literature review', *Personnel Psychology*, 31, 665–99, 1978.

Benyon, H.; Blackburn, R.M., *Perceptions of work: variations within a factory*. Cambridge: University Press; 1972.

Berlin, J.A.; Colditz, G.A. 'A meta-analysis of physical activity in the prevention of coronary heart disease', *American Journal of Epidemiology* (1990), 132 (4), pp. 612–28.

Bhagat, R. S. 'Effects of stressful life events upon individual performance effectiveness and work adjustment processes within organisational settings: a research model', *Academy of Management Review* (1983), 8, (4) pp. 660–71.

Biddle, S.J.H. 'Exercise and psychosocial health', *Research Quarterly for Exercise and Sport* (1995), 66 (4), pp. 292–97.

Blake, R.R. ; Mouton, J.S. *Solving costly organisational conflicts*. San Francisco: Josey-Bass, 1984.

Bonnet, M.H. 'Dealing with shift work: Physical fitness, temperature, and napping', *Work and Stress* (1990) 4(3), pp. 261–74.

Bortner, R. W.; and Rosenman, R. H. 'The measurement of a pattern A behaviour', *Journal of Chronic Disorders*, 20, (1967) pp. 525–33.

Bouchard, C.; Shepard, R.J.; Stephens, T.; Sutton, J.R.; McPherson, B.D. *Exercise, fitness and health: a consensus of current knowledge*. Champaign, IL., Human Kinetic Books; 1988.

Bradley, J.; Sutherland, V. 'Occupational Stress in Social Services: A Comparison of Social Workers and Home Help Staff'. *British Journal of Social Work*, 25, (1995), pp. 313–31.

Berridge, J.R.; Cooper, C.L. 'The employee assistance programme', *Personnel Review* (1994) 23 (7), pp. 4–20.

Breaugh, J.A. 'Predicting absenteeism from prior absenteeism and work attitudes, *Journal of Applied Psychology*, (1981), 36, pp. 1-18.

Breslow, L; Buell, P. 'Mortality from coronary heart disease & physical activity of work in California', *Journal of Chronic Diseases*, 11, 1960, pp. 615–26.

Briner, R.; Hockey, G.R. 'Operator stress and computer-based work', in C.L. Cooper and R Payne (eds.) *Causes, Coping and Consequences of Stress at Work*. Chichester: Wiley, 1988, pp. 115–140.

British Institute of Management, *The management of acquisitions and mergers*. Discussion Paper No. 8, Economics Department, September 1986.

British Retail Consortium, *Retail Crime Survey*: London: BRC, 1997.

Broadbent, D.E.; Little, F.A., 'Effects of noise reduction in a work situation', *Occupational Psychology*, (1960), 34, 133–40.

Brockner, J.M.; O'Malley, T.; Reed T.; Glynn, M. 'Threat of future layoffs, self esteem and survivors' reactions: Evidence from the laboratory and the field', *Strategic Management Journal*, 1993, 14, (special issue) pp. 153–66.

Brodsky, C.M. 'Long-term work stress', *Psychosomatics*, 25, 5 (1987) pp 361–68.

Buchan, A. 'Workplace stress – the legal view', in *The A-Z of Occupational Diseases*. Conference Proceedings, London: IBC UK Conferences, February, 1997, p. 15.

Buck, V. *Working under pressure*. London: Staples, 1972.

Buckingham, L. 'A headache that just won't go', *The Guardian*, 31 October, 1994.

Bulatao, E. Q., VandenBos, G.R. 'Workplace issues: its scope and the issues', in G.R. Vandenbos and E.Q.Bulatao (eds.) *Violence on the job*. Washington, DC: American Psychological Association, 1996.

Bunce, D. 'What factors are associated with the outcome of individual-focused worksite stress management interventions?', *Journal of Occupational and Organisational Psychology* (1997) 70 (1), pp. 1–17.

Burke, R. 'Organisational-level interventions to reduce occupational stressors', *Work and Stress* (1993) 7 (1), pp. 77–87.

Burke, R.J. 'Issues and implications for heathcare delivery systems', in J.C. Quick, R.S. Bhagat, J.E. Dalton and J.D. Quick (eds.) *Work stress; Health care systems in the workplace*. New York: Praeger; 1987, pp 27–49.

Bylinsky, G. 'How companies spy on employees', *Fortune* (1991), November, pp. 131–40.

Callan, V.J. 'Individual and organisation strategies for coping with organisational change', *Work and Stress* (1993) 7(1), pp. 63–75.

Cameron, K.S.; Kim, M.U.; Whetten, D.A. 'Organisational effects of decline and turbulence', *Administrative Science Quarterly* (1987), 32, pp. 222–40.

Campbell C. P.; Cheek G. D., 'Putting Training to Work', *Journal of European Industrial Training*, 13,4 (1978) pp. 32–6.

Cannon, W.B. 'Stresses, strain of homeostasisi', *American Journal of Medical Science*, 189 (1), pp. 1–14, (1935).

Carayon, P. 'Effect of electronic performance monitoring on job design and workers stress: Review of the literature and conceptual model', *Human Factors* (1993), 35 (3), pp. 385–95.

Cartwright, S.; Cooper, C.L. *Mergers and acquisitions: the human factor*. Oxford: Butterworth Heinemann; 1992.

Cartwright, S.; Cooper, C.L. 'The psychological impact of merger and acquisition on the individual; a study of building society managers', *Human Relations*, Vol. 3, 1993, pp. 327–47.

Cartwright, S,; Cooper, C.L. *Managing mergers, acquisitions and joint ventures.* Oxford: Butterworth Heinemann: 1996.

Cascio, W. F. 'On managing a virtual workplace', *The Occupational Psychologist*, No. 35, August 1998 pp. 5–11.

Cascio, W.F.; McEnvoy, G.M. 'Cumulative evidence of the relationship between employee age and job performance', *Journal of Applied Psychology*, 1989, 74, pp. 11–17.

Casey D. 'Transfer of Learning – There are two separate problems', in J. Beck and C. Cox (eds.) *Management Development: Advances in Practice and Theory*, UK: John Wiley; 1984.

Casey. D. *Managing Learning in Organizations*: Buckingham: Open University Press; 1993 p. 5.

Cervinka, R. 'Night shift dose and stress at work', *Ergonomics* (1993), 361(1–3), pp. 152–60.

Chalykoff, J.; Kochan, T.A. 'Computer-aided monitoring: Its influence on employee satisfaction and turnover', *Personnel Psychology* (1989), 40, pp. 807–34.

Chaston, T. 'Self-managed teams: Assessing the benefits for small service sector firms', *British Journal of Management* (1998) 9, pp. 1–12.

Chater, R.E.J.; Chater, C.V. 'Positive Actions: Towards a Strategic Approach, *Women in Management Review*, 7 (4), (1992) pp. 3–14.

Cherniss, C. *Staff burnout: Job stress in the human services.* Beverly Hills, CA: Sage; 1980.

Christian, P.; Lolas, F. 'The stress concept as problem for theoretical pathology, *Social Science and Medicine*, 21 (2), 1363–5, 1985.

Clarke, S. 'Presentees: New slaves of the office who run in fear', *Sunday Times*, 16 October 1994.

Cobb. S.; Rose, R.H. 'Hypertension, peptic ulcer and diabetes in air traffic controllers', *Journal of the Australian Medical Association* (1973), 224, pp. 489–92.

Cohen, A. 'Industrial noise, medical absence and accident record data on exposed workers', *Proceedings of the International Congress on Noise as a Public Health Problem*, W.D. Ward (ed.). Washington: US Environmental Protection Agency; 1974.

Cohen, A. 'The influence of a company hearing conservation program on extra-auditory problems in workers', *Journal of Safety Research* (1976), 8, pp. 146–62.

Cohen, B.G.F. 'Organisational factors affecting stress in the clerical worker', in B.F.G. Cohen (ed.). *Human Aspects in Office Automation*. Amsterdam: Elsevier; 1984.

Confederation of British Industry, *'Managing Absence: In sickness and in health'*. London: CBI; April, 1997.

Conrad, P. 'Who comes to worksite wellness programs? A preliminary review', *Journal of Occupational Medicine*, 29,4 (1987) pp. 317–20.

Cooper, C.L. *The Stress Check*. USA: Prentice Hall; 1981.

Cooper, C.L. 'The road to health in American firms', *New Society*, 1985 pp. 35–6.

Cooper, C.L. 'Hot under the collar', *The Times Higher Education Supplement*, 21 June 1996, p. 15.

Cooper, C.L. 'The psychological implications of the changing patterns of work', *RSA Journal*, 1/4 1998, pp. 74–8.

Cooper, C.L.; Bramwell, R. 'Predictive validity of the strain components of the occupational stress indicator', *Stress Medicine*, 8 (1992) pp. 57–60.

Cooper, C.L.; Cooper, R. D.; Eaker, L. H. *'Living with Stress'*. Harmondsworth: Penguin; 1988.

Cooper, C.L.; Davidson, M.D.; Robinson, P. 'Stress in the police service', *Journal of Occupational Medicine*, (1982), 24, pp. 30–6.

Cooper, C.L.; Faragher, B.; Rout, U. 'Mental health, job satisfaction and job stress among general practitioners' *British Medical Journal* (1989), 289, pp. 366–70

Cooper, C.L.; Jackson, S. *'Creating tomorrow's organisations; a handbook for future research in organizational behaviour'*. Chichester & New York: John Wiley & Sons; 1997.

Cooper, C.L.; Kelly, M. 'Stress among crane operators', *Journal of Occupational Medicine* (1984) 26(8), 575–78.

Cooper, C.L.; Marshall, J. *'Understanding Executive Stress'*. London: Macmillan; 1978.

Cooper, C.L.; Payne, R. *Causes ,Coping and Consequences of Stress at Work*. Chichester and New York: John Wiley & Sons; 1988.

Cooper, C. L.; Roden J. 'Mental health and satisfaction among tax officers', *Social Science and Medicine*, 21(7) 1985, pp. 747–51.

Cooper, C.L.; Sadri, G. 'The impact of stress counselling at work', in P.L. Perrewe (ed.) *Handbook on job stress (Special Issue) Journal of Social Behaviour and Personality*. 6,7 (1991), pp. 411–23.

Cooper, C. L.; Sutherland, V. J. 'The Stress of the Executive Lifestyle: Trends in the 1990s'. *Employee Relations*, 13, (4) 1991, pp. 3–7.

Cooper, C.L.; William, S. (eds.) *Creating Healthy Work Organisations*. Chichester: John Wiley; 1994.

Cooper, C.L.; Sloan, S.J.; Williams, S. *'Occupational Stress Indicator Management Guide'*. Windsor, England: ASE a Division of NFER-Nelson; 1988.

Cox, C. J.; Makin, P.J. 'Overcoming dependency with contingency contracting', *Leadership and Organizational Development Journal* (1994), 15 (5), pp. 21–6.

Cox, M.; Shephard, R.; Corey, P. 'Influence of an employee fitness programme upon fitness, productivity and absenteeism', *Ergonomics* (1981), 24 (10), pp 795-806.

Cox, T. *Stress*. London: Macmillan; 1985.

Cox, T, *'Stress research and stress management – putting theory to work'*, Contract Research Report 61/93. Sudbury: HSE Books, 1993.

Cox, T.; Gotts, G. *Manual for the development of well-being questionnaire*. Nottingham, Centre for Organisational Health and Development: University of Nottingham; 1988.

Cox, T.; Leather, P. 'The prevention of violence at work: application of a cognitive behaviour therapy', in C.L. Cooper and I.T. Robertson (eds.), *International Review of Industrial and Organisational Psychology*. Chichester: Wiley; 1994, 9, pp. 213–45.

Cox, T.; Gotts, G.; Boot, N.; Kerr, J.H. 'Physical exercise, employee fitness and the management of health at work', *Work and Stress* (1988), 1(2), pp. 71–7.

Crown, S; Crisp, A.H. *Manual of the Crown Crisp Experiential Index*. London: Hodder and Stoughton; 1979.

Crump, J.H.; Cooper, C.L.; Smith, M 'Investigating occupational stress: a methodological approach', *Journal of Occupational Behaviour* (1980), 1 (3), pp. 191–204.

Czeisler, C.A.; Moore-Ede, M.C.; Coleman, R.C. 'Rotating shift work schedules that disrupt sleep are improved by applying circadian principles', *Science* (1982), 217(30), pp. 460–2.

Dalton, D.R.; Mesch, D.J. 'The impact of flexible scheduling on employee attendance and turnover', *Administrative Science Quarterly* (1990), 35, pp. 370–87.

Daniel, J. 'Circadian patterns of changes in psychophysiological indicators of adaptation to shift work', *Studia Psychologica* (1990), 32, pp. 173–7.

Daniels, J. *The long hours campaign in workplace culture – long hours, high stress*. London: Women's National Commission Parents at Work; 1995.

Daus, D. 'Technology and the organisation of work' in A. Howard (ed.), *The Changing Nature of Work*. San Francisco: Josey Bass; 1991.

Daus, C. S.; Sanders, D.N.; Campbell, D.P. 'Consequences of alternate work schedules', in C.L. Cooper and I.T. Roberston, (eds.), *International Review of Industrial & Organisational Psychology*. 1998, 13, pp. 185–223.

Davidson, M.J. 'Restructuring Women's Employment in British Petroleum', in R. Pearson and D. Elias (eds.), *Women's Employment and Multinationals in Europe*. London: Macmillan; 1989, pp. 206–221.

Davidson, M.J.; Cooper, C.L. 'Occupational stress in female managers – a review of the literature', *Journal of Enterprise Management* (1981), 3, pp. 115–38.

Davidson, M.J.; Cooper, C.L. *Shattering the Glass Ceiling: The Woman Manager*. London: Paul Chapman; 1992.

Davidson, M.J.; Venoe, A. 'Stress and the policeman', in *White Collar and Professional Stress*. (C.L. Cooper and J Marshall, eds.). London: John Wiley; 1980.

Dayal, I.; Thomas, J.M. 'Operation KPE: Developing a new organisation', *Journal of Behavioural Science* (1968), 4, pp. 473–506.

DeFrank, R. S.; Cooper, C, L. 'Worksite Stress Management Interventions. Their Effectiveness and Conceptualisation', *Journal of Managerial Psychology 2*, 1 (1987), pp. 4–10.

DeTienne, K.B. 'Big brother is watching: computer monitoring and communication', *Transactions on Personal Communication* (1994), 37 (1), March pp. 5–10

Dibb Lupton Alsop. 'Handling stress at work'. London; DLA Business & Law Training; 11 February 1999.

Dickson, R. Leather, P.; Beale, D.; Cox, T. 'Intervention strategies to manage workplace violence', *Occupational Health Review* (1994), 50, pp. 15–18.

Dimsdale, J.E.; Herd, J.A. 'Variability of plasma lipids in response to emotional arousal', *Psychosomatic Medicine* (1982), 44, pp. 413–27.

van Doornen, L.P.; de Geus, E.J.C., 'Stress, physical activity and heart disease', *Work Stress* (1993), 7 (2), pp. 121–39.

Douglas, D. 'Healing the impact of bullying', *Counselling at Work* (1996), Winter, p. 7–8.

Dowall, J.; Bolter, C.; Flett, R.; Kammann, R. 'Psychological well-being and its relationship to fitness and activity levels', *Journal of Human Movement Studies* (1988), 14, pp. 39–45.

Drucker, P.F. *The effective executive*. London: Pan; 1966.

Duchon, J.C.; Smith, T.J. 'Extended work days and safety', *International Journal of Industrial Ergonomics* (1992), 11, pp. 37–49.

Duffy, C. A.; McGoldrick, A.E. 'Stress and the bus driver in the UK transport industry', *Work and Stress* (1990), 4, pp 17-27.

Dwyer, D.J., and Ganster, D.C., The effects of job demands and control on employee attendance and satisfaction, *Journal of Organisational Behaviour* (1991), 12, pp. 595–608.

Earley, C.P. 'Computer-generated performance feedback in the magazine-subscription industry', *Organizational Behaviour and Human Decision Processes* (1988), 41, pp. 50–64.

Earnshaw, J.; Cooper, C.L. 'Employee stress litigation', *Work and Stress*, 8,4 (1994), pp. 287–295.

Eisenman, E.J. 'Employee perceptions and supervisory behaviours in clerical VDT work performed on systems that allow electronic monitoring'. Report prepared for the OTA assessment', *The electronic supervisor: New technology, new tensions* (OTA-CIT-333). (Washington, DC: US Governnment Printing Office; 1986.

Elkin, A.J.; Rosch, P.J. 'Promoting mental health at the workplace: The prevention side of stress management', *Occupational Medicine: State of the Art Review*, 5,4 (1990) pp. 739–754.

Erera, I.P. 'Social support under conditions of ambiguity', *Human Relations*. 1992, 45, pp.247–61.

European Foundation for the Improvement of Living and Working Conditions, 'Preventing absenteeism in the workplace' (Luxembourg: Office for Official Publications of the European Communities, 1997).

European Foundation for the Improvement of Living and Working Conditions. *'Second European Survey on Working Conditions'*. Dublin, Ireland; European Foundation Office for Official Publications; 1997.

European Foundation for the Improvement of Living and Working Conditions, *Combating age barriers in employment: Research summary*. Luxembourg: Office for Official Publications of the European Communities; 1997.

Eysenck, H. J.; Eysenck, S. B. G. *'Manual of Eysenck Personality Inventory'*. UK: Hodder and Stoughton; 5th Edition, 1987.

Falkenberg, L.E. 'Employee fitness programs: their impact on the employee and the organisation', *Academy of Management Review* (1987), 12(3), pp. 511–22.

Ferrie, J. 'Labour market status, insecurity and health', *Journal of Health Psychology* (1997), Vol. 2(3).

Firth-Cozens, J.; Hardy, G.E. 'Occupational stress, clinical treatments and changes in job perceptions', *Journal of Occupational and Organisational Psychology* (1992), 65, pp. 81–8.

Flanagan, J. 'The critical incident technique', *Psychological Bulletin* (1954), 51, pp. 327–58.

Flannery, R.B. 'Violence in the workplace, 1970–1995: a review of the literature'. *Aggression and Violent Behaviour* (1996), 1, pp. 57–68.

Folkow, B. 'Psychosocial and central nervous influences in primary hypertension', *Circulation* (1987), 76 (1), pp. 119–20.

Foxon M. 'Transfer of Training- A Practical Application', *Journal of European Industrial Training* 11,3 (1978), pp. 17–20.

Frankenhauser, M.; Johansson, G. 'Stress at work: psychobiological and psychosocial aspects', *International Review of Applied Psychology* (1986), 25, 287–99.

French, J.R.P. 'Person-role fit', *Occupational Mental Health*, 3,1, 1973.

French, J.R.P.; Caplan, R.D. 'Psychosocial factors in coronary heart disease', *Industrial Medicine* (1970) 39, pp. 383–97.

French, J.R.P.; Caplan, R.D. 'Organisational stress and individual strain', in *'The failure of success'*. A.J. Marrow (ed.). New York: Amacon; 1973, pp. 30–66.

Friedman, M.D.; Rosenman, R.H. *Type A behaviour and your heart*. New York: Knopf; 1974.

Friedman, M.D.; Rosenman, R.H.; Carroll, V. 'Changes in serum cholesterol and blood clotting time in men subjected to cyclic variation of occupational stress', *Circulation* (1958), 17, pp. 852–61.

Fritchie, R.; Melling, M. *The business of assertiveness*. London: BBC Books; 1991.

Fulmer, R. 'Meeting the merger integration challenge with management development', *Journal of Management Development*, Vol. 5(4), 1986, pp. 7–16.

Ganster, D.C.; Mayes, B.T.; Sime, W.E.; Tharp, G.D. 'Managing occupational stress: a field experiment', *Journal of Applied Psychology* (1982) 67, pp. 533–42.

Gazda, G. *Human relations development: A manual for educators*. Boston: Allyn & Bacon; 1973, p. 34.

Goldberg, D.P.; Hillier, V.F. 'A scaled version of the General Health Questionnaire', *Psychological Medicine*, 9 (1979), pp. 139–45.

Goodell, H.; Wolf, S.; Rogers, F.B. 'Historical Perspective, Chapter 2', in *Occupational Stress. Health and performance at work*. S. Wolf and A.J. Finestone (eds.). (Littleton, Massachuetts: PSG Inc; 1986.

Grant, R.A.; Higgins, C.A.; Irving, R.H. 'Computerised performance monitoring: Are they costing you customers?', *Sloan Management Review* (1988, Spring), 29, pp. 39–45.

Graves, D. 'Individual reaction to a merger of two small firms of brokers in the re-insurance industry - a total population study', *Journal of Management Studies*, Vol. 18(1), 1981, pp. 89–113.

Griffen, R.K.; Baldwin, D.; Sumichrast, R.T. 'Self-management information', *Journal of Management Information Systems* (1994), Spring, 10(4), pp. 111–33

Griffith, T. 'Teaching big brother to be a team player: Computer monitoring and quality', *The Executive* (1993), 7, pp. 73–80.

Griffiths, A. 'Ageing, health and productivity: a challenge for the new millennium', *Work and Stress* (1997), 11(3), pp. 197–214.

Grover, S.L.; Crooker, K.J. 'Who appreciates family-responsive human resource policies: The impact of family-friendly policies on the organisational attachment of parents and non-parents', *Personnel Psychology* (195), 48, pp. 271–88.

Guppy, A.; Marsden, J. 'Assisting employees with drinking problems: changes in mental health, job perceptions and work performance', *Work and Stress* (1997), 11,4 pp. 341–50.

Guppy, A.; Weatherstone, L. 'Coping strategies, dysfunctional attitudes and psychological well-being in white collar public sector employees', *Work and Stress* (1997), 11(1), pp. 58–67,

Hackman J.R; Oldham, G. R. 'Motivation through the design of work: test of a theory', *Organisational Behaviour and Human Performance*, (1976) Vol. 16, pp. 250–79.

Haines, V.A.; Hurler, J.S.; Zimmer, C. 'Occupational stress, social support and the buffer hypothesis', *Work and Occupations* (1991), 18, pp 212–35.

Hall, D.T. *'Careers in organisations'*. Santa Monica: Goodyear; 1976.

Hall, P.D.; Norburn, D. 'The management factor in acquisition performance', *Leadership and Organizational Development Journal*, Vol. 8(3), 1987, pp. 23–30.

Halpern, S. 'Big boss is watching you', Details (1992, May), pp. 18–23.

Handy, C. *Understanding Organizations*. New York: Penguin; 1985.

Handy, C. *The age of paradox*. Boston, MA: Harvard Business School Press; 1994.

Harrison, R. 'When power conflicts trigger team spirit', *European Business* (1972), Spring, pp. 27–65.

Hart, K.E.; 'Managing Stress in Organisational Settings: A selective review of current theory and research', *Journal of Managerial Psychology*, 2(1) (1987) pp. 11–17.

Hartley, J. 'Challenge and change in employment relations: Issues for psychology, trade unions and managers' in L.E. Tetrick and J Barling (eds.), *Changing Employment Relations: Behavioural and social perspectives*. Washington, DC: AMA; 1995.

Harz, N. 'Aptitude testing – Is 'big-brother' watching?', *Data Management* (1985), July, pp. 21–2.

Haynes, S. G.; Feinleib, M.; Kannel, W.B. ' The relationship of psychosocial factors to coronary heart disease in the Framingham Study III. Eight-year incidence of coronary heart disease'. *American Journal of Epidemiology*, 111 (1980), pp. 34–58.

Hecker, H.L.; Lunde, D.T. 'On the diagnosis and treatment of chronically hostile individuals, in M.A.' Chesney and R.H. Rosenman (eds.), *Anger and hostility in cardiovascular and behavioural disorders*. Washington, DC: Taylor & Francis; 1985, pp. 227–40.

Health and Safety Executive, 'Casenotes - Employer liable for stress related illness', *Health, Safety and Environment Bulletin*, No. 229, January 1995, pp. 15–16.

Health and Safety Executive, '*Stress at work – A guide for employers*', HS(G)116, HSE Books, 1995.

Health and Safety Executive, 'Mental Health Trust settles widow's stress suicide claim', *Health and Safety Bulletin*, April 1998, 268, p. 7 .

Health and Safety Executive. *Health and Safety News Bulletin*. HSE, April,1998, 286, p. 7–9.

Health and Safety Executive. '1990 survey of self reported work related illness in England and Wales'. Health and Safety Commission, August, 1997 pp. 1–2.

Health Strategy Unit, '*Our Healthier Nation: a contract for health*'. London: HMSO; CM 3852, April 1998.

Heaney, C.A.; Price, R.H.; Rafferty, J. 'The caregiver support program: An intervention to increase employee coping and enhance mental health', in L. R. Murphy, J.J. Hurrell, Jr., Sauter, S.L., and Keita, G.P. (eds.) *Job Stress Interventions*. Washington, DC: American Psychological Association; 1995, pp. 93–108.

Hellesøy, Odd, H. *Work environment Statfjord Field*. Bergen: Universitestsforlaget; 1985.

Helz, J.W.; Templeton, B. 'Evidence of the role of psychosocial factors in diabetes mellitus: a review', *American Journal of Psychiatry* (1990), 147 (10), pp. 1275–82.

Highley, J.C.; Cooper, C.L. *An assessment of employee assistance and workplace programmes in British organisations*. Research Report No.167; HSE Books; 1998.

Hinkle, L.E. 'The concept of stress in the biological and social sciences', *Science, Medicine and Man*, 1,31–48, 1973.

Hirsch, P. *Pack your own parachute*. Reading, MA: Addison Wesley; 1989.

Hitt, H.; Harrison, J.; Ireland, R.D.; Best, A. 'Attributes of successful and unsuccessful acquisitions of US firms', *British Journal of Management*, Vol. 19, 1998, 91–114.

Hockey, G.R. 'Effect of loud noise on attentional selectivity', *Quarterly Journal of Occupational Medicine* (1982), 24, 445–51.

House, J.S. *Work stress and social support*. Reading, M.A.: Addison-Wesley; 1981.

Houtman, I.L.D.; Kompier, M.A.J. 'Courses on work stress: a growing market, but what about their quality?' in L.R. Murphy, J.J. Hurrell, S. Sauter and G.P. Keita (eds.) *Job Stress Interventions*. Washington DC: American Psychological Association, (1995) pp. 337–49.

Hunt, J. 'Managing the successful acquisition; a people question', *London Business School Journal*, Summer 1998, pp. 2–15.

Hurrell, J.J.; McLaney, A.M. 'Exposure to job stress: a new instrument.' *Scandinavian Journal of Work Environment and Health*, 14 (Suppl. 1) (1988), pp. 27–28

IHSM Consultants '*Creative career paths in the NHS*'. *Report Number 1 – Top Managers*. Study conducted for the NHS Women's Unit, NHS Executive, London, 1994.

ILO *Conditions of Work Digest – Preventing Stress at Work*. Geneva: International Labour Office 1992, Vol. 11 (2).

ILO *Safety and related issues pertaining to work on offshore petroleum installations*. Tripartite Meeting, Geneva: International Labour Office, 1993.

ILO *Psychosocial factors at work: Recognition and control*. Report of the joint ILO/WHO Committee on Occupational Health; Ninth Session. Geneva: International Labour Office, 1984.

ILO '*Manpower Planning and Development in the Petroleum Industry. Report No. III*'. ILO Petroleum Committee, Tenth Session: Geneva, 1986.

Industrial Cases Reports, '*Petch v. Customs and Excise Commission*', I.C.R. 789, 1993.

Industrial Relations Law Reports, '*Johnstone v. Bloomsbury Health Area Authority*' London: IRLR, No. 118, 1991.

Industrial Relations Law Reports, '*Mughal v. Reuters Limited*' I.R.L.R. 571, 1993.

Industrial Relations Law Reports, '*Waltons & Morse v. Dorrington*' (I.R.L.R. 448, 1997.

Industrial Society, *Maximising attendance*. Industrial Society, 1997.

Industrial Society, 'Sick notes; main causes of absence'. Cited *Personnel Today*, 27 March, 1997, 'Yardstick'.

Institute of Employment Studies, '*Stress big issue, but what are the problems?*' London: IES Report; 331, 1997.

Institute of Management. *Are managers under stress?: A survey of management morale*. IMS: Corby; 1996.

Institute for Social Research, '*Employee satisfaction; tracking European trends*'. London: ISR; 1995.

Irving, R. H.; Higgins, C.A.; Safayeni, F.R. 'Computerised performance monitoring systems: use and abuse'. *Communications of the ACM* (1986), 29, pp. 794–801.

Ivancevich, J.M.; Matteson, M.T. *Stress at work*. Glenview, Illinois: Foresman, Scott; 1980.

Ivancevich, J.M.; Matteson, M.T.; Freedman, S.M.; Phillips, J.S. 'Worksite stress management interventions', *American Psychologist*, 45, (1990) pp. 252–61.

Jackson, S.E. 'Participation in decision making as a strategy for reducing job-related strain', *Journal of Applied Psychology* (1983) 68, pp. 3–19.

Jacobson, D.A. 'A personological study of the job insecurity experience, *Social Behaviour* (1987) 2, pp. 143–55.

Jamal, M.; Baba, V.V. 'Shiftwork and department-type related to job stress, work attitudes and behavioural intentions: A study of nurses' *Journal of Organisation Behaviour* (1992), 13, pp. 449–64.

Jick, T. 'As the axe falls: Budget cuts and the experience of stress in organizations'. In T.A. Beehr and R.S. Bagat (eds.) *Human Stress and cognition in Organiszations: An integrated perspective*. New York: Wiley; 1985, pp. 83–114).

Johnstone, H. 'Woman is awarded £67,000 for stress', *The Times*, 6 July 1999, p 4.

Jones, D.M. 'Noise', in *Stress and fatigue in human performance*. R. Hockey (ed.), Chichester: John Wiley; 1983.

Kagan, A.; Levi, L. 'Adaptations of the psychosocial environment to mans' abilities and needs', *Society, stress and disease*, Vol. 1 (L. Levi, ed.). Oxford: University Press; 1971.

Kagan, N. I.; Kagan, (Klein) H.; Watson, M.G. 'Stress reduction in the workplace: The effectiveness of psychoeducational programs', *Journal of Counseling Psychology* (1995), 42 (1), pp. 71–8.

Kahn, R.L.; Wolfe, D.M.; Quinn, R.P.; Snoek, J.D.; Rosenthal R.A. *Organisational stress: studies in role conflict and ambiguity.* UK: John Wiley; 1964, p. 41.

Kaliterna, L.; Vidacek, S.; Prizmic, Z.; and Radosevic-Vidacek, B. 'Is tolerance to shiftwork predictable from individual difference measures?', *Work and Stress*, 1995, 9 (2/3), pp. 140–7,

Kanter, R.M. 'Transcending business boundaries: 12,000 world managers view change', *Harvard Business Review*, May–June, 1991 pp. 151–66.

Karasek, R.A. 'Job demands, job decision latitude, and mental strain: implications for job redesign', *Administrative Science Quarterly* (1979) 24, pp. 285–308.

Karasek, R.; Theorell, T. *'Healthy work; Stress, productivity and the reconstruction of working life'.* New York: Basic; 1990.

Karasek, R.; Theorell, T.; Schwartz, J.E.; Schnall, P.L.; Pieper, C.F.; Michele, J.L. 'Job characteristics in relation to the prevalence of myocardial infarction in the US Health Examination Survey (HES) and the Health and Nutrition Examination Survey (HANES)', *American Journal of Public Health* (1988) 78, pp. 910–18.

Kaye, A.; Sutton, M. 'Productivity and quality of working life for office principals and the implications for office automation', *Office: Technology and People* (1985), 2 (4), pp. 267–86.

Keenan, V.; Kerr, W. 'Psychological climate and accidents in an automotive plant, *Journal of Applied Psychology* (1951), 35(2), pp. 108–11.

Kelly, M.; Cooper, C.L. 'Stress among blue-collar workers. A case study of the steel industry', *Employee Relations* (1981), 3(2), pp. 6–9.

Kerr, J.H.; Vos, M.C.H. 'Employee fitness and general well-being', *Work and Stress* (1993) 7(2), pp. 179–90.

Kerr, W.A. 'Accident proneness of factory departments', *Journal of Applied Psychology* (1950), 34, pp. 167–70.

Keyes, J.B. 'Stress inoculation training for staff working with persons with mental retardation: A model program', in L. R. Murphy, J.J. Hurrell, Jr., Sauter, S.L., and Keita, G.P., (eds.) *Job Stress Interventions.* Washington, DC: American Psychological Association; 1995, pp. 45–56.

Kidwell, R. E. Jr.; Bennett, N. 'Employee reactions to electronic control systems: The role of procedural fairness', *Group and Organization Management* (1994), 19 (2), pp. 203–18.

Kizer, W.M. *The healthy workplace: a blueprint for corporate action.* New York: Wiley; 1987.

Kirkpatrick, D.T. 'Techniques for evaluating training programs, *American Society of Training Directors Journal* (1959), 13, pp. 3–9.

Knauth, P. 'The design of shift system', *Ergonomics* (1993), 36, pp. 15–28.

Knauth, R.; Rutenfranz, J. 'Development of criteria for the design of shiftwork systems', *Journal of Human Ergology* (1982), 11, Supplement, pp. 337–67.

Kobasa, S. 'Stressful life events, personality and health: an enquiry into hardiness', *Journal of Personality and Social Psychology.* (1979) 37(1) pp. 1–11.

Koep, S. 'The boss that never blinks', *Time* (1986), 28 July, pp. 46–7.

Kogut, B. 'A study of the life cycle of joint ventures', *Management International Review, Special Edition,* April 1988.

Kolbell, R.M. 'When relaxation is not enough', in L. R. Murphy, J.J. Hurrell, Jr., Sauter, S.L., and Keita, G.P. (eds.) *Job Stress Interventions.* Washington, DC: American Psychological Association; 1995, pp. 31–44.

Kornhauser, S.V. *Mental health of the industrial worker.* New York: Wiley; 1965.

Kundi, M.; Koller, M.; Stefan, H.; Lehner, L.; Kaindlsdorfer, S.; Rottenbücher. S. 'Attitude of nurses towards 8-hour and 12-hours systems', *Work and Stress,* 1995, Vol 9 (2/3), pp. 134–39.

Labour Force Survey. London: HMSO; 1994.

Lapper, R. 'Insurers fear stress claims will increase', *Financial Times,* 10 February 1994.

Lavie, P.; Kremerman, S.; Wiel, M. 'Sleep disorders and safety at work in industrial workers', *Accident Analysis and Prevention* (1982), 14 (4) pp. 311–14.

Lazarus, R.S. *Psychological stress and the coping process.* New York: McGraw-Hill; 1966.

Leather, P.; Beale, D.; Lawrence, C.; Dickson, R. 'Effects of exposure to occupational violence and the mediating impact of fear', *Work and Stress,* 1997, 11 (4) 329–40.

Levi, L. 'Definitions and the conceptual aspects of health in relation to work', in *Psychosocial factors at work and their relation to health.* R. Kalimo, M.A. El-Batawi, and C.L. Cooper, eds. Geneva: WHO; 1987.

Levine, D.I. 'Participation, productivity and the firm's environment', *California Management Review* (1990), 32(4), pp. 86–100.

Levinson, H. 'The abrasive personality', *Harvard Business Review* (1978) 56, May–June pp. 86–94.

Levitt, H.A. *Employers need to halt idle gossip among the workers.* National Post, 30 August 1999, p. D8.

Lewis, S.; Cooper, C.L. 'Balancing the home-work interface: A European perspective', *Human Resource Management* (1995), 5, pp. 289–305.

Lim, V.K. 'Job insecurity and its outcomes: Moderating effects of work-based and nonwork-based social support', *Human Relations* (1996) 49 (2), pp. 171–194.

Lim, V.K. 'Moderating effects of work-based support on the relationship between job security and its consequences', *Work and Stress* (1997), 11 (3), pp. 251–266.

Lind, E.A.; Tyler, T.R. *The social psychology of procedural justice.* New York: Plenum; 1988.

Lipin, S. 'Corporations' dreams converge on one idea: It's time to do a deal', *Wall Street Journal,* 26 February 1997, A1, A12.

Livy, B.; Vant, J. 'Formula for selecting roughnecks and roustabouts', *Personnel Management,* 1979, February.

Lobel, S.A.; Kossek, E.E. 'Human resource strategies to support diversity in work and personal lifestyles: Beyond the 'family-friendly' organisation', in E.E. Kossek and S.A. Lobel (eds.) *Managing Diversity: Human resource strategies for transforming the workplace*. Oxford: Blackwell; 1996, pp. 221–44.

Locke, E.A.; Feren, B.B.; McCaleb, V.M.; Shaw, K.N.; Denny, A.J. 'The relative effectiveness of four methods of motivating employee performance'. In K. Duncan, M Greenberg and D Wallis (eds.) *Changes in working life*. Chichester: Wiley; 1980, pp. 363–88.

Long, R.J. 'The application of microelectronics to the office: organisational and human implications', in N. Piercy, (ed.) *The Management Implications of New Information Technology*. London: Croom Helm; 1984.

Long, B.C.; Flood, K.R. 'Coping with work stress: psychological benefits of exercise', *Work and Stress* (1993), 7 (2), pp. 109–19.

Losococco, K.A.; Spitze, G. 'Working conditions, social support, and the well-being of female and male factory workers', *Journal of Health and Social Behaviour* (1990), 31, pp. 313–27.

Mackenzie, R.A. *The Time Trap*. New York: AMACON; 1972.

Majchrzak, A.; Borys, B. 'Computer-aided technology and work: moving the field forward', in C.L. Cooper and I. T. Robertson (eds.) *International Review of Industrial and Organisational Psychology*. Chichester: John Wiley; 1998, Vol. 13 pp. 305–54.

Mankin, D.; Bikson, T.; Gutek, B. 'Factors in successful implementation of computer-based office information systems: A review of the literature and suggestions for OBM research', *Journal of Organisational Behaviour Management* (1984), 6 (3/4), pp. 1–20.

Margolis, B.; Kroes, W; Quinn, R. 'Job stress, an unlisted occupational hazard', *Journal of Occupational Medicine* (1974) 1(16), pp. 659–661.

Marks M.L. 'The merger syndrome: the human side of corporate combinations', *Journal of Buyouts and Acquisitions*, January-February 1998, pp. 18–23.

Maruyama, S.; Kohno, K.; Morimoto, K. 'A study of preventive medicine in relation to mental health among middle-management employees (Part 2) – Effects of long working hours on lifestyles, perceived stress and working-life satisfaction among white-collar middle-management employees', *Japanese Journal of Hygiene* (1995), 50, pp. 849–60.

Maslow, A.H. 'A theory of motivation', *Psychological Review* (1943), Vol. 50, pp. 370–97.

Mattiasson, I.; Lindärde, R.; Hilsson, J.A.; Theorell, T. 'Threat of unemployment and cardiovascular risk factors: longitudinal study of quality of sleep and serum cholesterol concentrations in men threatened with redundancy', *British Medical Journal* (1990), 310, pp. 461–66.

McCall, T.M. 'The impact of long working hours on resident physicians', *New England Journal of Medicine* (1988), 319, pp. 775–8.

McCloy, E. 'Stress – a clinical perspective for managers', in *Occupational Stress – Causes and Victims*. Conference proceedings, Civil Service Occupational Health and Safety Agency; June, 1995.

McGrath, J.E. 'Stress and behaviour in organisations', in *Handbook of Industrial and Organisational Psychology* (ed. M.D. Dunette): Chicago: Rand McNally; 1976.

McGrath, R., Jnr. 'Organisationally induced helplessness: The antithesis of empowerment', *Quality Progress* (1994) 27(4) pp. 89–92.

McKay, S. *Workplace culture high stress*. Report of a seminar by the National Women's Commission; 1995.

McKenna, E. *Business Psychology & Organisational Behaviour: A students handbook*. Hillsdale, USA; Hove, UK: Lawrence Erlbaum; 1994.

McLean, A.A. *Mind, self and society*. Chicago: University of Chicago Press; 1979.

Miles, H.H.W.; Waldfogel, S.; Cobb, S. 'Psychosomatic study of 46 young men with coronary artery disease', *Psychosomatic Medicine* 16 1954, pp. 455–77.

Miles, R.H.; Perreault, W.D. 'Organisational role conflicts: Its antecedents and consequences', *Organisational behaviour and human performance*, (1976), 17, pp. 19–44.

Mitchie, S. 'Reducing absenteeism by stress management: valuation of a stress counselling service', *Work and Stress* (1996) 10, pp. 367–72.

Mitler, M.M. 'The realpolitik of narcolepsy and other disorders with impaired alertness', *Psycholosocial Aspects of Narcolepsey*. Birmingham, N.Y: Haworth Press; 1992.

Monk, T.; Folkard, S. 'Circadian rhythms and shiftwork', in R. Hockey (ed.) *Stress and fatigue in human performance*. Chichester and New York: John Wiley; 1983.

Monk, T.; Tepas, D. 'Shift work', in C.L. Cooper and M.J. Smith (eds.) *Job stress and the blue-collar workers*. Chichester and New York: Wiley; 1985.

Moore-Ede, M. *The twenty-four society*. Reading, M.A: Addison-Wesley; 1993..

Morrell, D.C.; Evans, M.E.; Roland, M.O. 'The "five minute" consultation: effect of time constraint on clinical content and patient satisfaction', *British Medical Journal* (1989), 292, pp. 870–73.

Moyle, P. 'Longitudinal influences of managerial support on employee well-being', *Work and Stress*. 1998 12 (1), pp. 29–49.

MSF. *Preventing Stress at Work: An MSF Guide*. College Hill Press: Bishop Stortford; UK: MSF Health and Safety Information No. 40, 1995, pp. 9–10.

MSF. *Bullying at work: how to tackle it: A guide for MSF representatives and members*. College Hill Press: Bishop Stortford; UK, 1995.

Munsterberg, H. *Psychology and industrial efficiency*. New York: Houghton and Mifflin; 1913.

Murphy, L.R. 'A review of organisational stress management research: Methodological considerations', in *Job Stress: From theory to suggestion*. USA: Haworth; 1987.

Murphy, L.R. 'Workplace interventions for stress reduction and prevention', in C.L. Cooper and R. Payne, *Causes, Coping and Consequences of Stress at Work*. New York: John Wiley; 1988, pp. 301–39.

Murchinsky, P.M. *Psychology Applied to Work. An introduction to industrial and organisational psychology*. Pacific Grove, California:Brooks/Cole; 1993.

Myerson, S. 'Doctors' methods of dealing with "ongoing" stress in general practice', *Medical Science Research* (1991), 19, pp. 267–69.

Nasar, J.L.; Jones, K.M. 'Landscapes of fear and stress', *Environment and Behaviour* (1997) 29, pp. 291–323.

Nebeker, D.M.; Tatum, B.C. 'The effects of computer monitoring, standards, and rewards on work performance, job satisfaction, and stress', *Journal of Applied Social Psychology* (1993), 23 (7), pp. 508–36.

Nelson, A.; Cooper, C.L. 'Uncertainty amidst change: The impact of privatization on employee satisfaction and well being', *Journal of Occupational and Organizational Psychology* (1995) 68, pp. 57–71.

Nemecek, J.; Granjean, E. 'Noise in landscaped offices', *Applied Ergonomics* (1973), 4, pp. 19–22.

Newell, H. and Dopson, S. 'Muddle in the middle: Organisational restructuring and middle management careers', *Personnel Review*, 1996, 25(4).

Newman, J.D.; Beeh, T. 'Personal and organisational strategies for handling job stress: a review of research and opinion', *Personnel Psychology* (1979) 32, pp. 1–43.

Nicholson, A. N.; Marks, J. *Insomnia: a guide for practitioners.* London: MTP Press; 1983.

Novaco, R.W. 'Training of probation counsellors for anger problems', *Journal of Counselling Psychology* (1980), 27, pp. 385–90.

Oborne, D.J. *Ergonomics at work.* (3rd edn.) Chichester: Wiley; 1994.

O'Driscoll, M.P.; Cooper, C.L. 'Coping with work-related stress: A critique of existing measures and proposal for an alternative methodology', *Journal of Occupational and Organisational Psychology* (1994), 67, pp. 343–54.

Ono, Y; Watanabe, S.; Kaneko, S.; Matsumoto, K.; Miyako, M. 'Working hours and fatigue of Japanese flight attendants', *Journal of Human Ergology* (1991), 20, pp. 155–64.

Osipow, S.H.; Spokane, A.R. '*A manual for measures of occupational stress, strain and coping*'. Odessa, Fl:Par, Inc.; 1983.

Osler, W. 'Angina pectoris', *Lancet*, (1910) I, 839 .

Pearlin, L.I.; Lieberman, M.A.; Menaghan, E.G.; Mullan, J.T. 'The stress response', *Journal of Health and Social Behaviour*, (1981), 22, 337–56.

Parkes, K, R.; Mendham, C.A.; von-Rabenau, C. 'Social support and the demand discretion model of job stress: tests of additive and interactive effects in two samples', *Journal of Vocational Behaviour* (1994), 44, pp. 91–113.

Perrewe, P.L.; Ganster, D.C. 'The impact of job demands and behavioural control on experienced job stress', *Journal of Organizational Behaviour* (1989) 10, pp. 213–29.

Peters, T.J.; Waterman, R.H. *In search of excellence: Lessons from America's best run companies.* New York: Harper Row; 1982.

Petticrew, M.; Fraser, J.M.; Regan, M.F. 'Adverse life events and risk of breast cancer: A meta-analysis', *British Journal of Health Psychology* (1999), 4, pp. 1–17.

Pierce, J.L.; Newstrom, J.W.; Dunham, R.B.; Barber, A.E. *Alternative work schedules.* Boston: Allyn & Bacon; 1989.

Piotrkowski, C.S.; Cohen, B.G.; Coray, K.E. 'Working conditions and well-being among women office workers', *Special issue: Occupational stress in human computer interaction. International Journal of the Human Computer Interaction* (1992), Vol. 4 (3), pp. 263–81.

Pincherle, G. 'Fitness for work', *Proceedings of the Royal Society of Medicine* (1972), 65 (4) pp. 321–4.

Porter, A.M.D.; Howie, J.G.R.; Levinson, A. 'A measurement of stress as it affects the work of the general practitioner', *Family Practice* (1985), 2, pp. 136–46.

Porter, A.M.D.; Howie, J.G.R.; Levinson, A. 'Stress and the General Practitioner', in R. Payne and J. Firth-Cozens (eds.), *Stress in Health Professionals.* Chichester: John Wiley; 1987 pp. 45–70).

Poulton, E.C. 'Blue collar stress', in *Stress at work*. C.L. Cooper, and R. Payne (eds.) Chichester and New York: John Wiley; 1978.

Powell, G.N.; Mainiero, L.A. 'Alternative work arrangements', *Journal of Occupational and Organisational Psychology* (1999),72(1), pp. 41–56.

Prossin, A. 'The ocean and occupational health', *Canadian Family Physician* (1983), 3 (23), pp. 1135–40.

Quick, J.C. 'Dyadic goal setting and role stress in field study', *Academy of Management Journal* (1979) 22, pp. 241–52.

Quick, J.C.; Quick, J.D. *Organisational stress and preventive management*. USA: McGraw-Hill; 1984.

Ramanthan, C.S. 'EAP's response to personal stress and productivity: implications for occupational social work', *Social Work* (1992) 37, pp. 232–39.

Ramsey, J.D. 'Heat and cold', in *Stress and fatigue in human performance*. Robert Hockey (ed.), (Chichester, New York: John Wiley; 1983).

Rees, D.; Cooper, C.L. 'A criterion-oriented validation of the OSI outcome measures on a sample of health services employees', *Stress Medicine*, 7 (1991) pp. 125–7.

Richards, J.H. 'Time management – a review', *Work and Stress* (1987), 1(1), pp. 73–78.

Robertson, I.T.; Cooper, C.L. 'The validity of the occupational stress indicator', *Work and Stress*, 4 (1990) pp. 29–39.

Roethlisberger, F.; Dickson, J.J. *Management and the worker*. Cambridge, Massachusetts: Harvard University Press; 1939.

Rogers, S. 'Reduce stress to work happier', *Canadian Living* (1998) November, p. 102.

Rosa, R.R.; Colligan, M.J.; Lewis, P. 'Extended workdays: Effects of 8-hours and 12-hour rotating shift schedules on performance, subjective sleep, sleep patterns, and psychosocial variables', *Work and Stress* (1989), 3(1), pp. 21–32.

Rosegger, R.; Rosegger, S. 'Health effects of tractor driving', *Journal of Agricultural Engineering Research* (1960), 5, pp. 241–75.

Rosenman, R.H. 'Health consequences of anger and implications for treatment' in M.A. Chesney and R.H. Rosenman (eds.) *Anger and hostility in cardiovascular and behavioural disorders*. Washington, DC: Taylor & Francis; 1985, pp. 103–25.

Rubery, J.; Smith, M.; Fagan, C. *Changing patterns of work and working-time in the European Union and the impact on gender provisions*. European Commission, April, 1995.

Russek H.I.; Zohman. 'Relative significance of heredity, diet and occupational stress in CHD of young adults', *American Journal of Medical Sciences*. v235, 1958, pp 226–75.

Ruys, T. 'Windowless offices'. MA Thesis, University of Washington, cited in D.J. Oborne, *Ergonomics at work* (Second edn), Chichester: Wiley; 1970.

Sainfort, P.C. 'Job design predictors of stress in automated offices', *Behaviour and Information Technology* (1990), 9, pp. 3–16.

Sand, R.H. 'OSHA pre-emption of state criminal prosecutions, fetal protection, and workers' compensation for emotional stress', *Employee Relations Law Journal* (1990), 15, pp. 441–7.

Sargent, L.D.; Terry, D.J. 'The effects of work control and job demands on employee adjustment and work performance', *Journal of Occupational and Organizational Psychology* (1998) 71, pp. 219–36.

Scase, R.; Goffee, R. *Reluctant managers, their work and lifestyles*. London: Unwin; 1989.

Schabracq, M.J.; Cooper, C.L. 'Flexibility of labour, well-being and stress', *International Journal of Stress Management* (1997) Vol. 4, pp. 259–74.

Schein, V.; Davidson, M.J. 'Think Manager – Think Male – Managerial Sex Typing among UK Business Students', *Management Development Review*, 6(3), (1993), pp. 24–8.

Schweiger, D.M.; DeNisi, A.A. 'Communication with employees following a merger: A longitudinal field experiment', *Academy of Management Journal* (1991), 24, pp. 110–35.

Scott, A.J. 'Chronobiological consideration in shiftworker sleep and performance and shiftwork scheduling', *Human Performance*, Special Issue (1994), 7(3), pp. 207–33.

Schuler, R.S. 'Definition and conceptualisation of stress in organisations', *Organisation Behaviour and Human Performance*, 25, 184–215, 1980.

Schweiger, D.M.; DeNisi, A.S. 'Communication with employees following a merger: A longitudinal field experiment', *Academy of Management Journal*, 1991, 34, pp. 110–35.

Schweiger, D.M.; Ivancevich, J.M. 'Human resources; the forgotten factor in mergers and acquisitions', *Personnel Administrator*, November 1985, pp. 47–61.

Schweiger,D.M.; Ivancevich, J.M.; Power, F.R. 'Executive actions for managing human resources before and after acquisitions', *Academy of Management Executive*, Vol. 2, 1987, pp. 127–38.

Selye, H. *The stress of life*. USA: McGraw-Hill; 1956.

Selye, H. *Stress without distress*. Philadelphia: J.B. Lippincott; 1974.

Selye, H. *Stress in health and disease*. London: Butterworth; 1976.

Selye, H. 'The stress concept: past, present and future', in *Stress Research* (C.L. Cooper, ed.). UK: John Wiley; 1983.

Sherizen, S. 'Work monitoring: Productivity gains at what cost to privacy', *Computer World* (1986), 20 (27), p. 55.

Shostack, A.B. *Blue-collar stress*. USA: Addison Wesley; 1980.

Siegrist, J. 'Working conditions and cardiovascular disease', *Safety and Health Practitioner, I* (1997), November, pp. 35–7.

Siegrist, J.; Peter, R.; Junge, A.; Cremer, P.; Seidel, D. 'Low status control, high effort at work and ischaemic heart disease: prospective evidence from blue collar men', *Social Science and Medicine* (1990), 31, pp. 1127–34.

Simpson, R. 'Presenteeism, power and organisational change: long hours as a career barrier and the impact on the working lives of women managers'. *British Journal of Management*, Vol. 9 (special issue) September 1998, pp. S37-S50.

Sinetar, M. ' Mergers, morale and productivity', *Personnel Journal*, Vol. 60, 1981, pp. 863–867.

Singer, G. 'New approaches to social factors in shiftwork' in M. Wallace (ed.) *Shiftwork and Health*. Bundoora, Australia: Brain, Behaviour and Research Institute; 1985.

Skipper, J.K.; Jung, F.D.; Coffrey, L.C. 'Nurses and shiftwork; Effects on physical health and mental depression', *Journal of Advanced Nursing* (1990), 15, pp. 835–42.

Smith, M.J.; Cohen, H.H.; Cleveland, R.; Cohen, A. 'Characteristics of successful safety programs', *Journal of Safety Research* (1978), 10, pp. 5–15.

Smith, L.; Totterdell, P.; Folkard, S. 'Shiftwork effects in nuclear power workers: a field study using portable computers', *Work and Stress* 1995, 9, (2/3), pp. 235–44.

Sparks, K.; Cooper, C.L.; Fried, Y.; Shirom, A. 'The effects of hours of work on health: A meta-analytic review', *Journal of Occupational and Organisational Psychology* (1997), 70, pp. 391–408.

Spurgeon, A.; Harrington, J.; Cooper, C.L. 'Health and safety problems associated with long working hours: review of the current problem', *Occupational and Environmental Medicine* (1997), 54 (6), June pp. 367–75.

Steer, R.; Rhodes, S. 'Major influences on employee attendance: a process model', *Journal of Applied Psychology* (1978), 63(4), pp. 391–407.

Sterns, H.; Alexander, R. 'Performance appraisal of the older worker', in H. Dennis (ed.) *Fourteen steps to managing an aging workforce*. Lexington, MA:Lexington Books; 1988, pp. 85–93.

Surry, J.; *Industrial accident research: A human engineering appraisal*. Canada: Ontario Department of Labour; 1968.

Susser, P.R. 'Electronic monitoring in the private sector. How closely should employers supervise their workers?, *Employee Relations Law Journal* (1988), 13, pp. 575–98.

Sutherland, V.J. 'Managing stress at the worksite', in P. Bennett, J. Weinman and P. Spurgeon (eds.) *Current Developments in Health Psychology*. London: Harwood Academic; 1990.

Sutherland, V.J. 'Stress and the new contract for general practitioners', *Journal of Managerial Psychology*, 10,3 (1995) pp. 17–28.

Sutherland, V.J.; Cooper, C.L. *'Man and Accidents Offshore: the costs of stress among workers on oil and gas rigs'*. London: Lloyd's List/Dietsmann 1986.

Sutherland, V. J.; Cooper, C. L. *'Understanding stress: a psychological perspective for health professionals'*. UK: Chapman and Hall; 1990.

Sutherland, V. J.; Cooper, C. L. 'Stress Personality and Accidents in the offshore environment', *Journal of Personality and Individual Differences*, 12(3). (1991), pp. 195–204

Sutherland, V. J.; Cooper, C. L. *Stress and accidents in the offshore oil and gas industry*. Houston; Texas: Gulf Publishing; 1991.

Sutherland, V.J.; Cooper, C.L. *Man and accidents offshore: The costs of stress among workers on oil and gas rigs*. London: Lloyd's List/Dietsmann; 1986.

Sutherland, V.J.; Cooper, C.L. 'Job stress, satisfaction and mental health among general practitioners before and after the introduction of the new contract', *British Medical Journal* (1992), 304, pp. 1545–48.

Sutherland, V.J.; Davidson, M.J. 'Stress among Construction Site Managers: A Preliminary Study', *Stress Medicine, 5*, (1989), pp. 221–35.

Sutherland, V.J.; Davidson, M. J. 'Using a stress audit: the construction site manager experience', *Work and Stress*, 7 (3), 1993, pp. 273–86.

Sutherland, V.J.; Davidson, M.J. 'Managing Diversity: Using an equal opportunities audit to maximise career potential and opportunities in UK bank', *European Journal of Work and Organizational Psychology*, (1996) 5,4, pp. 559–82.

Szwergold, J. 'How to juggle business demands … literally', *Human Resources Focus* (1994), Vol. 71 (6), June, p. 3.

Talbot, R.; Cooper, C.L.; Barrow S. 'Creativity and stress', *Creativity and Innovation Management,* 1 (4) Dec. 1992, pp. 183–93.

Terra, N. 'The prevention of job stress by redesigning jobs and implementing self-regulating teams' in L. R. Murphy, J.J. Hurrell, Jr., Sauter, S.L., and Keita, G.P. (eds.) *Job Stress Interventions*. Washington, DC: American Psychological Association; 1995, pp. 265–82).

Toffler, A. *Future Shock*. UK: Pan; 1970.

Trade Union of Congress. *Part-time working in Britain: Analysis of trends in part-time work and the characteristics of part-time workers in 1994*. London: TUC; 1994.

Uehata, Tetsunojo. 'Long working hours and occupational stress-related cardiovascular attacks among middle-aged workers in Japan', *Journal of Human Ergology*, 20 (2), 1991, pp. 147–53.

Ulleberg, P.; Rundmo, T. 'Job stress, social support and absenteeism among offshore personnel', *Work and Stress* (1997), 11 (3), pp. 215–228.

Unger, H. 'The people trauma of major mergers', *Journal of Industrial Management*, 1986, pp. 10–17.

Verrier, J.R. 'Mechanisms of behaviourally induced arrhythmias', *Circulation* (1989), 76 (Suppl. 1), pp. 48–56.

US Congress, Office of Technology Assessment. *The electronic supervisor; New technology, new tensions, OTA-CIT-333*. Washington, DC: US Government Printing Office; 1987.

Wajcman, J., 'Women and men managers: Careers and equal opportunities', in R. Crompton, D. Gallie and K. Purcell (eds.) *Changing forms of employment*. London: Routledge, 1996, pp. 259–277.

Waldman, D.; Avolio, B. 'A meta-analysis of age differences in job performance', *Journal of Applied Psychology*, 1986, 71, 33–8.

Wall, T.D.; Clegg, C.W. 'A longitudinal study of group work redesign', *Journal of Occupational Behaviour* (1981), 2, pp. 31–49.

Wall, T.D.; Jackson, P.R.; Mullarkey, S.; Parker, S.K. 'The demands- control model of job strain: A more specific test', *Journal of Occupational and Organisational Psychology* (1996) 69, pp. 153–66.

Walsh, J.P. 'Top management turnover following mergers and acquisitions', *Strategic Management Journal*, Vol. 9, 1988, pp. 173–83.

Wardwell, W.I.; Hyman, M.; Bahnson, C.B. 'Stress and coronary disease in three field studies', *Journal of Chronic Diseases* (1964), 17, pp. 73–84.

Warr, P. 'Age and job performance', in J. Snell and R. Cremer (eds.) *Work and aging. A European perspective*. Basingstoke: Taylor and Francis; 1995, pp. 309–22.

Warr, P, Cook J.; Wall, T. 'Scales for the measurement of some work attitudes and aspects of psychological wellbeing', *Journal of Occupational Psychology*, 52 (1979) 129–48.

Warr, P.; Wall, T. *Work and well being*. Harmondsworth: Penguin; 1985.

Warshaw, L.J. *Managing Stress*, Reading, Massachusets: Addison Wesley; 1979.

Watzlawick, P.; Beavin, J.H.; Jackson, D.D. *Pragmatics of Human Communication*. London: Faber & Faber; 1968.

Welch, B.L. 'Extra-auditory health effects of industrial noise: Survey of foreign literature', *Aerospace Medical Research Laboratory, Aerospace Medical Division, Air Force Systems Command*. Wright Patterson; 1979, June.

Whatmore, L.; Cartwright; Cooper, C.L. 'Evaluation of a stress management programme in the public sector', in M. Kompier and C. Cooper, (eds.) *Preventing Stress, Improving Productivity: European case studies in the workplace*. London: Routledge; 1999, pp. 149–74.

Wheatley, M. *The future of middle management*. Institute of Management, Corby; 1992.

Whitfield, A. 'Many mental health nurses stressed out', *Health and Safety Bulletin, 262*, October, 1997.

Wing, R.R.; Blair, E.H.; Epstein, L.H.; McDermott, M.D. 'Psychological stress and glucose metabolism in obese and normal-weight subjects: a possible mechanism for differences in stress-induced eating', *Health Psychology* (1990), 9 (6), pp. 693–700.

WHO, *Psychosocial factors and health: Monitoring the psychosocial work environment and workers' health*. Geneva: World Health Organisation, 1984.

Wilkinson, R. 'Some factors influencing the effect of environmental stressors upon performance', *Psychological Bulletin* (1969), 72, pp. 260–72.

Williams, C, 'Implications for employer's liability insurance – what premiums will you have to pay?' in *'An employer's guide to stress at work litigation'*, IBC UK Conferences, London: May; 1997.

Wood, S. 'The transformation of work'. London: Unwin Hyman; 1989.

Wolf, S.; Wolff, H.G. *Gastric function: an experimental study of a man and his stomach*. New York: Oxford University Press; 1943.

Wolf, S.G. cited, H. Lewis, H. Griswold, and H. Underwood (eds.) *Stress and Heart Disease: Modern Concepts of Cardiovascular Disease*. New York: American Heart Association; 1960 (29), pp. 559–603.

Wirral, L.; Cooper, C.L *'IM-UMIST, Quality of working life survey'*. London: Institute of Management; 1997.

Wright, P.K.; Bourne, D.A. *Manufacturing Intelligence*. Reading, MA: Addison-Wesley; 1988.

Wynne, R.; Clarkin, N. *Under construction: Building for health in the EC workplace*. Dublin: European Foundation for the Improvement of Living and Working Conditions; 1992.

Wynne, R.; Clarkin, N.; Cox, T.; Griffiths, A. *Guidance on the prevention of violence at work*. European Commission; 1995.

Zemke, R. 'Rethinking the rush to team up', *Training* (1993), p. 61.

Index